Ecclesiological Investigations

Series Editor

Gerard Mannion

Volume 2

Christian Community Now

Ecclesiological Investigations brings together quality research and inspiring debates in ecclesiology worldwide from a network of international scholars, research centres and projects in the field.

Other titles in the series:

Receiving: The Nature and Mission of the Church
Comparative Ecclesiology
Church and Religious 'Other'

Christian Community Now

ECCLESIOLOGICAL INVESTIGATIONS

Paul M. Collins
Gerard Mannion
Gareth Powell
Kenneth Wilson

t&t clark

Published by T&T Clark
A Continuum imprint
The Tower Buildig, 11 York Road, London SE1 7NX
80 Maiden Lane, Suite 704, New York, NY 10038

www.continuumbooks.com

British Library Cataloguing-in-Publication Data
A catalogue record for this book is available from the British Library

Typeset by Data Standards Limited, Frome, Somerset
Printed on acid-free paper in Great Britain by Biddles Ltd, King's Lynn, Norfolk

ISBN-10: HB 0567032426
ISBN-13: HB 9780567032423

CONTENTS

WELCOME TO ECCLESIOLOGICAL INVESTIGATIONS: *A NEW INTERNATIONAL RESEARCH NETWORK*

Gerard Mannion

This volume encapsulates the fruit of three years of ecumenical conversation between four Christians for whom the many questions demanded of the church today have proved fascinating and enlightening in equal measure. When we began to meet we hoped something positive and constructive would emerge from the meetings, aside from their instant conviviality and good-humoured nature. Yet none of us had anticipated just how widely and how quickly these conversations would grow into a conversation that would traverse not simply ecclesial but also continental boundaries and which would take on a life of its own, fired by an energy and enthusiasm that seemed infectious and which was demonstrative of true catholicity and communion in action. The initial conversations of four people emerged into a much wider constellation of conversations, indeed, into the establishment of a new international research network, 'Ecclesiological Investigations'.

The Network has been established to bring people together in open and pluralistic conversation and collaboration. The abiding ethos of the Network is that the church must be inclusive if it is to be relevant and if it is truly to fulfil its (God's) mission. Conversations about the nature, role and purpose of the Church today are increasingly preoccupying not just theologians, but the faithful, pastors and church leaders alike. The Network's mission is to provide encouragement, resources and facilitation for such dialogue. Here I briefly provide some background to the emergence and mission of this Network and warmly extend an invitation to others to join and sponsor its work.

Catholicity in Action: The St Deiniol's First International Conference

Theologians and activists from four different continents and from many different churches gathered at the St Deiniol's Library in Wales between 12 and 15 January 2007 to discuss the issues and themes of greatest importance to the church of today and of the future, including explorations concerning the nature and role of the church. The event marked the First Conference of the Ecclesiological Investigations International Research Network.

This conference was a landmark event for the new Network and followed on from another initiative exploring the nature and role of the Church which has proved very successful indeed, namely the establishment of the new Ecclesiological Investigations Group of the American Academy of Religion, which staged its first sessions in Washington DC at the end of November 2006. This saw 150 people attend the first session on 'The Nature and Mission of the Church: Ecclesial Reality and Ecumenical Horizons for the 21st Century', with much discussion being generated in relation to the recently issued document of the World Council of Churches. And 130 attend the second session on 'Comparative Ecclesiology: Critical Investigations', exploring the nature, scope and promise of this new method in general and the pioneering work of Roger Haight SJ, in particular.

The Mission of the Ecclesiological Investigations Research Network

The mission statement of this new Network states that it seeks to serve as a hub for national and international collaboration in ecclesiology, drawing together other groups and networks, initiating research ventures and providing administrative support as well as acting as a funding magnet to support conversations, research and education in this field. The abiding ethos of the Network will be that the Church must be inclusive if it is to be relevant and if it is truly to fulfil its mission. Finally, the task of this international Network is to foster and facilitate open and pluralistic conversation and collaboration.

The Network's Five Fundamental Aims

1. The establishment of partnerships between scholars, research projects and research centres across the world.
2. The development of virtual, textual and actual conversation between the many persons and groups involved in research and debate about ecclesiology.
3. Organising and sharing in colloquia, symposia and conferences.
4. Encouraging joint teaching, exchanges of postgraduate students and faculty.
5. Publishing this new and ongoing series of volumes on Ecclesiological Investigations.

Some Background

As indicated, the Network has emerged from small beginnings. In 2002, questions concerning the nature, role and contemporary life of the church led four scholars to begin a series of meetings to present and discuss a series of papers on a wide variety of ecclesiological themes. Hence there emerged a three-year research initiative and series of conversations involving Paul Collins, Gerard Mannion, Gareth Powell and Kenneth Wilson. They initially met under the auspices of

Chichester University and hence the group took as their name 'The Chichester Group', which brought together an Anglican, a Roman Catholic and two Methodists. The present volume that you hold in your hands was, itself, the direct result of these discussions.

In Summer 2005 invitations were sent out to numerous UK persons to form a small steering group to help establish a broader network of people and institutions involved in the field of ecclesiology. The group's chief aims included the intention to focus upon ecclesiology from the standpoint of different Christian denominations and from differing international and cultural perspectives (ecumenical and comparative intentions). The group was to share an openness to and celebration of the pluralistic reality in the midst of which the Churches today find themselves living (pluralistic intentions). The work of the group would deal with the challenges facing churches today (praxis-oriented intentions). A major new publication series formed a key part of the new group's intentions, along with the establishment of study days and teaching initiatives pertaining to the church (educational intentions). A limited amount of funding was raised for the initial meetings of this group. Members from a wide variety of church and organisational backgrounds agreed to join the steering group.

The outcome was the establishment of a partnership involving five institutions in which the Centre for the Study of the Contemporary Ecclesiology (originally located at Liverpool Hope University) has played a leading role. Links were established with numerous other centres and institutions pursuing similar aims across the international community. In addition to this research centre, the five initial UK partners were thus the Department of Theology, Chichester University; Durham University's Research Centre for Contemporary Catholic Studies; Heythrop College; London; and Ripon College Cuddesdon, Oxford. Further international partner institutions have since been added to their number, including from Canada (St Michael's College, Toronto); the USA (Boston College); Belgium (Catholic University of Leuven); and three from India (Old Orthodox Seminary, Kottayam; The University of Calicut; and the Tamil Nadu Theological Seminary, Madurai). Most recently the Queen's Ecumenical Foundation, Birmingham and the Milltown Institute, Dublin have also joined this expanding group. From this there has emerged the Ecclesiological Investigations Research Network.

In November 2005, at Old Saint Joseph's Parish Hall, Philadelphia, a reception was held to launch the proposed New Ecclesiology Program Group of the American Academy of Religion, sponsored by Liverpool Hope University and organized by Paul Collins, Michael Fahey and Gerard Mannion and with much support from elsewhere. In December that year the Academy approved the proposals. The new group also took the title Ecclesiological Investigations and has been established to provide a ready platform and further series of opportunities for dialogue for all those involved in the field of the study of the church in its numerous forms.

From such beginnings, the American Academy of Religion (AAR) Group has progressed from strength to strength. In 2007 its sessions explored 'Communion and Otherness: Contemporary Challenges of "Impaired Communion" ' and 'The Church and its Many Asian Faces/Perspectives on Transnational Communion'.

Thus the Network has already made significant and swift progress which has brought new attention to the importance of the study of ecclesiology for our times.

Network Initiatives to Date

The Network has already made significant and swift progress which has brought new attention to the importance of the study of ecclesiology for our times. In addition to the popular new program unit of the AAR, a new seminar of the UK Society for the Study of Theology, also focusing upon Ecclesiology, was established at the 2007 annual conference at Girton College, Cambridge University and a twice-yearly series of 'Study Days in Ecclesiology' for research students and other interested parties in the field have been taking take place since 2006 with the first three being staged in the UK and the next due to take place in Ireland in 2008, followed by further events throughout Europe with analogous and events anticipated across other continents. Discussions with T&T Clark International led to the launch of this new series of publications for the Network, the first four volumes being published in the first half of 2008.[1]

Obviously, the series seeks to help fulfil the broader aims and objectives of the network itself and involves collaboration amongst a wide range of international scholars and research centres and projects across the field of ecclesiological enquiry. This includes work in historical, collaborative, denominational, methodological, ecumenical, inter-faith, conceptual, thematic and inter-disciplinary forms of ecclesiological enquiry, as well as studies of particular traditions, developments and debates pertinent to the broad field.

Not only does the series seek to publish the very best of research presented to the network's various meetings, conferences and colloquia, it also seeks to be a visibly identifiable publication outlet for quality research in ecclesiology worldwide, tapping into a truly global network of research groups, projects, church organisations and practitioners, experts and scholars in the field. The series also aims to encourage and indeed commission collaborative volumes and 'cutting edge' monographs in the field, as well as textbooks that will further enhance knowledge, understanding and dialogue in the field The series also seeks to offer a home to thematic collections of essays and conferences proceedings from numerous additional groups and research centres in the field. Thus, in particular, the series seeks to incorporate the best of the scholarly papers presented at the AAR Program Group papers, the annual Ecclesiological Investigations International Conference, and from similar gatherings of theological and ecclesial scholars from around the globe. It will also seek to reflect the wider debates generated in relation to such papers and meetings.

The Network and Series alike are in partnership with the journal *Ecclesiology*, edited by Paul Avis, which the Network endorses as a further worthy and most fruitful outlet for ongoing ecclesiological enquiry. The January 2008 issue

(Volume 4, no. 2) was especially devoted to the new Network, featuring, in particular, several papers presented at the first international conference in 2007.

Developing the International Network

Thus the Ecclesiological Investigations Network has been established to gather people together regularly to discuss issues and themes of interest and concern in contemporary ecclesiology. The plan is to spread the work of this group wider to embrace other partners in the international scene further afield. We are hence hoping to dovetail the work of the network with the efforts of the AAR program group to continue to establish broader and inclusive conversations and networks in ecclesiology and to further raise the profile of the sub-discipline.

Each partner institution involved in the network to date brings considerable and diverse gifts and expertise to the network. These international partners are institutions of the highest quality in which groundbreaking study and research in ecclesiology have been pursued for many years now. The geographical and social contexts in which their work is carried out, as well as the demonstrative societal benefits of such work, can only inform and enhance the work of institutions elsewhere and the network in general alike. Furthermore, the initial conference sought to help mechanisms to be developed which will ensure that the experiences and insights of all international partners gain exposure, scrutiny and a wider hearing than might otherwise be possible.

The rapid progress made in this initial work in building the foundations for this Network demonstrates that it is very much needed, can serve the requisite communities and scholars alike in a wide variety of ways, and will not simply enhance the standing of the discipline in the academic community across the globe, but might also, through bringing people and communities together in ongoing conversation and partnership, have a major positive impact on the lives of those communities that form the subject-matter which ecclesiology is engaged in studying.

The Network will be also be groundbreaking in that in all its activities it seeks to build partnerships, collaboration and understanding, in contrast to the competitive ethos that prevails in much of the contemporary academic world. Collaboration over and against competition will be its guiding principle.

Intended and Enduring Collaborative Legacy

The ethos behind the initial mission statement of the Network entails a firm commitment to exploring issues pertaining to pluralism, both religious and otherwise, as well as towards ethical debates of national, international and intercontinental relevance from the outset. Such endeavours offer further scope for the Network's lasting legacy to be positive in numerous ways. The Network seeks to cut across a variety of disciplinary, cultural, religious and geographical boundaries. Finally, it is worth emphasizing that it is also a key aim of the network to involve particular partners from those regions of the world which have extremely limited access to funding to facilitate their participation in the broader international network.

In January 2008, the Network's second international conference, taking the theme 'Church in Pluralist Contexts' was hosted at Old St Joseph's Orthodox Seminary in Kerala, India (thanks to Fr K. M. George) and was enormously successful in launching the work of the Network in earnest on the South Asian continent, with the vast majority of contributors being from the region itself. Of equal significance and success was the linked conference in Trichur at the University of Calicut (thanks to the Chair of Christian Studies, Professor Paul Pulikkan) on Inculturation and Church. Paul M. Collins is owed a great debt of gratitude for his tireless efforts in overseeing the organization of these events.

The Key to the Future: Major Funding and Support

The next major task for the Network's steering group is to secure the substantial funding necessary in order that all the initial faith, hope and charity comes to long-lasting fruition. This will require a coalition of funding organisations, institutions and individuals to help ensure the open, pluralistic and collaborative vision can bear much ongoing fruit in future.

We invite all institutions, charities, organisations and individuals who are passionate about and committed to the life and mission of the church today and tomorrow, who believe in a church of churches that is called into being to bear witness to the gospel and to serve the wider human family through tireless work towards the kingdom ends of justice, peace and righteousness, to join and sponsor the collegial and collaborative work of this new Network.

Pluralism is not an ideology; rather it is first of all a descriptive term for the way things are, for reality. At the same time it is also the name for the healthiest and most appropriate response to the way things are, as opposed to turning away from and attempting to deny that reality in various modes of self-delusion and community delusion. Pluralism is all around us and inescapable. But why would anyone seek to escape the riches of the diverse gifts God gives humanity to share? You are warmly invited to join this ecumenical inter-continental conversation and we look forward to your participation and contribution. Let us close this welcome with the wise words of Gregory Baum from 1969, a scholar whose very life and work, in many ways, embody the ethos of our new Network,

> The doctrines of the Church, therefore, make known to us not only the wonderful things God works in the Christian community but the wonderful things [God] performs in the entire human family. The doctrines of the Church become for us the key for the understanding of human life and history; they make known to us the destructive powers at work in human society and the redemptive presence of God to the community of man ... Wherever people come together to solve their problems, enter into conversation and open themselves to one another and to their neighbors, the Holy Spirit is present, aiding them to avoid the traps into which they are tempted to fall and initiating them into new insight and fellowship. ... In other words, the self-

communication of God, which has become concrete and visible in the man Jesus, to whom the Church gives witness by her faith, orientates the whole of human history towards growth and reconciliation.[2]

Note

1. In addition to the present volume, these are, *The Nature and Mission of the Church: Ecclesial Reality and Ecumenical Horizons for the 21st Century*, eds. Paul Collins and Michael Fahey; *Church and Religious Other: Essays on Truth, Unity and Diversity*, ed. Gerard Mannion, and *Comparative Ecclesiology: Critical Investigations*, ed. Gerard Mannion.
2. Gregory Baum, 'The Church as Hermeneutical principle', part III of his *Faith and Doctrine*, New York, Newman press, 1969, 112–13.

Acknowledgements

Our deep gratitude must be expressed to many. First of all to Jane Leek and all at the Derwent Charitable Consultancy for providing a home for the meetings which led to this volume and eventually to the establishment of a new international ecumenical research network in ecclesiology – mighty oaks from little acorns indeed! Certainly not small was the subsequent financial assistance and encouragement provided through Derwent to facilitate that network's coming into being.

Our gratitude also to Mark Chapman for carefully reading through an earlier draft of the volume and for his dedicated commitment to the Ecclesiological Investigations International Research Network and to Michael Fahey, not simply for his gracious Foreword and ongoing commitment to ecumenical ecclesiological explorations but for his help in establishing the AAR ecclesiology group and his service to this as co-chair. We are also deeply grateful for his ongoing work towards furthering the development of the wider international network and towards helping to establish and promote this series, itself. We are sincerely grateful, also, to the other members of the AAR Group steering committee, namely, Michael Attridge, Julie Clague, our own Paul M. Collins, Peter De Mey and Amy Plantinga Pauw, and to all who have supported and attended the group in any shape or form.

Many further thanks are due also to Tom Kraft for believing in this series and its enormous potential, to Dominic Mattos and all at T&T Clark/Continuum.

Above all, a continent-hopping very big thank you to all the members of the Ecclesiological Investigations International Research Network itself – particularly members of the steering group and of the editorial executive committee and advisory board of this new series. Your belief, encouragement and inspiration have made it a reality in a world and at a time when open and pluralistic dialogue and discussion across the churches and far beyond have never been more necessary.

LIST OF CONTRIBUTORS

Paul M. Collins is Reader in Theology at the University of Chichester. A priest of the Church of England, he worked in theological education for 20 years at Chichester Theological College, then at the Queen's Foundation Birmingham and presently the University of Chichester. He serves the Ecclesiological Investigations International Research Network in many ways, being a member of the steering committee, the editorial committee of the T&T Clark publication series and of the AAR Group Committee. His research interests include the doctrines of the Trinity, *Theosis*, the Church and inculturation, especially in South India. His major publications include, *Trinitarian Theology West and East* (OUP, 2001), *Context, Culture and Worship: The Quest for Indian-ness*, (ISPCK, 2006), *Christian Inculturation in India* (Ashgate, 2007). The outcome of his research project in India is also available in database recently made available on the web: http://inculturation.chi.ac.uk/index.cfm He is currently a member of the Faith and Order Advisory Group of the Church of England.

Gerard Mannion serves as chair of the Ecclesiological Investigations International Research Network and is presently a Visiting Senior Fellow of the Katholieke Universiteit Leuven in Belgium. He studied at the universities of Cambridge and Oxford, previously lectured at church colleges of the universities of Oxford and Leeds and was Associate Professor of Ecclesiology and Ethics at Liverpool Hope University. The founding director of the Centre for the Study of Contemporary Ecclesiology, he is also editor of the Ecclesiological Investigations publications series, as well as being co-chair of the Ecclesiology Program Group of the American Academy of Religion. He has authored, edited and co-edited volumes on numerous issues in both ecclesiology and ethics, as well as published various other writings on differing aspects of systematic theology and philosophy, elsewhere. A Roman Catholic layman, he also serves on the UK Catholic Theology Commission on Social Justice. His most recent publications include *Ecclesiology and Postmodernity: Questions for the Church in Our Time* (Liturgical Press, 2007) and *The Routledge Companion to the Christian Church* (2007, ed. with Lewis Mudge).

Gareth Powell, studied at Westminster College, Oxford, the Queen's Theological Foundation and the University of Birmingham and the Ecumenical Institute,

Bossey, in Switzerland. A Methodist minister, he is currently Methodist chaplain to Cardiff University. He has a wide experience of the issues that arise in ecumenical debate as a member of the Methodist–Roman Catholic Conversations and chair of the Methodist Church Committee for Local Ecumenical Development. He is currently pursuing a PhD in Methodism and canon law. Gareth also serves on the Steering Committee of the Ecclesiological Investigations International Research Network and the editorial committee of the T&T Clark Ecclesiological Investigations series.

Kenneth Wilson lectured in philosophy and theology at Wesley College and Bristol University; he was Principal of Westminster College, Oxford from 1981–96 and a member of the Faculty of Theology in the University of Oxford. In 1996 he established the research centre at The Queens Foundation in Birmingham. His current research interests are the role of theological enquiry in public debate and ecclesiology. He is a member of Ecclesiological Investigations and deputy chair of a research project, Learning for Life, which is focused upon character education. He is a member of both the steering committee of the Ecclesiological Investigations International Research Network and the editorial committee of the T&T Clark Ecclesiological Investigations series. Since 2004 he has been Visiting Fellow of the University of Chichester, Senior Research Fellow of Christ Church University, Canterbury, and chair of the Ammerdown Trust. Publications include *Learning to Hope* (2005). He is a Methodist minister.

PREFACE

This coauthored volume is the outcome of an ecumenical speaking and listening that has involved a continuing conversation between four theologians over a period of more than two years. The scholars are active members of three mainline churches in the UK: Anglican, Methodist and Roman Catholic. They propose that the church will live as it grows in self-understanding in the light of the claim that its purpose is to focus attention on God, Creator, Redeemer and living presence.

In so doing they address key debates in the US and European contexts, as well as dealing with matters of pressing concern in the wider global church. What does it mean to say that the church in itself and on behalf of the world bears witness to and celebrates the presence of God in contemporary ethics, worship, governance and mission? The individual human being knows himself or herself to be a person only by recognizing the total environment in which he or she lives, which includes persons, the physical world and God. So also with the church, the authors argue: it is set in an environment of God, and the human and physical world of everyday experience.

The proleptic understanding of the church offered here is now, by the grace of God, inclusive of all people and all that is good and desirable. It is in stark contrast to the limited and beleaguered perspectives offered in the currently fashionable positions widely associated with certain theological approaches elsewhere. The *missio dei* of the church, the authors argue, is to celebrate the joy of the world in the presence of the redemptive creativity of God, Father, Son and Holy Spirit. The Church is not an invasion force but a spiritual sign of the Divine Presence. This truly ecumenical perspective is that same conviction which holds together Marie-Dominique Chenu, a neglected influence on Vatican II, and Methodism's father-in-God, John Wesley: the world is indeed our parish.

The authors have sought to bridge the gap between theoretical and practical theology, and ecclesiology itself.

Paul Collins, Gerard Mannion, Gareth Powell, Kenneth Wilson
(*The Feast of St Augustine of Canterbury*)

INTRODUCTION

This volume is the product of a conversation between four theologians whose ecclesial provenance is variously Roman Catholic, Anglican and Methodist. We met over the course of nearly three years in London in a room kindly provided through the good offices of the Derwent Charitable Consultancy. Out of those conversations have emerged not simply this modest volume, which is an attempt to construct a truly ecumenical and truly *theo*-logical ecclesiology, but also an intercontinental research network in the field which has already made rapid progress in bringing together disparate and distant voices to engage in discourse and constructive dialogue about the communities called Church. So also is this publication series itself the product of those initial conversations within sight of Hyde Park Corner and Marble Arch (officially the beginning of the M1 motorway!) and not a great distance from where the Tyburn martyrs died for their faith in times when eucherial divisions inflicted deep woulds upon the body of Christ.

Ecclesiology – discourse about the church – is a lively subject of current debate, both academically and from the point of view of the ordinary believer trying to find paths and places in which to nourish the desire for and experience of God. Personal and institutional interests brought us together: we found that we were concerned, both personally and theologically, about the content of many contemporary discussions about the nature of the church and the consequent impression that the church gave to the world regarding the purpose 'being' church.

There have, for example, recently been many official reports that purport to be about ecclesiology, but on reflection they seemed to us to be as much concerned with social anthropology and the resolution of cultural issues as they were with theology and the particular branch of theology, ecclesiology, which most concerned us. For example, take *Women Bishops in the Church of England*,[1] *Mission-Shaped Church*[2] and *The Windsor Report*[3]: each arises out of what some perceive as a threat to the Church of England or is focused upon a fear for the survival of the institution. Or consider again the encyclicals *Redemptoris Missio*,[4] *Ut Unum Sint*,[5] and the statements issuing from the Congregation for the Doctrine of the Faith (CDF), such as the *Instruction on the Ecclesial Vocation of the Theologian*,[6] and *Dominus Jesus*.[7] In many respects, all can be interpreted as being, to an unhelpful degree, self-regarding.

Of course it is not surprising: the search for survival strategies is an instinctive reaction when an institution feels itself under threat. And indeed there is real anxiety on the part of all churches about their parlous state. A report on the numbers who participate in the life of the church in the United Kingdom suggests that the community of faith is shrinking so fast that by 2040, there could be twice as many Muslims worshipping in the mosque on a Friday as there would be Christians in church on Sunday.

Notwithstanding the many concerns that are certainly significant, we have found ourselves unimpressed by the fear of imminent disaster for the church. For we believe ecclesiology is above all a theological task. Our attention has therefore been on God whose work is world-focused not church-contained. The church's task is to witness to God and to God's presence. It is God, we therefore believe, who should be and must be the focus of the church's worship, teaching and life. Since God is the redemptive Creator of all that is, and since God has given Godself in Christ to making a success of that creating, we cannot conceive of a time when God will abandon this world to its own devices.

We are therefore unable to associate the actual size of a worshipping community with success or failure. God cannot fail and be God. As we understand it, were God to fail, then God, as we understand God, would have denied God's own nature, as 'Gracious Presence', which is impossible. Were this to happen, it would not be the church that had failed, but the faith of the community of faith that would have turned out to be unwarranted. Hence to give all one's ingenious attention to maintaining the church is essentially a non-Christian activity. The task of the Christian, and the church, is to focus upon God, God's giving of God's self to the world and the celebration of God's presence with his world. From that we may gain the confidence, hope and joy, which will encourage personal faith, the faith of the church and the life of the world. 'God so loved the world ...' Any ecclesiology will have to be built on that confidence. It is in the light of such considerations that what we have to say, quite naturally and properly, takes on a trinitarian form.

God, to whom we give attention, nourishes faith through God's presence in the world that God is creating and to which God has given God's self. We therefore expect to encounter God in God's world, where the church is set, not in the Church alone. To believe otherwise poses serious questions with regard to one's understanding of the Christian doctrines of creation and providence. Of course, the institutional church has too often presumed a role based upon a false confidence that is overweaning, thereby bringing attention on itself rather than directing the world's attention to God. We have to learn to be patient and to live with uncertainties. The necessity for ecclesial humility is, therefore, a theme, which permeates the following chapters.

Notwithstanding this, as people of hope, we celebrate on behalf of the whole of creation God's presence, for incarnation means that the universe has assumed without contradiction all that God is for us in Jesus whom we call the Christ. We remember this every time that we offer in eucharistic celebration the world and all that is to God. God takes the bread and wine and makes it for us the food of our salvation. The very fact that it is God who is present in Christ means that we can have – not paradoxically but really – joy in the presence of the Crucified. The church is grounded in the hope that God has overcome the world and all its evil, which is what we mean by resurrection.

In all this we thus discern something of what many Christian communities understand to be the sacramental nature and task of the Church: that it should be both a sign and a mediation of the gracious and loving divine self-communication to the world. For if such self-communication, such loving grace, were limited to the confines of the church, then ecclesiology becomes nothing more than soteriological tautology. But if so, then fundamentals of our theo-logy fall down at crucial junctures. As Gutierrez famously said, 'By preaching the Gospel message, by its sacraments, and by the charity of its members, the Church proclaims and shelters the gift of the Kingdom of God in the heart of human history.'[8]

The implication we explore is that the Church has continuously to reinterpret her self-understanding in the wider world of Christian faith, and in the knowledge that she always has to relearn what it means to present the world to God, and to celebrate God's presence in the world. There are serious moral questions to be considered, for the church is at the very least a moral community – the trinitarian and sacramental aspects of its being could entail nothing less.

The question of what it is to be the church present in creation is investigated through an exploration of context and of the experience of worship. The implications for governance and for the exercise of authority both within the church and by the church in the world are understood to be both crucial and difficult. Finally we have given some consideration in conclusion to the gift of mission. The art of conversation, initiated by God with God's creation, taken up on behalf of the world by the community of faith, is now to be continued by the church with the world. The community that is actually involved cannot be defined at any moment of time: hence the importance that the church work so as to be always open to the world and to God (we underline the fact that catholicity implies the broadest perspective on ecumenicity, and the life of the Spirit).

In all, then, this collective volume, both in form and content, is an exercise in affirming catholicity, as opposed to going down the route of any narrow self-regarding ecclesial groups to be found anew today across all denominations. Their inward-looking, repristinated 'siege mentality' is, we believe, counterproductive in our postmodern, pluralistic times.

We seek to offer a theo-logical ecclesiology, via a series of reflections upon aspects of God and ecclesial being today. In doing so, we are conscious that we set down a challenge to those self-regarding and self-congratulatory ecclesial outlooks that purport to be ecclesiology today but which, on closer inspection, might actually fall far short of meeting the basic requirements of such. The words of Keith Ward capture the mission of contemporary ecclesiological discourse well:

> The Christian faith is that God begins that enabling and healing action in history, and does so in some way and to some extent in every part of history. Some parts of the historical process will naturally be capable of channelling the healing actions of God more clearly and effectively than others ... The role of the church is to witness to the meaning of history, to the fact that history is given its fullest meaning and brought to

completion in God, and that all conscious creatures can share in the awareness of that meaning and completion.[9]

That all four authors are European males really is more accident than design, but we are nonetheless conscious of the limited and contextualized nature of our perspectives. Hence this is one of the reasons why we have since opened up our conversation further and look to doing so still more in the future.

Part I. *Attending to the Creator*

In this first part of the book the authors set out their belief that the world and the church are grounded in and take their life from God, Creator, Redeemer and Living Presence. The volume as a whole is shaped in such a way as to present this reality. The church's life, its work and its nature are of no more significance than a mutual admiration society, apart from the intention to make clear the divine gift of the world and its delightful God-given capacity to grow in faith for the world's sake.

The essential purpose of the church, which stems from its divine origin, is to give attention to God, which is explored in Chapter 1. This is not a means to passivity; neither is it a matter of 'looking at' and being transported by the experience to another dimension. Giving attention to God has many aspects: it is, for example, focused in the eucharist, where the Church, on behalf of all people and the whole of creation, celebrates the living presence of God in Christ and, filled with God's grace, is sent out into the world to do God's will, that is to live in the world as God's people.

Giving attention to God is not confined to 'religious' occasions, but involves the sanctification of one's experience of living in the world and learning about it. It is therefore concerned with scientific enquiry and technical innovation, with historical understanding and artistic creation, because by committing ourselves to them we equip ourselves to share the spirit of God's creativity, provided, that is, we do it redemptively. All this is explored in the Chapter 2, 'The World as Creation'.

Part II. *Encountering Christ*

In Part 2 we explore the implications for ecclesiology of developments in the modern, and now postmodern, world through a christological lens.

Hence Chapter 3, 'The Enlightenment and Certainty', discusses the meaning and relevance of certainty in the post-Enlightenment world we now enjoy, and attempts to evaluate its importance for the church's self-understanding. A positive appreciation of the nature of humility in the work and life of Jesus Christ is a necessary condition for the church's current self-understanding. Through engaging with a variety of thinkers from Aquinas through to Foucault and Derrida, the chapter works towards the conclusion that the church – as a life-giving community – must learn the virtue of humility, intellectual, moral and spiritual.

These themes are explored further in Chapter 4, 'Hermeneutical Investigations: Discerning Contemporary Christian Community', which begins by noting that a fundamental refusal to engage in probing and self-critical ecclesiological hermeneutics has been a marked feature of much ecclesiological thinking across numerous denominations in recent decades. It is a product of the rise of inward-looking and neo-exclusivistic ecclesiologies, which are in the ascendancy throughout the Christian church. It suggests there is a need for Christians, in each generation and especially in the present era, to ensure that the Gospel is allowed to provide a hermeneutic of the Church. The chapter turns to examine critically the ecumenical movement's hermeneutical 'turn' in *A Treasure in Earthen Vessels* and moves on to mention some recent studies in hermeneutics and ecclesiology.

Finally, this middle section ends with Chapter 5, a profound meditation on 'Joy in the Presence of the Crucified', which explores why in a world wracked with pain it is the reasonable duty of the church on behalf of the world to be a body of pure joy. Discussion of the relationship between nature and grace, the human and the divine, has been a major source of conflict between the many Christian traditions. We now see that the separation, though not perhaps the difference, is exaggerated; as Rahner says, there is no such thing as *ungraced* nature. The implications of this are explored with reference to the understanding of the world as 'creation'.

Part III. *Living in the Spirit*

In this third section, we address areas of ecclesiology, which might be termed 'applied' or 'practical' theology. However, no attempt is made to produce a blueprint for the churches, or indeed a road-map whence they should journey. Part 3 is entitled 'Living in the Spirit' and we see this essentially as an attempt to discuss areas of living the Christian life by the Christian community, in relation to the work of the person of the Holy Spirit. The reader should not here expect a detailed and specific work of pneumatology. Rather we have sought to expound areas of life of the Christian community, which one would naturally assume are guided and prospered by the person of the Holy Spirit. Thus the trinitarian structuring of our conversation is directed in this section to the 'subjectivity' of the persons of the community, as well as of the community itself. The four topics of our investigation: ethics, context, worship and governance each in turn address a particular aspect of that 'subjectivity' enlivened by the person of the Spirit. The essays on ethics and context both deal with broadly ranging aspects of current discourse in these areas, while those on worship and governance look at particular aspects of those features of the life of the churches. These four essays seek to investigate how the churches continue to respond to tradition in the light of contemporary influences and pressures upon the Christian community. While not attempting to provide a road-map, they do set out parameters and potentialities, which the churches might expect and explore were they to take up aspects of our conversation. In particular the possible responses to trajectories in contemporary philosophical discourse are explored, in the hope that the churches may find ways of discovering new strengths in exploring, pursuing and applying these responses.

Finally the book concludes with a short excursus on the *missio dei* (Mission of God), as much a promise of further conversation as the conclusion of the present one.

Notes

1. *Women Bishops in the Church of England?* (London: Church House Publishing, 2004).
2. *Mission-shaped Church* (London: Church House Publishing, 2004).
3. *The Windsor Report: The Lambeth Commission on Communion* (London: The Anglican Communion Office, 2004).
4. *Redemptionis Missio*, Pope John Paul II 8th Encyclical, 8 December 1990, to celebrate the 25th Anniversary of the Vatican II statement on Mission.
5. *Ut Unum Sint* (1995).
6. *Instruction on the Ecclesial Vocation of the Theologian* (Rome: 1990).
7. *Dominus Jesus*, 2000.
8. Gustavo Gutierrez, *Theology of Liberation* (London: SCM Press, 1974), p. 11.
9. Keith Ward, *Religion and Community* (Oxford: Clarendon, 2000), pp. 328–9.

PART I

ATTENDING TO THE CREATOR

Chapter 1

GIVING ATTENTION TO GOD

Kenneth Wilson

Introduction

The purpose of the church is, on behalf of all creation, to 'give attention to God'. This is a task that has to be learned by every member of the community of faith. It is a task, too, for which the community of faith has regularly to be rescued from error, complacency and indifference. Nothing human is free from the possibility of decay and dissolution so, just as Terence declared himself to be indifferent to nothing human, Christians should take this debilitating feature of human experience into account when thinking of their faith.[1] The church will find it important to remind itself regularly of its purpose and nature. Of course, it is not easy for it since the very same anxious condition of human nature will encourage even the church to pursue and accept easy solutions rather than continue in hard work and careful thought. Hence the importance of keeping questions about God in the forefront of the church's mind.

What does the Christian community of faith mean when it refers to God? What does it mean when it says that it wants to give attention to God? Of course, if the church is serious when it says it wants to give attention to God, it must do everything in its power to become conscious of what in fact by its actions it is trying to do. If one wants to be taken seriously the current politically correct term is 'transparency'. In this connection the word seems fine: the nature of the church's words and life needs to be transparent, if the world is to see Jesus and be drawn into the conversation which will reveal the presence of God, Father, Son and Holy Spirit.

There was a time when all, or almost all, systematic theologies began with a section on God; it is now more commonly the case for the volume to begin with a discussion of the human experience of God, especially as found in the life and worship of the church, and only then to turn in conclusion to a discussion of the Being of God. There is, it is true, merit in this approach. However, in contrast with the many hundreds of references to God in the New Testament, there are only two, or at most four, to the church universal – at any rate using the word, 'ecclesia'.[2] This in itself suggests that we would do well from time to time to begin what we want to say about the church with a discussion of the term 'God'.

There is no denying that the life, teaching, death, resurrection and ascension of Jesus whom we call the Christ is at the centre of the faith of the Church. Christology is the essential dimension of Christian doctrine, because paying attention to Jesus is a way of beginning to pay appropriate attention to the divine in our lives. Yet, no one could argue that human interest in or reflection about God, let alone conversation about God or perhaps even with God, began with Jesus. Indeed, without first having some desire to pay attention to 'God', stimulated perhaps by some shared perception of the divine – even some understanding of the nature of God, what it means to refer to God and to want God would be completely unintelligible.

Actually, in such circumstances, it is hard to see how reflection on the life and work of Jesus Christ could be of more than moral significance. Even that possibility is destroyed by the beastly portrayal of the 'brave' Jesus in Mel Gibson's film *The Passion of the Christ*, for here the irrelevant intrusion of 'realistic' pain, keeps earthbound any possible moral transformation which might ensue through the stimulus of the imagination.[3] But putting that thought on one side, the Christian is not a morally superior person and whatever the church is, it is not a society for the improvement of morals. It is called by Christ to the much more ambitious purpose of bearing witness to the truth, above all to the truth that is God.

One might say that Jesus was the occasion of 'a giant leap for mankind', in the sense that he transformed the context and location for 'conversation about God' by anticipating in his own 'story-ing' a new grammar and a new linguistic framework, the sharing of which could provoke anyone to an impossible awareness of God's presence in the ordinary events of everyday life. Of course, when one comes to see that 'The world is charged with the grandeur of God',[4] one is inclined to think of it in a new light and to give 'added value' to one's self and one's neighbours. One may come to see the world as a creation rather than a happenstance with all the potential that such an insight offers. The result may be new opportunities for thinking and acting well. But they will be the consequence of the vision, not the purpose of it.

Interestingly, we say of the church, that Christ *called* it into existence; that is exactly right. It is the conversation of Jesus with the tradition(s) of faith into which he was born, to which he reintroduced his disciples and who in turn became the Church. They were intrigued by his priorities and by the ways in which he talked about them, so much so indeed that they continued the conversation amongst themselves after his death, and after what they mysteriously came to talk of as his resurrection and ascension. By his conversation, it turned out, Jesus had helped them all in anticipation, to come to terms with the events of his life. Moreover their understanding grew further as they talked their language out with the wider community notwithstanding its own diverse perspectives on God and the nature of human life. The disciples found themselves trying to remember Jesus's words, to tell his stories and to begin again and again their conversation with him, knowing that by so doing they were actually revivifying, refreshing and expanding their own conversation with God. The conversation of the church, the community 'called' into being by Jesus, continued and continues to stimulate the same sort of 'awareness of the presence of God' as Jesus himself found as he talked and lived out the consequences of his own talking.

The conversation cannot be conducted in a static language, though there is always the tendency for a new language that offers the possibility of revelation to become fixed, as if the mere repetition of formulas was itself all that was required for it to continue to be revelatory. It is always risky to engage in conversation, but it is a risk that has to be taken if one's understanding is to grow and one's experience to be extended. It is hard to live up to one's words, and to do what one says one wants to do. More difficult still is to be what one says one wants to be. It is a normal condition of the life of the church that it falls short of the glory of God: hence the significance of refocusing on God, who God is, and how God acts.

Fitness for purpose

Any manager will tell you that the prime question about any organization, or any division of it, concerns its fitness for purpose. Given the fact that the church has been in existence for two millennia or thereabouts, one can hardly say that in human terms it has been a failure. But this does not of itself deal with questions regarding the church's fitness for purpose. Let us consider some.

The churches, all of them, are short of clergy. But it would be a brave person who suggested that a church that was short of clergy was unfit for purpose, if it was mindful of the fact that its purpose was to focus on God. So the diversion of resources to improve recruitment to the ordained ministry, even if successful, will not of itself improve the capacity of the church to fulfil its purpose. One might suppose, for example, that matters of quality, of education, of pastoral support, of remuneration and conditions of service would be important to consider. But in so doing one might find that the church had refocused its sense of purpose, so that instead of giving attention to God, it was actually giving attention to the clergy. The need for the institutional church to fill slots, to put a priest or minister into a parish, may have been a constituent element in the slackening of selection procedures for selection, with the unfortunate consequence that unsuitable candidates entered the priesthood, with all that that has led to in sheer incompetence and actual abuse. It is no comfort to recognize that the church has suffered from bad publicity, warranted or not, in previous eras.[5]

All churches are short of money. The consequence is that many look shabby in comparison with those striking temples of mammon, the supermarkets, or the pleasant ambience of most homes. Moreover, there are churches with admirable ideas for the fulfilment of their social purpose, the housing of the homeless, the care of drug addicts, the loneliness of the elderly and the encouragement of family life. The demands on churches for their assistance in the community are huge and growing, notwithstanding the serious anxieties of the churches in respect of the support of the clergy and other fulltime church workers in employment and in retirement. But there is no necessary connection between the possession of adequate finance and the fulfilment of the purpose of the church, if that purpose is to give attention to God. This is certainly the case if what the world perceives is the church 'trying to get' more money to pay its bills.

The churches in the Western world are losing congregational strength: numbers of worshippers are falling. Indeed, even the involvement of the church with those central moments of human life, birth, marriage and death, is reducing rapidly. In order to regain the interest of the ever-growing wider community, the churches need to be seen to be more attractive, more successful; they need more young people, more families and greater relevance. The importance of this can be dressed up in theological terms by pointing to the fact that the church must be a missionary church. But again, there seems to be no necessary connection between large congregations, successful membership drives, more popular worship occasions, or an increase in the number of marriages in church and the purpose of the church, which is to focus attention on God.

The churches, all of them, are looking for ways to restructure themselves in order precisely to make themselves more fit for purpose. A policy of centralization has been pursued in the Anglican and Methodist Churches so that targets can be defined, monitored and accounted for and the performance of the clergy regularly assessed. The consequence has often been loss of communication with the ordinary member, and the destruction of those things which have no line on which to enter them in the machine-read reports, but which are of the essence of being 'church'. The problem is a familiar one. How do we report the advance in wisdom amongst a school's sixth form? How do we devise a set of criteria for moral excellence and develop a comparative system for reporting the achievement of students? The problems of giving an honest and full account of the life of a school are notorious, especially when the dimensions of comparison are introduced: it is even more difficult to do so in the life of a Christian community of faith, the real purpose of which is to focus attention on God.

None of this is intended to imply that clergy are unimportant, that money does not matter, that the number of those engaged with the church is irrelevant or that styles of management are of no significance. On the contrary they, and many other matters, such as the condition of the churchyard and the quality of the singing are of very great importance. What, however, is vital to understand is that none of them is of the slightest value if the one thing that matters is missing, namely the desire to focus attention on God by ensuring that God is at the heart of Christian conversation. If we say as churches, and as Christians, that what we want is God, we must be seen to be trying to get God.

All too frequently the churches lose sight of their primary focus; they are then justly accused of being at best inconsistent and at worst hypocritical.

The existence of God

In one way or another the question of God and of God's existence has featured in human conversation since time immemorial. It is prominent in the Hebrew Bible though there it is a practical issue, not a philosophical problem. How is this?

One can be misled into thinking that the stories of creation are intended to answer the question, 'Who created the world?', or even, 'How was the world created?' They are not. What puzzled the Hebrew in his whole being was not the existence of the universe *per se* but his own existence as a human being with feelings, affections, understandings, ambitions and imaginings. Who were human beings and how could they be as they were in the world where they found themselves, apparently privileged in comparison with other creatures? Especially was this the case because the world that they enjoyed seemed on the one hand hard and indifferent to their concerns, and on the other delightfully fruitful in the ways in which it provided for their physical needs, stimulated their imagination and their curiosity. They came to terms with their perplexities by telling stories rather than by stating answers. Their approach was dynamic not static, their story developing and never-ending.

It seemed to the Hebrews that their sense of themselves was perfectly natural, and not the product of extraneous forces or influences. They needed a story that could in principle account for everything, not one that simply 'explained' their personal experience of their humanity. So the story they developed and found most illuminating was one that suggested that the world they shared with all life, both plants and creatures, was the engaging gift of a Being whose presence transformed their ordinary experience. They came to understand that the personal reality they knew in themselves and for themselves was the true reality and not the result of a foreign or misleading irruption into a world of blind fate. What they felt about themselves had not come about by accident but was, if you like, the very purpose of the world's being. It is worth noting that the creation of matter is not a dimension of the story; the focus is the bringing of order out of chaos. Their own sense of 'ordering' as human beings in the context of the disorder they all too frequently experienced as the world, was one dimension of this; their own experience of 'ordering' in their personal/social lives was another of equal importance.

Initially the story was set in the context of their tribal history and confined to their experience of themselves as Hebrew people; only later as they developed their story did they come to see that there was no true account of themselves that did not include all people. Actually, as we can see when we read the stories of creation in Genesis and their elaboration in the Old Testament, the story became more inclusive as they came to realize that there was nothing at all which they could reasonably exclude from the range of their creative telling of stories; the Being, whom they called Yahweh or God was not a creator, but *the* Creator. God created everything, both the heavens and the earth.

This was the God on whom they could focus, whose loving kindness had made them what they were, put them where they were, and given them a world to enjoy in which they could flourish as persons together. They and everything that contributed to their lives in any way were included in God's story.

Ultimate mystery?

But are we not ahead of ourselves? We are already assuming that the term 'God' means something when we know that in a major tradition of Christian theological reflection the only thing of which we can be sure is that we know nothing of God apart from the basic fact of God's existence and the truth of certain negative propositions. Thus whatever God is, God is not an object like other objects of human experience; God is not confined by the temporal world; God does not occupy space/time. 'God is the ultimate mystery, we can only know what God is not.'[6]

As a means of denying the transcendental deduction this is an unexceptionable assertion. God is indeed the ultimate mystery in the sense that God cannot be pigeonholed. If God is as the Hebrew story of creation in Genesis suggests, and it is reasonable to develop a conversation about the world of human experience that includes God, there can only be one God. And, of course, if there is only one member of a class and the class is itself unique, then while one may induct some understanding of the Being who is God, one cannot deduce without doubt the truth of any claim about God. To invite a person to share in the telling of a story and by so doing to get inside the narrative so as to be able to chance one's arm in continuing the story for one's self, is exactly how some insights into the 'character' of God can be discerned. It is discernment, not deduction that is required. But then as human beings we shall be shaped by what we have come to see for ourselves rather than by what we are required to learn by mere deduction. After all, as with a computer so also with the human mind: there is no privileged position for deductive knowledge, its value depends not only upon the rules of deduction but on the truth of the basic propositions to which the rules of deduction are applied; rubbish in means rubbish out.

But there is something to add of logical and factual significance. For if there is God, and if and only if there is but one God, the Hebrew story, now further developing in the Jewish and Christian traditions, will be right to judge that everything else that exists is contingent upon the Being who is God. Thus, the disturbing imperative under which the author of St John's gospel struggles to make sense of the fact of Jesus, the Christ. If Jesus is the person whom 'St John' thinks he is, then the explanation is not merely contingent upon local historical circumstances: far from it, the birth, life, death and resurrection of Jesus Christ was in some mysterious sense necessarily the work of God. In order to make room for this 'revelation' he finds himself driven back to the beginning, indeed to creation. He is therefore even required to think through all over again his understanding of God and God's relationship with the world: a mighty task for any Jew. He was familiar with Jewish traditions, and to some extent with the world of Greek philosophy, yet they were simply inadequate to contain what he wanted to say. And so in the first chapter of the gospel the author tries another approach and with imaginative insight affirms the presence of the Word with God in anticipation of creation. All that was made was made through the Word, that is, through Jesus whom we call the Christ.[7] God's eternal loving commitment of

God's self to the world 'St John' knew, was fully expressed in the Incarnation, in Christ.

The universal point is implicitly and subtly made by the marvellous entry in the index of Timothy McDermott's concise translation of the *Summa* – GOD, pp.1–600. The volume has 600 pages *in toto*. Quite! There is, of course, not one proposition that can be asserted as true of God without careful discussion and serious enquiry; but there are things to be said which merit serious reflection, one just needs a lot of space to say anything about God, Creator, Redeemer and Friend.[8] Hence it is important to tell the story to get the conversation going – again.

Herbert McCabe begins his essay 'Creation' in the following way:

> In my view to assert that God exists is to claim the right and need to carry on any activity, to be engaged in research, and I think this throws light on what we are doing if we try to prove the existence of God. To prove the existence of God is to prove that some questions still need asking, that the world poses these questions for us.[9]

The stories regarding the creation take basic human questions with the seriousness they deserve. What is it to be human? What is it to be a person? Why am I so curious about my experience and its meaning? Who am I? These questions are transformed, but not solved, when we take the fact of God's existence to be a dimension of the world's nature, and a feature of human life; a contemporary telling of the stories will continue to address the same questions.

The activity of God

The subject is confusing. How can God, who is not material, let alone a physical being, act in a world that is nothing if not a physical world? In the simple terms of cause and effect suggested by the question it is unanswerable and indeed, as Gilbert Ryle would say, a category mistake. God is not able to operate cranes or drive buses. The wrong approach is being taken: it is not a matter of cause and effect, but of discernment, understanding and practice.

The Hebrew story of creation does not suggest that God is doing something in the sense of intervening in a world that is foreign to God. On the contrary, as we have seen, it implies that the whole of what humanity is and experiences is open to the ordering of God's affectionate will. The claim that God's will is affectionate is implicit in the writer's claim that 'God saw everything that he had made, and, behold, it was very good.'[10] Moreover, God's 'doing' in relation to creating is the same as God's being in relation to creation: God cannot be if God is not doing. In an important sense, therefore, God's self is conceived in active terms: a point made clear because all the words used of God in creating are verbs.

The question of Jesus, and of the relationship of Jesus to God is of the essence of the story for Christians. This 'new' activity of God seals the Church's understanding of God. It is also to be noted that it is a thoroughly active perception of God's involvement with the world and therefore of a piece with the Old Testament story. Jesus lives out a life in obedience to God's will. He can be said in a unique way to have wanted God, and to have given his whole life to the business of 'trying to get' God. The fact that, as the church believes, nothing prevented him from achieving his purpose, which was to fulfil God's purpose for the world, shows once and for all that the world is indeed very good. The self-awareness which prompted the Hebrews to tell their story of creation is drawn to our attention as we also become conscious of those deep desires for goodness, truth, love and community which potentially well up in every human being. They are indeed the essence of the world's nature, and why it can rightly be called God's creation. Christians believe that the story of Jesus is the continuation of the story of God. As they begin to share the story they begin to lay down the foundations of a life of faith.

From the point of view of God, of course, it cannot be said that at some time in the history of God Jesus came into being. It is therefore true to say that Jesus, the Son of God, was pre-existent in the sense that what the church knows Jesus is in and for the world, is precisely who God is in his creating. Jesus, however, became part of creation and lived out his life in our history, thus declaring the presence of the Eternal God with God's whole creation and giving it new meaning. No matter what, as it were, since God is God, Creator and Redeemer, human nature will flourish. The church, by seeking to enjoy life in Christ by giving attention to God, is able to give form to her desire for God by engaging in conversation with him.

God as God is in God's self: the Holy Trinity

We are in a position now to claim that the fact of the possibility of this conversation is evidence of the triune nature of God. God's nature is to do, to create. God is Father, in the sense that historically the term has been used to express God's caring creativity. God is Son, in the sense that God actually shares the world of human experience in such a way that he reveals the true nature of human being and the commitment of God to make its fulfilment possible. God is Holy Spirit, in the sense that human experience bears witness to this possibility with sufficient regularity and persistence as to convince that creation is indeed imbued with the presence of God. God is who God is. As one might simply say, if you want God you will know that you already have God, for the wanting is itself prompted by the God who is wholly present as God, the Holy Spirit.

Rahner's restructuring of his theology around the central doctrine of the Trinity is illuminating here.[11] The Word is the other through which God expresses God's self; the Word therefore anticipates creation, but in such a way as to be clear that it is always God's intention to incarnate the Word and to build the human appreciation of what it is to be a human person around this divine reality. The economic and the immanent Trinity are one and the same person; there is no distinction between God as God is, and God as God is for his creation.

The doctrine of the Trinity is one way in which the out-flowing nature of God's being in the grace of active love is expressed in the church's understanding of God.

In Greek Orthodoxy the term *perichoresis* is used to refer to the coinherence of the persons of the Divine Trinity. That is to say, one cannot refer to one person of the Trinity without referring to them all, and yet each person has an identity that is consistently personal. What is more, by talking of the Trinity in terms of personhood it is intended to make plain the fact that their gracious mutuality of affection is not self-absorbing but always concerned to give attention to that which is other, because the well-being of the other for the other's own sake is what makes God to be God. It is not only possible for God to give attention to that which is other than God's self, it is God's nature.

God and love: reflexivity and coherence

The demands of such a God are not impossible, but they are large. They are personal in the best sense of that term; they involve our relationships with God, with ourselves, with one another and with the whole world. For if, as the church claims, human being is made in the image of God, it must be possible for human beings to follow Christ and give attention to the other.

Of course, were God's nature not love, it would not merely be difficult but simply impossible to do God's will. The natural imagination of the human mind works both to exaggerate the duties that have to be done and to limit the range of opportunity and choice that is open to us to fulfil those we have. This condition might be called 'sinful', since it covers the tendency to withhold the expression of affection to another if, as we often do, we anticipate the hurt we would experience were we to be rejected. For, make no mistake about it, in the event of such rejection it is the gift of the self that is rejected, not some physical boon. The feeling that inhibits affectionate behaviour is therefore thoroughly understandable even if in the light of what is implied about God and God's work in creation, it is unreasonable. When we believe, moreover, we can see the unreasonableness.

The sharp 'Kantian' insight of the marvellous spiritual director, Jean Pierre de Caussade, SJ (1675–1751) frees us to be ourselves. Our Lord's call to perfection must be a possibility, he urges, because he indeed calls us to it. Hence the importance of learning to discern God's will for us. As de Caussade wrote, 'If the state of your health does not permit you to go to Mass you are not required to go.'[12] Sound advice if there ever was any, which requires to be understood at many levels, not excluding the proper questions it raises about the nature of the Mass. But doing God's will is not always a grand matter; it may mean no more, but no less, than writing the letter we have intended for too long to write to a grandfather, or to pay the gas bill.

There is of course no room for complacency. One is equally inclined to ignore opportunities that will increase opportunities to do God's will. The church can never tire in well-doing and regularly needs to be roused from its lethargy. Like all other human institutions it is inclined to define its targets such that they can be achieved by the minimum effort. The purpose of the church is to give attention to God so that it can be reminded that it is suffused with God's loving presence and motivated to share in the establishment of the reign of God.

'Giving attention to God'

To give attention to something is not to be absorbed by it but to discern the true nature of what it is to which one is giving attention, so that what one gives attention to is liberated to nourish, sustain and inform one's own person. To attend to something properly is therefore not to any extent to confuse one's self with what one is attending to. In this context it is vital to underline the fact that God is not 'an object of worship'; God is not an object in any sense of the term. God is to be engaged with by giving attention to the stories which speak of God as creating and redeeming; to give attention to them is to attend to them and try to take up the conversation for ourselves. If we do this we will be 'trying to get' God, and can be said indeed to want God.

In the most focused sense, the storying with God is what is done in the Eucharist. Here Christ celebrates with all God's people, past, present and future,[13] on behalf of all creation, the continuing promise implicit in God's presence with God's people in God's world. The Church here does what God says (and does) and is sent out in the power of the spirit to love and serve the Lord.

The possibilities of conversation

A great deal has been made in this essay of the notion of conversation. If one thinks of it as merely 'utterance' in the sense of saying words, one is mistaken. For example, in an essay familiar to many French schoolchildren, Montaigne writes, 'Just as our mind is strengthened by contact with vigorous and well-ordered minds, so too it is impossible to overstate how much it loses and deteriorates by the continuous commerce and contact we have with mean and ailing ones'.[14] It is another case of 'rubbish in, rubbish out', and the search for excellence that is associated with intelligent engagement in conversation, whether with the minds of others gained through books and the arts, or in conversation with friends and associates. The implication is that by sharing in the conversation of the church with God one opens one's whole self to the possibility of personal transformation after the pattern of Christ.

Michael Oakeshott refers to education as 'The invitation to disentangle oneself, for a time, from the urgencies of the here and now and to listen to the conversations in which human beings forever seek to understand themselves'.[15] In my view this is a good way to approach one dimension of the way in which we come to understand what it is to be human and, *therefore,* Christian. For this to happen, there has to be both space and time. We as members of the community of faith, the church, provide in worship, in reflection and in prayer the time and space in which God can become part of our conversation and we can become part of God's conversation in Trinity. The amazing sensitivity that is found in the experience comes from the fact that a conversation involving God is not hierarchical. We are talked with, not down to; hence the appropriateness of the term 'conversation'. We are not simply told things; actually, given our human nature, we could not simply be told things, because in order to be able to hear and do what is being said, we have to exercise judgement if we are to come to understand it for ourselves. Of course, the non-hierarchical nature of the conversation with God is expressed perfectly in Jesus Christ, the incarnation of God.

The generosity that this implies on the part of God is to a degree covered by what Oakeshott has to say about a liberal education in which the many modes of experience engage with one another as individual personalities in a culture.

> Perhaps we may think of these components of a culture as voices, each the expression of a distinct and conditional understanding of the world and a distinct idiom of human self-understanding, and of the culture itself as these voices joined, in a conversation – an endless unrehearsed intellectual adventure in which, in imagination, we enter into a variety of modes of understanding the world and ourselves and are not disconcerted by the differences or dismayed by the inconclusiveness of it all. And perhaps we may recognise liberal learning as, above all else, an education in imagination, an initiation into the art of this conversation in which we learn to recognise the voices; to distinguish their different modes of utterance, to acquire the intellectual and moral habits appropriate to this conversational relationship and thus to make our *début dans la vie humaine*.[16]

The inclusiveness of this conversation, God and the world, makes for the possibility of eternal life.

Conclusion

To want God is to try to get God. If we do seek God, we shall find God. The research that is required involves us in joining in the creatively redemptive conversation of God with God's world.

> Blessing and honour, and thanksgiving and praise,
>   More than we can utter
>   More than we can conceive
> Be unto thee, O holy and glorious Trinity,
>   Father, Son, and Holy Spirit,
> By all angels, all men, all creatures,
>   For ever and ever.
>   (Lancelot Andrews)

Notes

1. 'Homo sum; humani nil a me alienum puto.' Terence, *Heautontimorumenos*, 1. i. 25.
2. Cf. Mt. 16.18; Col. 1.18; and possibly 1 Cor. 12.28; Eph. 1.21.
3. There is an illuminating review of the film by Peter Aspden in *FT Magazine*, 45 (6 March 2004): 8.
4. Gerard Manley Hopkins, 'God's Grandeur', *Poems of Gerard Manley Hopkins*, ed. Robert Bridges, 2nd edn with a critical introduction by Charles Williams (Oxford: Oxford University Press, 1937), p. 26.

5. The experience of the young St Francis de Sales was of a shocking situation in Paris during 1582–86. Bremond, quoting Amelote, refers to priests of the time as those, 'whose very name had become shameful and infamous and hardly used save to describe an ignorant and debauched person'. This account may be an exaggeration of the actual situation, but there is sufficient truth to take it seriously.

6. Thomas Aquinas, Qu. 3.

7. I accept the view of Raymond E. Brown, that while the *authority* that forms the basis of the gospel may very well be St John, he is unlikely to have been the writer. The school of St John incorporated much material from many sources into the 'finished' product, including the early Christian hymn found in Jn 1.1–18. The process, far from diminishing the significance of the gospel, enhances it because of the role of conversation in bringing it into existence. Cf. Raymond E. Brown, *The Gospel According to John*, vol. 1 (London: Geoffrey Chapman, 1971), pp. i–xii.

8. Timothy McDermott, *Summa Theologiae: A Concise Translation* (London: Eyre & Spottiswoode, 1989), p. 643.

9. Herbert McCabe, *God Matters*, (London: Geoffrey Chapman, 1987), p. 2.

10. Gen. 1.31ᵃ (AV).

11. Karl Rahner, 'Remarks on the Treatise *de Trinitate*', *Theological Investigations*, vol. 4 (London: Darton, Longman & Todd, 1966), pp. lxxxvii–civ.

12. Jean Pierre de Caussade, *Abandonment to Divine Providence*, trans. E. J. Strickland (Exeter: Catholic Records Press, 1922), p. 4.

13. As I understand the expression, this is what 'the Communion of Saints' means. The doctrine will repay particular study given its potential relevance to the transformation of individual human experience through the Internet and the implications of our global economy.

14. Michel de Montaigne, *The Complete Essays*, trans. M. A. Screech (London: Penguin Books, 1991), p. 1045.

15. Efraim Podoksik, *In Defence of Modernity: Vision and Philosophy in Michael Oakeshott* (Exeter: Imprint Academic, 2003), p. 211.

16. Michael Oakeshott, *The Voice of Liberal Learning* (New Haven, CT, and London: Yale University Press, 1989), pp. 38–9.

Chapter 2

THE WORLD AS CREATION: THE GOD-GIVEN CONTEXT OF GOD'S GLORY

Kenneth Wilson

Introduction

A great deal of our Western culture assumes that the Christian religion involves a belief that something foreign was introduced into our world at a particular point in history. Many people find absolutely no evidence for this and are therefore unbelieving. Furthermore, since our normal assumption is that evidence, if it is to be reasonable, will be empirical, by which we tend to mean essentially scientific, the chance of coming across evidence for this foreign element is not merely unlikely but impossible. Thought of in this way, however, many Christian believers, far from disagreeing, will be eager to confirm the view since they themselves ground their faith on direct revelation of God that by definition is beyond scientific enquiry and certainly involves the introduction of something from outside our normal experience. A church, based upon such an uninformative and uninterpretable belief, will at best be no more than a shelter from the wintry blasts of ordinary experience, a rescue machine saving souls from devilish storms, a *navis* adrift on the sea of life. Its apparent attractiveness to some is intelligible even to unbelievers, but irrelevant because unreal, unnatural and a consequence of self-deception.

Such a church, uncurious, un-enquiring and unlearned in human experience, keen only to add to its number, evolves fissiparously as it attempts to defend herself, while in every branch claiming to be the true vine or at least a part of it. In the absence of any open desire among church structures for real knowledge and wisdom, an innate desire for self-preservation leads each branch of the church to turn on others or on the world, or on both, or occasionally to seek allies from amongst themselves for the same reason. It is, as sociologists of organizations can only too easily demonstrate, a recipe for self-destruction.

This introverted ecclesiology is not the whole truth. Many theologians and some Churches reject it. It is, however, held by very many Christians and, I dare to say, is part of the common belief of the majority of those who are not. The purpose of this essay is to challenge this view and to affirm a more generous, open and delightful perspective on the nature, purpose and life of the church.

Beginning with God: identity, continuity and change

Any ecclesiology worth its salt has to begin with God, above all with what we believe to be true of God as God is in God's self. It is, of course, a conventional assumption of some theologies that nothing can be asserted of God as God is in God's self. At any rate nothing can be asserted, it is claimed, the truth or falsity of which can be reasonably debated. This seems to me to be plainly false. In a fine piece of ethical analysis, Robert Merrihew Adams argues with reference to Plato's *Symposium* that our experience of the beautiful as we know it in beautiful things, relationships or persons, is an experience of real beauty because it participates in a transcendent Beauty, distinguished from ordinary human experience of the beautiful by being eternal, unchangingly and unqualifiedly beautiful. The same may be said, he suggests, again with reference to Plato, only this time to the *Republic*, in connection with the more general excellence of the Good, of which beauty is at least a dimension. When we come across something as good, we recognize it to be so because it participates in a transcendent Good. The Good like Beauty is eternal, unchangingly and unqualifiedly Good. It is not to be confused with usefulness or happiness; it is above all a goodness that is worthy of love and admiration. Conceived of in this way, the Good is instantiated in the person of the Divine, God, who is therefore the unique source of all that is good and true and beautiful. Anything less would not be God. God would not be God if God were conceived of as cruel, suspicious, envious, or as suffering from major psychological disorders for which God needed to seek psychiatric help. It is by learning to appreciate the good, the true and the beautiful in ordinary everyday life, that we begin to participate intentionally or not in the reality that is the Divine.[1]

What is suggested here does not provide of course anything approaching a proof of the necessary existence of God; what it does is indicate what some of the necessary conditions are for God to be God. God must, of God's self, in God's aseity, independent of all other conditions and agents, be the instantiation of everything that is excellent, which we normally refer to as the Good. Whether God exists is a matter of experience not merely of logic, though if Colin McGinn is right it will interestingly be reasonable to say that when we predicate existence of any object or person including God we are indeed referring to a property even in the case of the existence of God, of God's instantiation.[2] This makes the further investigation of the qualities of God a potentially illuminating matter; indeed it could well give further stimulus to the study of the ontological argument in some of its various forms.

A striking feature of this conception of God is its coherence with the God of Christianity. God is person, eternal, unsurpassable in the excellences that are instantiated in God's nature, and unchanging. These are qualities of God, as Christians understand God that must influence the way we understand the coherence of the classical attributes of God. For reasons that are more to do with human psychology than they are with coherent thinking about the nature of God, conversation on the attributes tends always to begin with omnipotence. After all, it is natural for a human being to imagine that if only she had more power, she would be able to ignore the persons, powers, defects and deficiencies that prevent her from getting her own way. However, it is not clear that God getting God's own way whatever the circumstances, is consistent with the qualities of excellence that are properly attributed to God. 'Getting one's way' is often a sign of weakness, in the sense that it might indicate that a person is unwilling to engage in conversation about the desirability of the purpose she is intent upon achieving, about the range and depth of the knowledge and experience on which she is drawing to make her judgement, or more particularly the means by which it could best be achieved. There could, and in most situations should, be other situations of which the agent should be aware, most particularly including her knowledge of herself. If she knew herself better, she might be more willing to take other views into account, and learn to share responsibility, a *sine qua non* of effectively achieving any worthwhile purpose

In the case of God we must assume that if God is the source of all excellence, God's nature is such that it is not simply fulfilled by God getting God's own way. If God has a worthwhile project (and given the goodness of God we have to assume that any project which God had would be good) God will only achieve it by seeking the responsible partnership of at least one other.

Since knowledge, especially but not exclusively self-knowledge, is a key element in responsible judgement we would be wise to begin the discussion of the attributes of God with omniscience rather than with omnipotence. The understanding of what one means when one says of God that God is omniscient may also be influenced by natural human psychological reaction because one may be driven by the belief that if only we learned a little bit more we would know everything. It is easier, however, to gain insight from the human situation to deepen our understanding regarding omniscience when predicated of God than it is omnipotence. We are aware of our own ignorance and the vulnerability that flows from it. This knowledge arises from the many times when we have found ourselves behaving in ways we considered well-judged at the time but have subsequently come to understand were uncomfortably false to our own natures and where we did not do ourselves justice. It makes perfectly good sense in the light of experience to say that we have come to know ourselves better. The fact that we do not know ourselves completely and are unlikely ever to do so is a root reason of many of the mistaken judgements that we make; however, the fact that we can recognize our mistakes and bring into our consciousness our capacity for self-deception provides for the possibility of a growing awareness of our true natures. If God is the Good, in the sense that God is the fountain of all excellences, then such a claim cannot be made of God. Whatever else God knows God must know God's self if God is eternal, unchanging and only capable of acting in conformity with God's own nature. There can be no dimension of God's self that unforeseen circumstances could bring to light, and no aspects of God's self that are potentially in conflict with one another. God knows God's self utterly. God is at peace with God's self, a truth which Christian theology refers to as the Trinity, God in three persons.

The question arises as to whether God knows the future. Does God know all that is capable of being learned? Does God have information such that human persons are denied freedom to choose with regard to their own futures? For many the answer is obvious; if God is omniscient then God knows all that has happened, and will happen. Moreover, in order to be in possession of the past and future in this way, God must know everything that could be learned about the nature of creation, and since it is God's creation that is hardly surprising. However, it seems to me, the question is misleading, given that the primary context of God's knowing is God's knowledge of God's self. Indeed, the question is beside the point. Given that God knows God's self utterly and absolutely, whatever the circumstances as they transpire God will behave according to God's nature as the source of all that is Good, the instantiation of all excellencies, and thus bring about the perfection of God's purposes.

If, as I believe, God who instantiates the Good is omniscient in the sense outlined, it is reasonable to claim that God is indeed also omnipotent. The heart of God's omnipotence is that God is in charge of God's self and therefore responsible for God's own behaviour including God's motives: for this to be the case it is a necessary and sufficient condition that God is omniscient. Nothing has power over God in the sense that it could force God to act in a way that is contrary to God's nature. This is entirely consistent with the realization that because God is the instantiation of the Good, there are things which it would not be appropriate for God to do and which indeed in a significant sense it is impossible for God to do. For instance, it would be impossible for God to hate someone and attempt to destroy him. It would be impossible for God to intervene in a process in a radical new way in the light of God's discovery that things were not going according to plan. Hence, of course, Karl Rahner is correct when he affirms that the order of creation and the order of redemption historically are one and the same.[3] God's nature is to create redemptively; redemption is, as it were, God's method in creation.

God, who is Omniscient and Omnipotent, is therefore completely free precisely because God is not determined in God's origin or nature. God is God. So God's creating is an entirely free choice, unqualified and unconstrained by anything other than God's own nature. Furthermore, in creating, the only thing that God has in fact to give is God's very own self. To give oneself is what is meant fundamentally when one understands what it means to love someone. Hence the Christian claim that God in creating gives God's self in love to the other in order to make possible the success of the other. In doing this God reveals not only God's nature but also the nature of the other which God's love is bringing into being. Person can only give the presence of personal self to that which is itself capable of receiving personal life, which is why the Christian claims that the essence of the creation to which God has given God's self is itself personal. God is not, of course, described in Genesis as creating matter: the origin of matter is a scientific enquiry of very considerable interest and complexity, with which contemporary cosmologists are making steady if not dramatic progress.

Self-giving in love is not a simple matter. It carries with it the personal intention of bearing the burdens of the beloved in the sense of sympathetic understanding and responsible sharing. But exactly how the Creator and the creation can have such an intimate relationship while at the same time being so distinctly 'One' and

'Another' has been the source of much destructive as well as fruitful theological enquiry. The way that this is understood in Christian theology is precisely to bring into the open the fundamental misunderstanding that was alluded to in the introduction to this essay. There can be no question of intervention from outside, yet there can be no confusion either of the 'One' and 'Another'. It is at this point that christology becomes central to Christian faith and, as we shall see in a later section, to our understanding of the nature of the Church.

Jesus is the incarnation of God. He was born of a woman, suffered under Pontius Pilate, was crucified, dead and buried; on the third day he rose again, according to the Scriptures, and ascended into heaven where he sits on the right hand of God the Father Almighty. If we eliminate external intervention, magic and self-deception, what can we make of this poetic story? I suggest that by it we are affirming and making poetically explicit what has been implicit in the account of God and the world, creator and creation that has been developed above. Namely, that the Divine which many are mistakenly trying to find a way of reintroducing from outside has never in fact been absent. The contrary supposition, on which much of our life is based, is false and misleading.

The world, as created by God, is a world in which the totality of what it is for God to be God can be presumed without threat to the nature of what it is to be Creator and creation. Specifically, what it is for God to be God, namely personal being in full self-giving to the 'other', is capable of instantiation in all its glory. Indeed, it is impossible for the reality of this truth to be expunged. Hence, the birth, life, death, resurrection and ascension of Jesus whom we call the Christ, is in its singleness the final witness to the presence of God with God's world and with God's people. And if God is present in creation and in the person of Jesus, then no person can truthfully deny the reality of the same possibility for his or her life; any and every life can be lived in a fully personal manner whatever the experience to the contrary. We say that such a life is lived 'in Christ' in order to remind ourselves constantly of the deep fact of real knowledge in the context of the illusions which tempt us to live as if it was not true, thereby achieving what we believe falsely to be a competitive advantage. No more than it is for God, is the living of a life of self-giving love an easy work for human being.

God, as God is seen in Christ, is precisely the 'One' who is capable of sympathetic understanding and shared responsibility with 'Another', namely God's world, for the sake of the world's well-being. Actually in being this 'One', Jesus reveals the 'Other' the Divine nature of the world of which he is a dimension, and God's presence in creating as redemptive in its method. This is not in a most profound sense at all new. How could it be, since God's omniscience is such that God knew when freely choosing to create that God's nature was such that God was that loving presence which could and would bear the pain of constant redemptive creativity? The Old Testament calls it 'loving-kindness'; the New Testament talks of God's will being done on earth as it is in heaven; indeed, Jesus asks his disciples to pray that this be the case.

Such self-giving in love is a covenant in the sense that all the implied suffering of shared involvement with bringing about change for the better God willingly bears and invites human being to share. The Holy Spirit that God pours out on the world is the life-giving focus that God brings to the world at all times as evidence of God's presence. It is the personal presence which, in terms of Christian theology, makes possible the recognition of the beautiful that we enjoy as instantiating the Beauty that is eternal, and the good that we experience as embodying the Good, which are all in God, the instantiation of all excellences.

God is the 'One' who in relation with 'Another' is that God whose identity confirms in the unchangeable nature of God's eternal continuity the real presence of the possibility of change for 'Another', God's creation.

Creating, making and fulfilling

Word derivations are not always useful guides to the meaning of a concept since in principle they often offer no more than an introduction to the history of a word's use. However, in the case of the concept of creation the strands that lie behind the developing usage of the word 'create' in Christian theology do seem to be helpful.

The word found most frequently in the Septuagint and the New Testament is '*ktizein*' (perhaps the root *kshi* in Sanskrit) which carries the meaning of founding a city or colony, or of making habitable. (One should remember that colonies have founders and therefore have personal origins.) It carries a good deal of weight since it is common in Greek literature from Homer and Pindar to Herodotus and Thucydides. The Vulgate eschews *condere*, which would be the natural equivalent of *ktizein*, and prefers '*creare*', to beget, which seems to emphasize even more the personal nature of the activity which informs the emerging Christian understanding of the doctrine of creation. It does, however, give rise to or sustain the misleading tradition that identifies a primary association of Divine creation with event and beginning. Our contemporary understanding of the process of parenting gives additional perspectives that help to contextualize the significance of the term as process and participation. The word is used widely in the Romance languages. The Germanic languages use *Schöpfung*, which is best interpreted as meaning 'shape' or 'give form to'. In English usage the primary use of 'shape' is given as 'create, fashion or form', but interestingly, although still used of God, by the seventeenth century there is evidence that this is thought inappropriate.[4]

There is quite properly nothing here to support the notion of *creatio ex nihilo* so widely held by some to be the core meaning of the doctrine of creation. The origin of matter is outside the speculation of the Genesis story. The expression *ex nihilo*, when taken to imply this mistaken perspective, is better understood as having come into common use in theology as a consequence of the natural determination, already alluded to above, to base an understanding of God on the assumption that God's primary attribute is omnipotence. God's power includes the bringing into being of matter; this can be questioned while still letting 'God be God'. The story of creation as recounted in Genesis does of course employ the verb, *ba'ra'*, a verb almost uniquely used of the activity of God in creating: this fact has on occasions been used as a means of smuggling in the notion of *creatio ex nihilo*. It is as if, since only God can *ba'ra'*, there must be something unique about God's creating which sets it apart from all other creative activity, and this is only capable of being understood if we assume that God created the world in every perspective out of nothing; but this is not necessarily so. In any case, even the stories in Genesis do not talk of 'nothing' but of Chaos; the traditions discuss the context in which God works to bring into being the human being, made (*ba'ra*) in God's image.

Properly interpreted, the doctrine of *creatio ex nihilo* would be consistent with the underlying perspective that the divine nature is such that there is not anything that can cause God to be other than God is and therefore nothing that can cause God to behave in a way that is contrary to God's nature. Indeed, to build any understanding of God upon the assumption that 'God' could legitimately be the last term of a causal sequence of however many terms is to make not so much an empirical but a logical mistake. And, as we have seen, this fact about God's nature depends first and foremost upon the fact that God knows who God is utterly. Thus it is reasonable, as Jesus asks, that his disciples pray,

Our Father who art in heaven,
Hallowed be thy name,
Thy kingdom come,
Thy will be done
On earth as it is in heaven'
(Mt. 6.10)

with the genuine expectation and hope that 'neither death, nor life, nor angels, nor principalities, nor things present, nor things to come, nor powers, nor height, nor depth, nor anything else in all creation, will be able to separate us from the love of God in Christ Jesus' (Rom. 8. 38–39).

Hence the Chalcedonian Creed begins, 'We believe in one God, the Father almighty, maker of heaven and earth, of all things visible and invisible.' There is simply no thing of any kind in any conceivable place that can change God.

The implication of the claim that God creates is that since it *is* God, person, the source of Good, indeed of all excellences, who creates, and since God is present with the creation in Christ and in the Holy Spirit, it is undeniable that the world in which human being is evolving is, in all its dimensions of time and space, capable of being lovingly humanized, made habitable, and encultured with all the goodness that is God. The environment already exists which makes this possibility capable of fulfilment: that environment is indeed the result of God's gracious *creatio ex nihilo*, for apart from the activity of God there would be no real possibility that the world was of such a kind that it could be humanized – that is, made whole in and through Christ.

The good news is, therefore, that the fundamentally beneficent feelings towards the world and to other people that arise within all human beings are capable of fulfilment in sympathetic and cooperative action for the good of all: they are worth sustaining, encouraging and developing, so that we enjoy more and more the world which God has made possible, is making possible and will always make possible. In acknowledging a basic desire to do good, and recognizing it as something we want to do, it is appropriate that we should organize ourselves so that we can seriously set about trying to do.[5] Human being instantiates, as in a mirror darkly, the Good that is God, learns to love God for who God is and allows nothing to prevent the fulfilment of God's will for God's world. Indeed the Gospel is that nothing can frustrate it, in the end.

The bad news is that human beings can all too easily be discouraged in their pursuit of the Good and lose touch with any sense of personal value that gives sense and meaning to their lives. The result is that in the face of disappointment, misunderstanding and frustration they often give in to a sense of failure and abandon the attempt to do the good that they know in their hearts they desire. Actually the temptation to give up trying can be as strong when things are going well as it can when things are going badly. After all, if one has achieved notwithstanding the failures of others, enough human and material capital to survive with the opportunity of modest enjoyment, it will always be tempting to give in and to settle for what one has. At such moments of self-concern one will be focused upon oneself and not upon the transforming presence of God in Christ, with the consequence that one loses that sense of the Good that informs all that is worthwhile about the world: the upshot is that one will lose the will to give attention to the needs of others and the common good. But this common experience underlines the fact that anything that is personally worthwhile has to be worked at continuously. It was a teacher of mine who reminded his pupils again and again, 'if things are not getting better, you can bet your bottom dollar that they are getting worse'. It is true of everything, whether one is considering playing a rugby match, learning Latin, gardening, playing the violin or working to improve one's appreciation of Dante's *Divina Commedia*. If something is worthwhile, then it is worth learning to do it better.

On the other hand, when things go badly one is inclined to blame the world and to lose touch with the 'ground of our being'. Then one begins to think that the good which one thought one desired is either uninstantiatable, mere wish-fulfilment or at the very best only to be achieved in the face of enormous evil as a result of one's own efforts – usually at the expense of others. 'Competitive advantage' is what one seeks when one arrives at this position rather than the courage and personal awareness that will enable one to accept responsibility, bear witness to the truth in Christ and continue to try to reveal the presence of the loving God in the ordinary business of living.

It is important to remember that God did not promise that success would be easy. Success for human being comes through the work involved in the realization of eternal personal values – which is how one must interpret the fulfilment of God's purpose. That can never be easy. Indeed, how could it be? By definition all personal achievement, for human being as well as for God – is the consequence of collaborative enterprise: it is not even something which God could choose to do of God's self for God's self in God's own 'private' self, and in God's 'private' time. For this to be possible at all, there is required the revelation of God's self, the recognition on the part of God that the work was worth all of God's self, and the commitment of God's self to ensure that it would be done whatever the short-term but very real pain of suffering and misunderstanding. The key to it all was the knowledge of God's self that God has. In order to be able to cooperate with God to fulfil God's delightful purpose for the world, it will be necessary for human being to be able to grow in self-knowledge in order to know what it is genuinely to be 'persons-in relation' with the consequent analogous possibility of responsible self-giving in redemptive creating. The Christian gospel is that this is the case: we can come increasingly to know ourselves and share in the fulfilment of God's purpose for God's world.

Coming to know ourselves implies responding to the metaphysical impulse to 'make sense of things as a whole', to hold all our experience together. For many theologians this impulse has been regarded as an authentic if not the authentic religious aspiration.[6] It has a hollow ring in many contemporary ears because it suggests the possibility of a 'Grand Narrative', which postmodernism despises; and all who have been brutalized by the imposition of any ideology fear with much justice. However, this is to miss the point. The Grand Narrative in question here, if indeed there is such a thing, is better thought of as the active quest on the part of 'persons in relation' to uncover meaning and hold themselves together with regard to their experience, so that the story they tell 'makes sense'. This is a lifetime's work, and for the human race a journeying enquiry that will take the whole of time. But it is possible to make progress, and it is possible to anticipate success. This is the Kingdom of God: it is implicit in the claim of Christians that the world is a creation and not a happenstance.

The education of the world: finding one's self

There are at least five dimensions to satisfying the metaphysical impulse to 'make sense of things', a human enquiry towards 'coming to know one's self'. It is a process of learning that we may call 'the education of the world'. These dimensions are the physical world of sense data, the human story in historical time, the world of the imagination in all its aspects, the social and personal lives of human beings individually and in community – the ways we come to be responsible for ourselves and one another, and the larger personal world including the previous dimensions in which we attempt to pull things together understood as including God's real presence.

I shall have something briefly to say about each of them, but the first and most important thing to emphasize is that while each of these can independently be taken to be a complete account of the world of human experience, they overlap and interact, and actually constitute one world of human experience, which it is the intriguing task of the human being (mind, body and soul) to enter into, come to know, understand and enjoy for its own sake. The process whereby one comes to a growing knowledge of one's self is precisely constituted by the way or ways in which one works to make a coherent whole of our total experience. The process culminates in a narrative, constantly revised, developed and rethought that human beings tell themselves in order to place themselves in what they call 'the scheme of things'. And the preferred story as it evolves in the telling is discovered to be neither entirely consistent nor coherent, thus producing the stimulus to take steps to enquire for further insight. It is a hard and demanding task to work to accommodate new experience, new knowledge, new hopes and new ambitions.

Indeed it is in fact a hard business to recognize experience as new, for the natural impulse is to domesticate and package it in familiar material.[7] Change has never been easy for human beings to accommodate, yet positive movement in love towards the God who is the source of all that is 'the Good', is what enables human beings to find themselves as loving persons.

The apparent paradox is that in order to find our own selves we are required to work with others and especially to learn how best to give attention to their stories: not even this personal task of finding our selves is a thoroughly private affair. It involves a willingness to risk revealing ourselves, itself something that can be painful in its own right: the world as I struggle to understand it interrogates me as much as I interrogate the world. 'What does this mean?' invites the question, 'Who am I if I am beginning to understand what this means?' Perhaps it is in this essential capacity to be aware of our selves even as we seek to reveal our selves that we show ourselves to be made in the image of God.

I turn now to the many dimensions of the story: first, the day-to-day world of ordinary physical experience. A moment's reflection enables one to recognize that the day-to-day world of matter is far from ordinary. The physical world is certainly mysterious: it fills one with awe. Its biodiversity is truly astonishing. Of all known animals 85 per cent are arthropods: there are over 1.5 million known species of insect, with many more discovered and classified each year. Are there really 70 sextrillion stars in the universe, more than all the grains of sand on all the beaches of the world? How exactly does the physical biochemistry of the brain relate to the subtleties of understanding, feeling, self-consciousness and imagination thrown up in the human mind in all its dimensions? Can we learn how to supply the entire world's energy and water needs?

The questions have answers because, as we are just beginning to understand through the physical sciences, the world is open to reasonable enquiry through experiment and careful analysis of data. The results moreover can be used so as to offer the possibility of untold wealth, a term which is simply misunderstood if it is reduced to money, a mere medium of exchange. True wealth will come as the knowledge we gain delivers hope to all of that personal life which is God's purpose for the world.

However, we are also increasingly aware that we shall only be able to enjoy the wealth of our knowledge in comfort if we learn to treasure and share it. For that to occur we will have to learn to value knowledge and sharing for their own sakes. It appears we have some way to go in these regards; our experience tells us that our well-being is not simply a matter of commanding the physical resources of the world. The destruction of the community of humankind and nature mythologized in the story of the Fall, with its impression of a judgemental God, is replaced in the New Testament by a vision of a life-giving Tree of knowledge whose leaves are for the healing of the nations. What can be done will be done (Rev. 22.2). Understanding the world of human experience is not only a matter of coming to terms with the 'other' of the world but with ourselves as human beings with physical dimensions that are also aspects of the world.

Secondly, I turn to the story of the human race: it is in historical time exciting and depressing, disturbing and encouraging. We at last understand that no story of human being could be complete which did not include an account of the intimate relationship which human being has with the material world. We constitute an integral part of it; some would say the human race constitutes its most advanced expression in evolutionary terms. This is increasingly open to enquiry. But while the current understanding of the physical world including the human race is clearly a most important dimension of the human story, it does not itself provide all the clues to who or what we are. Groups, tribes, families, communities, societies, classes, races, nations, etc. have wanted to take into account their interpretation of their relationship with the physical world and to tell their own stories with regard to their own sense of identity and in relation to one another. They have developed their own myths in order to explain their origins or justify their claims to power. Such myths are far from meaningless; they help a group (however constituted) to find itself in the telling of its story and its continuation in its own time.

Historical enquiry, for long unique in the panoply of intellectual disciplines by dint of having no discrete technical language though obviously drawing on those of many others, has begun to open up these worlds of experience to internal and comparative analysis. The very nature of its language facilitates the historian's ability to get at a total picture of human life in the world. The picture is always changing because the perspective from which the historian writes is inevitably partial because of the historian's own personal experience and life situation, but also necessarily partial in the sense that each day adds enormously to the number of perspectives which can be brought to bear on any event or series of them. 'Explanations' evolve as the time-line grows, the political geography of the environment changes, technical resources increase to enable new sources of evidence to be better examined, and historians by dint of novel and imaginative approaches bring fresh insights to bear on otherwise familiar material. Above all the community of historical scholarship that informs debate will by its conversation stimulate leaps of understanding and temporize in coming to terms with previously accepted conclusions.

Moreover, in writing or reading what historians write, the question of meaning is bound to be raised. Can the forces of history be directed by the conscious choice of appropriate policies? Are there inevitabilities implicit so that all human being can sensibly do is to adjust behaviour in their light? Does our knowledge and experience of the human story show human being to be anything other than an animal like other animals? Historical enquiry does not solve the human enquiry but gives rise to another dimension of questioning; to avoid it is paradoxically to shorten the horizon and limit our vision.[8]

Thirdly, the history of human being includes many attempts, through the development of social, economic and political structures by means of which individual societies have sought to become responsible for their lives together. Attempts have been made to classify them, analyse them comparatively, and trace their development, the most distinguished perhaps by S. E. Finer, though sadly he did not live long enough to bring his retirement project to its intended conclusion.[9] In principle he regards the history of government as an account of the evolution of the state with its structures for decision-making usually organized round the palace, the forum, the nobility or the church. These hardly ever exist in their pure form, but the classification helps to organize not merely the Western experience but all systems of government. The rashness of Finer's claim has been questioned in principle as well as in detail. However, the point I wish to emphasize is that wherever in the world there has been a human society, it has sought to organize itself in one way or another in order to be responsible, accountable and effective. In political terms the accountability may be to a God, to a palace or court which all too frequently attribute their power to a God, a nobility or an aristocracy which attributed its privileges to an assumed superiority of intelligence, racial distinctiveness, or the providential and inevitable course of events, or to the people. Even in the latter case, the people may not be thought of as all the people, but defined in such a way as to exclude (for example) women, the poor, children, people of other tribes or races, etc.

The fundamental question seems to revolve around the following considerations: How can we, consistent with the myriad ways that a state might choose to define itself, be true to our traditions, maintain our authority and work in our own interests? Given the situation in which we find ourselves, and the future as we imagine it at any one time to be, how far can we do this of and for ourselves? How far do we have to assume that one person's good will necessarily need to take into account the desires and interests of all other persons and communities? How far does a well-run nation have to take account of the needs of other nations if it is to be successful in the long term? To what extent, indeed, can we ignore the well-being of the physical world of which we increasingly realize we are an integral element?

From time to time, societies will be able to learn from experience and as a result of conscious learning and the accidental course of events, evolve fruitfully; at others they will find themselves dominated by ideologies that preclude the possibility of questioning the worthwhileness of their own institutions, relationships and policies. In one sense it may be argued that the history of political institutions is concerned with the evolution of attempts to regulate and bring into effective partnership the needs of the community and the needs of the individual. This question is one that has always to be faced since there is no obvious answer that will suit all times and all circumstances.

Particular dimensions of strategic planning and political accountability are facilitated by the development of economics. Since there are certain basic goods that every human being needs and a constantly fluctuating relationship between the availability of these resources and the number who demand them in a competitive environment, it was vital that we found means whereby to calculate reasonably accurately the relationship of supply and demand. The result has been huge technical changes in the patterns of investment, the means of production and distribution that have provoked the current debate about the respective virtues of centrally planned and capitalist economies. It is important to keep this question in mind because whereas there are goods such as defence and public order which it is difficult to place in private hands, the role and relationship of the public and private in other areas of life such as health and education, capital investment, financial regulation, scientific research or land-ownership will always be a matter of debate. Maintaining the possibility of choosing between different approaches at different periods of history and in different societies will be important for the future well-being of the human race. Ideological approaches to these problems are no more likely to be illuminating for our economic and social welfare than fundamentalist theologies are for creative religious faith.

Moreover, if we are to develop political, economic and social institutions capable of meeting the needs of all, the contemporary reawakening of the sense of being a global society, with the special dimension of a global economic system brought about by rapid technological change, requires us to ask the question in a profoundly new way. There will be no complete solution, only the continuous possibility of taking account of new approaches and new possibilities in the light of a sense of failure, as at each period of history some people and some nations find themselves excluded from sharing in the common good.[10] 'Could do better', will be the regular report on every economic system, whether global, national or local. In order to realize its genuine humanity, the human race will always be looking for new strategies.

If the human story has been facilitated by knowledge of the physical world, of the history of human societies, and by the ways in which from time to time human societies have sought to meet their needs by becoming accountable for themselves and their world, then it has been transformed by the visionary stimuli offered by the human imagination. If the worlds of nature, or human history, or the processes of human management of their own affairs, while independent for useful pedagogical and intellectual purposes, can only be told sensibly when put together, the worlds of the imagination have to be seen as intimately working at every level of consciousness in all the processes of learning and reflection to offer insight, fresh questions and new dimensions as yet unexplored. There would be no scientific explanations, no mathematical equations, no understanding of history or of economic development without the imagination. Indeed it would be true to say that human beings would be unable to engage in intelligent rational enquiry at all, were it not for the comparative perspectives thrown up by the working of the human imagination.

It would be easy to fall for the view that the imagination is a vehicle of deception because it proposes impossible combinations that can seduce us into chancing our arm with unreasonable experiment. However, it is the very fact that the exercise of the imagination can bring dimensions of our experience into relation with one another which otherwise we would have kept apart that makes for original insight, and glimpses of new worlds of experience in which to place what we already know with all the potential for transformed understanding. We have seen the value of this many times. For example, in the way Darwin put the evidence together which led to the reformulation of the theory of evolution, now consistently tested, challenged and in process of being proven in practice; or the way in which Wiles pursued his schoolboy dream of solving Fermat's last theorem.

And this is apart from what we usually call art. The French Impressionist painter Claude Monet (1840–1926) opens up not just a superficially entertaining world of colour, but by the use of colour remakes the world we perceive, and questions our understanding of it. He makes its translucent nature clearer than it was before. The German Expressionist painter Ernst Ludwig Kirchner (1880–1945), in response to developments in science, literature and philosophy, shows us (particularly in his city works) a heightened awareness of individual and community. The threat to individual integrity and therefore the very possibility of art is revealed in his awful self-portrait in uniform with his right hand amputated. The English sculptor Henry Moore (1898–1986) focused on the integrity of the relationship between mind and matter, emotion and form, through his technical skill in (as he thought), 'liberating' his sculptures from the stone in which they were imprisoned or getting them to flow from his hand onto the paper. This is especially so in his many presentations of Mother and Child.[11]

But the reality of art is not confined to the intellectual dimension. Poetry, music, drama, the novel, as well as painting, sculpture and garden design, invite an intrinsic intimacy through the interpenetrative expression of and release of feeling. In a significant sense a work of art, whatever the medium, may be said to be a revelation of the artist; he or she gives himself or herself to the work. And this is done with particular abandon because in the last resort there is nothing the artist can do to determine the response of the listener, viewer, reader or performer to the work. Indeed, the more artists attempt to control readers or viewers, the less likely they are to show them anything. The primary reason is that the attempt to control inhibits the ability to reveal, on which depends absolutely the possibility of creating a real work of art.

It is apparent that one needs care in handling this dimension of human nature. Plato appreciated the potential danger. He wished to exclude art from the curriculum of the Guardians' education because for Plato, a picture was a copy of a representation and therefore likely to be doubly misleading. The peril was therefore all the more threatening, since the artist was inclined to attempt to speak directly to a person's feelings, thus bypassing the intellect and causing behaviour which was instinctive and not thought through by the intellect.[12]

Wordsworth, while well understanding this danger, believed on the contrary that the imagination offered the most wholesome and whole fulfilment of effective thinking. He wrote of

> Imagination, which, in truth,
> Is but another name for absolute power
> And clearest insight, amplitude of mind,
> And Reason in her most exalted mood.[13]

The imagination shows the wonderful liberty – and therefore power – with which the human mind is endowed. It is true that through its unlimited capacity for untutored speculation the imagination can destroy the possibility of true judgement and tempt us to run after false gods. It needs to be disciplined, ordered and inspired by focusing ourselves on the abundant desire for the life-giving target of God as found in truth, beauty and justice. The Good, which is God, needs to be kept in mind so that the love of God will allow us to bring to bear the power of the imagination to remove the bonds of fear and loneliness that will otherwise frustrate our fundamental desire to do what is lovely and of good report.[14]

Wordsworth understood this. Hence in the passage partly quoted above he wrote: -

By love subsists
All lasting grandeur, by pervading love;
That gone, we are as dust. – Behold the fields
In balmy spring-time full of rising flowers
And joyous creatures; see that pair, the lamb
And the lamb's mother, and their tender ways
Shall touch thee to the heart; thou callest this love,
And not inaptly so, for love it is,
Far as it carries thee. In some green bower
Rest, and be not alone, but have thou there
The One who is thy choice of all the world:
There linger, listening, gazing, with delight
Impassioned, but delight how pitiable!
Unless this love by a still higher love
Be hallowed, love that breathes not without awe;
Love that adores, but on the knees of prayer,
By heaven inspired; that frees from chains the soul,
Bearing, in union with the purest, best,
Of earth-born passions, on the wings of praise
A mutual tribute to the Almighty's Throne.

This spiritual Love acts not nor can exist
Without Imagination, which, in truth,
Is but another name for absolute power
And clearest insight, amplitude of mind,
And Reason in her most exalted mood.
This faculty hath been the feeding source
Of our long labour: we have traced the stream
From the blind cavern whence is faintly heard
Its natal murmur; followed it to light
And open day; accompanied its course
Among the ways of Nature, for a time
Lost sight of it bewildered and engulphed:
Then given it greeting as it rose once more
In strength, reflecting from its placid breast
The works of man and face of human life;
And lastly, from its progress have we drawn
Faith in life endless, the sustaining thought
Of human Being, Eternity, and God.

Imagination having been our theme,
So also hath that intellectual Love,
For they are each in each, and cannot stand
Individually.[15]

Fourthly, there are the questions that are raised about us. What is this humanity, given that a human being is capable of understanding the world through the careful organization of sense data? What is the human brain that it can not only organize the data of the senses but also so imagine an extension of the human capacity to 'experience' the world and make sense of the data by devising machines. What is the significance, if any, of the stories that we tell to situate ourselves in space and time? How is it that we can so organize ourselves together that we are capable in principle of acting responsibly and bringing about changes that improve our lives? What are we, if we can enjoy the world fully and grow in knowledge of ourselves as a result?

There are many approaches, philosophical, psychological, sociological amongst them, all of which have something to contribute to the discussion, yet there always remains the question of the total person, and of the total human experience. Colin McGinn claims that the human mind is constituted to raise questions about human nature which it is vitally important to go on asking because they are irreducible features of the human situation, but which the human mind is simply not equipped to answer.[16]

I can understand this point of view, and indeed share it to a degree. However, the questions point to dimensions of what it is to be human which we have to come to terms with. There is, for example, the awareness of others, which arouses a new sense of one's own self, and promotes the desire to appreciate another person as person, not as object or thing precisely because the encounter with the other person has made one aware that one is one's self and not a thing or an object. The impression we have goes even beyond this into the essentially moral world of relationships because of the sense we have as persons, that persons are to be respected, loved and collaborated with, which stimulates further questions of our selves and of the selves of others. What is it to be a good human person and not just an effectively successful human body? There is a wholeness about the self which we recognize to be brittle, vulnerable and easily diminished by destructive experience. Moreover, once broken, it is extremely hard to put the self back together: it is, it seems, beyond the power of any individual on his own and depends upon another person beginning to treat the 'broken' person as a whole person once more. Healing does not simply require the treatment of a symptom, but the enlivening of a person through personal relationship so that he or she can begin all over again to take responsibility for himself or herself.

Denis Donoghue takes a similar view regarding the nature of Beauty. In the presence of a beautiful object or person we are drawn first of all, quite simply to appreciate it: only then do we set about the task of wondering why. The conversation we have with ourselves and share with others is better regarded as an attempt to enhance our capacity to enjoy Beauty and recognize it rather than analyse it.[17] For this to be a realistic understanding we have to learn to give attention to the wholeness that is Beauty, in such a way that it will reveal itself and nourish our capacity for the affection that alone gives life to what is essentially beautiful, and the fulfilment of ourselves as persons whole and entire.

Lastly, there is the perspective in which we try to hold things together. The desire to do this is a natural impulse rather than an acquired characteristic: a matter of nature rather than nurture. Most persons if not all, apply themselves to the task of holding things together, of making coherent sense of their lives in one way or another. Sometimes, of course, one can be drawn to a reductionist solution so that a part is taken and defined as the whole: scientism, aestheticism, historical determinism would all be cases in point. But even here the very fact that the partial approach is defined as the whole bears testimony to the importance of satisfying the impulse to glimpse the whole.

Ruskin felt passionately about this, and frequently bore testimony to it in his lectures: 'Not only is there only one way of *doing* things rightly, but there is only one way of *seeing* them, and that is, seeing the whole of them, without any choice, or more intense perception of one point than another, owing to our special idiosyncrasies'.[18] Learning to appreciate fine art involves the whole person, he said, since: 'FINE ART is that in which the hand, the head and the *heart* of man go together'.[19]

The context in which the Christian tradition places itself is one that includes God, God's redemptively creative presence in Jesus, whom we call the Christ, and the transformation that this promises through the presence of the Holy Spirit. In raw intellectual terms the Trinity, as thus alluded to, provokes the insight that human fulfilment rests on knowledge, experience and skill. The Christian claim and hope is that these in turn are only possible for human kind because they reflect and share in the work of God, Father, Son and Holy Spirit, who is committed to the success of God's world. The ambitious curiosity, desire to experiment and will to acquire the skills necessary for the imaginative application of what one learns with which we find ourselves endowed, are evidence of the God-given nature of what it is to be human. The innate desire of every human being to be an affectionate person reflects the fact that the Person who is God is indeed capable of finding expression in the world; we are not deceived in following our best instincts.

The whole perspective of human vitality provided by the Christian faith is both an explanation of how and why it is possible to understand the world, why we want to find ways of cooperating in order to make it more personally fulfilling and why we take delight in what is beautiful and just, and a vision that we can work towards. It is not of course a complete picture, let alone a final account of it; the story of God's redemptive creativity is in progress because we are a part of it. We cooperate with it, or frustrate it by the way in which we use our growing knowledge of the world, build developable institutions, social, economic and political, through which we can grow in accountability, tell stories about our human history, exercise our imaginations and become responsible for our past, present and future through attending to the sense of ourselves which emerges when we put all these dimensions together in a larger picture.

The church: celebration of the Kingdom

At this point, the question may well be asked: 'What has this to do with the nature of the church?' To which one might reply: 'Everything, for the institution in which Christians hold all this together in the presence of God, celebrate the truth of it, formally and informally, and on behalf of all people and all creation offer it to God in expectation of being made whole is the One, Holy, Catholic and Apostolic

Church.' In the church, Christians enjoy the unity they long for, and work for the unity yet to be achieved. The church is the community of conversation, shared with the whole world and including all things, begun by God in creation, encouraged by God in Christ, and sustained by God in the Holy Spirit. The Trinity of hope, on which the church is focused and in which humanity shares through knowledge, experience and skill is God, Father, Son and Holy Spirit.

The Christian faith affirms God to be the absolute Good. God is Personal Being, wholly committed in love with all its cost to the success of what God has begun in creating, whose world must therefore be personal since it has received God's whole personal revelation in Christ. Whatever the experience we may endure on a day-to-day basis, the world in which we are set is a God-given environment capable of being transformed after the pattern of the life of Christ. This is what the church is called to be – the lively and present society transforming the world after the pattern of Christ.

The church is a community of faithful people, past, present and future, which in the context of the real world of ordinary human experience believes that this transformation is not only possible but also under way because it began in creation. The church in its dynamic life incorporates an intellectual, aesthetic and moral dimension; the community of faith is learning about God's world, enjoying God's world and living God's life in the world. Its approach is to take advantage of the results of all well-founded enquiries and, while knowing perfectly well that the task is never-ending, to reflect upon their significance for faith. In talking of faith in this way, the church means to attend to the question, 'Given that this is how we have best to think through and interpret our experience in this God-given world, how can we so live as to enhance our capacity as human beings to live personal lives together?' For the intention of the church is to live so as to become consciously aware in community and personal life, of the Good, the Just and the Beautiful in which unconsciously, it believes, all persons share because of the nature of the Creation as revealed by God in Christ. In doing this, it will be able to become more response-able and therefore more responsible for working in partnership with God's redemptive creativity and even to provide the opportunity whereby others may become conscious of the same truth, and desire to join in bringing to fruition the purpose of God.

The action of the church is, first, to celebrate this world of God's making in all its dimensions and give thanks to God for it. This is in contradistinction to William Blake's conviction, based upon his own interpretation of his experience, that the spiritual world was superior in every respect to the material and capable of being known independently of the physical world. Thus he could write:

Since all the riches of this world
May be gifts from the Devil and earthly kings,
I should suspect that I worshipp'd the devil
If I thank'd my God for worldly things.[20]

Since he thought the world innately barbarous and destructive of the real human nature that was profoundly love, he thanked his God that:

The Angel that presided o'er my birth,
Said, 'Little creature, formed of joy and mirth,
Go, love without the help of anything on earth.'[21]

An ecclesiology to be true to the nature of God in the church must be based upon a contrary assumption. Notwithstanding the fact that it makes room for the spiritual, the earthly and earthy church is the embodiment in the world of the work effected by God in Christ, whom it receives as the incarnation of the living God. Through its holy life, encouraged by the Spirit, all persons are called to see that the world we want is the world we can have. It underlines the fact that the work which we do in coming to terms with our world, in trying to understanding our physical environment, telling the human story to ourselves and one another, learning how to become responsible for the well-being of our world, ourselves and one another, enjoying the stimulus, beauty and delight (and sometimes embarrassment) of our imaginations, is a beginning of that gaining of self-consciousness which enables us to share in God's self-giving which is God's redemptive creativity. It is in this capacity for self-giving of ourselves in order to share in the revelation of the personal nature of the world and others, that we may be said to share the *imago dei*. The church is indeed in no way separate from the world, but the self-conscious focus of all the world's endeavour, its knowledge, its history, its self-conscious awareness, its affectionate ambition, its beauty, its fear, its love, its joy and sadness, in those who want to try to work with the intention of translating their experience into the wholeness of Christ.

The sacramental life, especially as found in the eucharist, is the fullest expression of this affirmation. For it is in the sacramental life that there is affirmed the goodness and beauty of creation, God's redemptive creativity, God's real presence, the intelligibility of human experience, the possibility of intelligent moral purpose, and the assurance that life for and with God in Christ, is ultimately life pure and simple in the eternal presence of God. The reading of Scripture brings a congregation in touch with some of the dimensions of the conversation that God engages in with the creation: a conversation that is developed by the preaching in the minds and hearts of those present. The story is performed in the church's representative offering in Christ of the world and all that it is, past, present and future; there can be no doubt that there is involved in this celebration all that the human being is and can become. The making real of the possibility of human faithfulness to God's redemptive creativity, is the foundation of the sending-out into the world to do God's will. The eucharist is a genuine – real – 'bringing to mind' of the fact of God's presence with God's people, in the knowledge of which there is nothing that can frustrate us in the end. 'If God is for us, who is against us?' (Rom. 8.31).

The eucharist is, of course, also a judgement on the church and the world because in celebrating our common humanity as creatures in the presence of the Creator, we will, through God's grace, both be enabled to recognize the injustice of our actual relationships and given the grace to renew them.

The church, through its worship, puts itself in the right position to be able to give full attention to the person of God, to know itself forgiven and so to gain nourishment from the divine self-giving that education through experience of the world offers. Because all can know in some measure, whether consciously and unconsciously, the God of truth and justice and beauty, and because everything that is good or true or beautiful, shares in the reality of God, the church can willingly cooperate with all persons of goodwill, of whatever faith or none, to reveal the love of God. However, in order to have the courage to do this honestly, it has self-consciously to work at its own life, its thinking, its behaviour, its institutions and its theology, in order that they instantiate more affectionately, more inclusively, the love of God in Christ. There is no final solution; no continuing city, no comfortable resting-place for the church apart from Christ, for the work is always directed towards God who makes all things new.

However, the church, grounded in the reality of Jesus's humanity as well as sharing in the divine nature of Christ *is*, like the world of God's creation, perfectible not perfected. The church therefore (apparently paradoxically, but in fact really) shares fully in the world's failure; it is easily discouraged and inclined to fall back on a forlorn attempt to seize power in order to achieve its purposes, rather than to bear witness to God's self-emptying in love. It is only when it recognizes this seductive stance to be a delusion that it is driven back in sacramental celebration to stand before God as creature in the presence of the Creator; then it is at its most powerful. It is impossible for the broken church to put itself together; it is as impossible for the church to do so in its own strength as it is for any broken human being. Hence in eucharistic celebration, before the church is able to make its confession, it is reminded of the transforming beauty of God's real presence and loved back to life. God's presence is not conditional upon the Church's confession, but the very condition of the possibility that the church is able to make a confession. Paradoxically, however, it is only when the church is honestly aware of its own need, that it is driven to a position to be able to recognize the presence of God in Christ, and only then is it in a position to ask questions about what it means. As Donoghue says in his account of Beauty: one becomes aware of being in the presence of something beautiful before asking oneself what is beautiful about it. So also the church itself becomes aware of being in the presence of God before it asks what it means and tries to find the language in which to engage others in conversation about it. Christ is the church's one foundation, not the fact of the church a necessary condition of the presence of Christ.

The church only exists because God in Christ has shown the personal nature of God's creative purpose. The church only exists because St Peter and the disciples saw the face of God in Jesus. The church only exists because St Paul was driven to his knees by the presence of God in the Risen Christ. The church, as a divine and human society, in conversation with the Father through the Son and in the Holy Spirit, can rightly be said to be the Body of Christ. It is the community of God representatively inclusive of all people, all created thing, and all true relationships. The church does not make things happen; it points to the truth of God in Christ whereby all can know that everything has already happened that needs to happen if all people are to enjoy the fulfilling of God's purpose in God's creation. In its joyful celebration of God's presence with God's people, it cannot but celebrate God's presence with all of God's world and all God's people. It offers all to God in

Christ in thanksgiving, in joy, in hope, in full confidence of the things that are to come.

Conclusion: celebration in peace and joy

If the reality of the church's life is indeed as I claim, all the greater is the pity of the church's present fearful condition in that it does not apparently act as if it is true. But if it is true, as I believe, there is no reason why we cannot learn to do so, and thus become truly the church, the Body of Christ. For it to be the case we must encourage one another to think a little harder about what it means to acknowledge that we are aware of being in God's presence in the world. We must want to grow in understanding of the world's nature as creation. We shall have to give more attention to the conversations whereby we come to appreciate increasingly the wholeness of things. We shall have to try harder to be ourselves for Christ's sake. In becoming more response-able we will also want to become more responsible, thus making for a more just world. We shall have to listen more graciously to one another. We shall have to attend with greater seriousness to our histories, both communal and personal. We shall need to become more tolerant and more realistic about our personal desires, misleading and destructive as they often are.

For this to be possible we shall have to enjoy ourselves rather more than we do: we shall have to follow the psalmist and 'taste and see that the Lord *is* good' (Ps. 34.8a). We shall have to learn what it is to trust and love one another more: every healthy person actually wants to do this. We shall have to learn to love and not despise ourselves: God already loves us in Christ.

The life of the church is where these things can be learned, where God is trusted and where we can be ourselves. To recognize this and participate in its life is to be able to celebrate the fact of our humanity and our experience of the beauty of the world in peace and joy: it is to look on the face of God in Christ and live.

Notes

1. Robert Merrihew Adams, *Finite and Infinite Goods* (New York: Oxford University Press, 1999), pp. 13–49.
2. Colin McGinn, *Logical Properties* (Oxford: Clarendon Press, 2000), pp. 15–51.
3. Karl Rahner, 'The Order of Redemption within the Order of Creation', *The Christian Commitment* (New York: Sheed & Ward, 1963), pp. 38–74.
4. Cf. '*God makes and the Tailor shapes*', s.v. *shape*, Oxford English Dictionary.
5. It is intriguing that Anscombe should say that the primitive sign of wanting is 'trying to get'. Elizabeth Anscombe, *Intention* (Oxford: Basil Blackwell, 1957), p. 67.
6. John Macmurray, John Baillie and John Oman would be cases in point. It is significant that Macmurray's Gifford Lectures, '*The Self as Agent*', and '*Persons in Relation*' should recently have been republished with new introductions (Oxford: Humanities Press, 1991). Cf. Adam Hood, *Baillie, Oman and Macmurray: Experience and Religious Belief* (Aldershot: Ashgate, 2003). To this idiosyncratic Scottish group of twentieth-century theologians, should be added, for example, Karl Rahner and Bernard Lonergan, from their widely contrasting perspectives.

7. Kuhn was surely right when he pointed out how the professional world of the scientist, so apparently open to new ideas and 'progress', was actually organized by the very way in which peer group review took place to make it difficult for radically new ideas even to gain publication. In one sense the fact that it is hard would be a good thing if it meant that radical ideas receive careful scrutiny, but Kuhn's view was that this was not always the case (cf. F. Kuhn and S. Thomas, *The Structure of Scientific Revolutions* [Chicago, IL: Chicago University Press, 1962]). Of course, theology, which so many (especially those who are without faith?) regard as incapable of development, and nothing more than a system organized to rule out the possibility of genuine thought, finds it even more difficult to make room for the possibility of development, let alone radical ideas. But in theology, as in any other form of human imaginative enquiry that seeks to come to terms with ordinary changing human experience, the possibility of new insights leading to new conceptualization is always likely.

8. For a stimulating contemporary reflection see J. C. D. Clark, *Our Shadowed Present: Modernism, Postmodernism and History* (London: Atlantic Books, 2003).

9. S. E. Finer, *The History of Government*, 3 vols (Oxford: Oxford University Press, 1997).

10. Globalization is not new, neither is a global economy: what is new is the combination of technological innovation, political authority, economic power, cultural imperialism and military might to such an extent in one power that a genuinely global empire is imaginable. The danger is that many will assume it to be inevitable, whereas in fact it is ultimately impossible to bring to fruition because of the inventiveness, freedom of conscience and self-consciousness of the human person.

11. See catalogue to the exhibition, *Mother and Child: The Art of Henry Moore* (Hempstead, NY: Hofstra Museum, 1987). Moore's focus on the theme was life-long: it is represented amongst his first and last works.

12. Plato, *Republic*, Bk X.

13. William Wordsworth, *The Prelude*, ed. J. C. Maxwell (Harmondsworth: Penguin, 1971), Bk xiv, l. 190.

14. St Paul in his letter to the Philippians, talks of 'having the same mind which was in Christ'; he is anxious to underline the fact that such a commitment, while fulfilling of our human nature because it is in conformity with the will of God, makes huge demands on us as well as on God (cf. Phil. 11.1–13).

15. Wordsworth, *The Prelude*, ll. 168–209

16. Colin McGinn, *Problems in Philosophy: The Limits of Enquiry* (Oxford: Basil Blackwell, 1991).

17. Denis Donoghue, *Speaking of Beauty* (Newhaven, CT, and London: Yale University Press, 2003), pp. 21–56.

18. John Ruskin, 'The Two Paths', lecture ii, in John Ruskin, *Sesame and Lilies* (London: J. M. Dent, Everyman Library, 1907; repr. 1944), p. 120.

19. Ruskin, 'The Two Paths', p. 118.

20. William Blake, Gnomic Verses, in *Complete Writings of William Blake*, ed. Geoffrey Keynes (Oxford: Oxford University Press, 1966), p. 557.

21. Blake, *Gnomic Verses*, p. 557.

PART II

ENCOUNTERING CHRIST

Chapter 3

THE ENLIGHTENMENT AND CERTAINTY: THE HUMILITY OF THE CHURCH

Kenneth Wilson

Introduction

'Logic is a Greek discovery'.[1] The laws of thought, the rules of argument, even when carried through as cogently as Aristotle described them and later logicians have developed them, do not of themselves guarantee the truth of their conclusions. Certainty requires more than can be provided by mere perspicuous argument.

On what else could the foundations of knowledge be based? The Pre-Socratics believed that the solution lay in the identification of some fundamental matter, allusion to which was essential if any explanation was to be reasonable. There was serious argument but no agreement about what it could be. Thales believed the base material to be water, Heraclitus fire, Anaximenes air. Parmenides held an apparently contemporary view: thought and speech must have an object. He believed therefore that the existence of a single, unchanging, coherent world could safely be assumed and, potentially, fully explored, given the coherence of meaningful discourse. Such securities, of course, raise as many questions as they resolve; certainties in any fundamental sense seem lost in mystery.

However, later Greek philosophers, Socrates himself, Plato and Aristotle for example, nevertheless considered that there were matters of which they believed themselves to be certain, beyond a peradventure. What they required to explain to their own satisfaction was how, in a world where change was (apparently) the normal day-to-day experience in life, there could be such a thing as stability, even certainty. To what could this consistency be attributed?

Plato claimed that the accuracy of human perception, of which he had no doubt materially, was attributable to the soul's pre-existence in a world where there was intimate knowledge of things-in-themselves. Thus the appearance of, for example, a dog or a table, in ordinary perception, triggered the percipient to recollect the *real* dog or table that the soul had previously known. For Aristotle, the only thing of which one could be (reasonably) certain, is the existence of a physical individual, for example a horse or a chair, for it is from the fact of such individuals that we are, by means of language and attention to the rules of logic, able to sort experiences into classes which it is necessary to do if our understanding of the world is to grow.

Such certainties underlie the possibility of intelligible change, a matter that was very familiar to Aristotle given his illuminating attention to the study of biology.

When we come to recent discussion we find ourselves in a totally different world. Richard Rorty is regarded by many to have revolutionized the study of philosophy. He, as he points out, is said to have abandoned any search for truth and in place of the traditional distinction between reality and appearance he wishes to substitute useful and useless.[2] In place of epistemology, the search for the foundations of knowledge, he would like to talk of hermeneutics; this is not, he avers, in order to replace epistemology with a new discipline, but rather to preserve the assumption that there is no one useful foundation on which to base certain knowledge. This seemingly conversational point should not be dismissed as swiftly as some would like: it should be taken with the greatest seriousness. In a post-Enlightenment world, where any suggestion of a 'grand narrative' in any sense, is fundamentally questioned, the possibility of identifying, even of sensibly looking for, 'the foundations of knowledge' is itself open to dispute. Moreover, surely philosophical enquiry can be valuable if it is useful.

By the same token, the status of theological enquiry and the role of religion would surely be enhanced and not diminished if it could also be shown to be useful. Of course, this would require a reconsideration of the nature of certainty and truth as (commonly) applied in religion, but it would not imply the unreasonableness of holding a point of view sincerely and firmly.

Unreasonable religious certainty has been the occasion of much human misery over the centuries, and it still is. A recent letter to the press points to the inconvenient public assumptions that undermine the possibility of intelligent public discussion of religion in general and Christianity in particular.[3]

> It is entirely laudable that all of us should seek to be accepting and understanding of difference in all walks of life. However, a fact which political correctness will not address is that religions and religious creeds by their very nature are mind control systems with absolutist claims. Whether the source of revelation is the Talmud, the Gospels or the Koran, each one claims final and unique truth, which automatically means the others at best are partial, at worst, false, and thus no possible agreement can be reached.
>
> Fundamentalism is only one step further along this disastrous road. Creeds, religions and belief systems close the mind. Enslavement to holy books and their commands automatically closes the mind, and enmity for other creeds is thus never far away.[4]

Careful attention to a creed, a religion or a belief system requires precisely that one be not *enslaved* to any of them. Obedience implies understanding, understanding implies intelligent enquiry, and intelligent enquiry requires freedom to enquire.

The purpose of this essay is to discuss the meaning and relevance of certainty in the post-Enlightenment world that we now enjoy, and to evaluate its importance for the church's self-understanding. I shall argue that the church in its claim to embody truth, especially the truth of God as revealed in Christ, will do well to embody the virtue of humility as evinced in the life and work of Jesus. The church as the Body of Christ must live his bodily life as well as celebrate the fruits of his death.

Revelation and experience

In the minds of many Christians, and even more in the minds of those who are not Christians, revelation implies above all the guarantee by supernatural means of the truth of statements that would otherwise at best be beyond investigation, at worst obviously false to any reasonable person. In fact, it is nothing of the kind.

Two things need to be stated clearly. First, revelation implies a dynamic relationship between persons, experience of which offers the possibility of learning things that are beyond conclusive and final resolution by enquiry. In this sense it is a 'whole experience' that cannot be meaningfully fragmented into parts, because in principle there are none. Hence of course, for the Christian, as for Jew and Muslim, God is one, indivisible and unchanging, knowledge of whom is *therefore* capable of growth. Indeed, properly understood, no person is divisible, human or divine: to consider it so is a category mistake. The experience of being in love, for example, is a mutual experience of wholeness, which nevertheless offers each person growth in understanding, self-awareness and delight.

Secondly, therefore, revelation is the doctrine that, far from guaranteeing the truth of some proposition or experience mysteriously communicated, draws attention to the fact that whatever one believes one knows there is more to learn, so much more indeed that what one thought one knew may turn out in the end to be so hopelessly inadequate as to have been misleading. Whether this approach to the doctrine is true of religions other than Christianity, Islam for example, is open to question.

I turn to a brief consideration of Aquinas (?1225–74). The Angelic Doctor, while he acknowledged the primacy of revelation gave due weight in his consideration of theology to human intellectual capacities and underscored the importance of philosophy and the sciences for theology. He understood that revelation attached itself to life by virtue of human experience, while experience would be meaningless apart from revelation. Revelation and experience were in a significant manner coherent and interdependent. Moreover, given that God in God's nature assumes all the perfections, and that God must therefore above all be good, Aquinas found it inconceivable that God would 'keep his knowledge of himself to himself and never give himself intimately, for goodness of itself is generous'.[5]

Two aspects of revelation are clear to Aquinas, without God's intention to reveal God's self, human being would have no knowledge of God. However, without the aid of the senses and the mind, human being would not be able to recognize what it is to have revealed knowledge of God. It is as if the doctrine of revelation for Aquinas is a dimension of pastoral theology. God of God's own nature is such that God wills to be known. Humankind of its nature is of such a kind that it desires to know all the perfections – that is to know and love God. Human enquiry, however, even if possible in principle, would take so much time that few human beings would have the possibility of making progress towards God; in making God's self available, God therefore both acknowledges the gap between the human and the divine, and in so doing bridges it.

These are the grounds for the development of the doctrines of the Incarnation and the Trinity. Far from providing certainties by means of revelation, these doctrines are questions continuously stimulating human enquiry about the nature and meaning of the experience provided by the senses and the consequent wholeness of the relationship suggested to the mind between human being and the 'ground' of the totality of the world with which human being is coming to terms in the process of living life. The doctrine of revelation recognizes the dynamic nature of the relationship that underlies the willingness of God to be known and the natural desire of humankind to know God. The only certainty here is the certainty of the possibility of wisdom and that, in Thomist terms, means the possibility by grace of *scientia divina*.[6]

St Robert Bellarmine (1542–1621) was a major figure of the Counter-Reformation and a theologian of considerable stature. The truth of revelation was axiomatic as far as he was concerned. But his approach to controversy and its meaning was reasonableness, courtesy and sound judgement; he did not seek simply to slay opponents with power and prejudice. His intelligent engagement with Galileo is a case in point. There may be certainty in the biblical revelation, but its meaning may require careful discernment because the form of expression may be according to the ordinary way of speaking and not itself therefore a technical statement to be taken literally. The sun may truly, for example, be said in common speech to move, but the implication that it moves round a stationary earth could still turn out to be false.[7] Bellarmine understood that the language of the Bible was open to interpretation. Moreover, while Galileo, given his naïvely realist approach to scientific hypotheses, was unable to accept that what he had discovered might be open to revision in the light of new evidence, Bellarmine believed that all scientific enquiry remained tentative.

In respect of political theory too, Bellarmine held to reason. It is true that the Pope has an authority to care for human souls that is derived directly from God: indeed the Pope alone has an authority that is directly God-given. But this does not mean that papal authority can legitimately be exercised over everything and everyone. Therefore, for example, he did not support the doctrine of the divine right of kings, rather holding that the authority of the civil power came in the first place directly from the people; he rejected any suggestion that the Pope could legitimately wield direct political power in the secular domain, or that a king was in some sense the vicar of the Pope since his authority was derived from him. Indeed, the Pope's secular authority was indirect, Bellarmine believed, and he could only intervene justly in the affairs of a civil power if the souls of the people were endangered by the actions of the civil authority. But in such cases, too, the people themselves were free to withdraw their allegiance and revolt.

Descartes

It is a matter of controversy whether Descartes should be regarded as the first of the modern philosophers or the last of the medieval: while he is something of both, he is more the modern thinker than the medieval scholastic. His interest in the emergence of scientific understanding introduced him to the untrustworthiness of the empirical world and related questions. He became possessed by a radical doubt that he sought to resolve by establishing human knowledge on unshakeable and secure grounds. Moreover, while in the event his approach to the problems of radical doubt led him to ground his confidence in what he knew on the existence of God, the manner in which he tackled the problem and the nature of the world that he took as the focus of his enquiry were certainly modern.

While it is true to say that the medieval period had from time to time been aware of the importance of careful observation in any discussion about the natural world, it is to the seventeenth century that we must look for the pre-eminence of science as we have come to know and value it.[8] Descartes' intrigued puzzling was stimulated by his familiarity with the success of the scientific method, above all with the insights which flowed from the application of mathematics to human enquiry about the world, and the nature of the world which the method was uncovering. Since from his Christian conviction he believed that there was but one world, he was driven to look for ways of holding experience together in one explanatory system.[9]

He had two aspects to bring together. On the one hand he was impressed by the certainties of mathematics and on the other, by the dubieties and, as he saw it, the potential, perhaps devilish, deceptions of empirical experience. Indeed, so impressed was he by the indubitability of mathematical enquiry, that he was driven to look for analogous certainties on which to ground his knowledge of the material world. He found the basic certainty of existence in his sense of himself as a thinking person when he was thinking, the so-called *cogito ergo sum* (I am thinking and so I must exist). Moreover, so certain was he of the perfection of this thought when he thought it that he could not bring himself to doubt it: he certainly existed. But whence the source of such perfection of perception since he knew himself to be susceptible to the possibility of deception at every point? Only God, the source of all perfections, could be the origin of such perfection, and since God is indivisibly one, he had from the knowledge of the certainty of his own existence certain knowledge of the existence of God, too.

There was still the perplexity of holding together what has become known as *Cartesian duality*: body and mind, the material and the spiritual. A human being was both body and spirit, though oddly body was, according to Descartes, not necessary to him as a thinking being. However, since spirit occupies neither space nor time, and material was defined as having extension, a 'natural' means of linking them had to be imagined. Descartes found – not by empirical enquiry! – or at least proposed, that the link was in the pineal gland, where the minute activity of the spirit acted coherently upon the body like a pilot in a ship.

The feel of Descartes' argumentation is clearly modern, but there is a reluctance to challenge orthodox religious belief, and occasionally even an explicit reference to the authority of the Church. A case in point is his response to Arnaud on transubstantiation. Arnaud accuses Descartes of conflict with the traditional doctrine of the Eucharist because he does not recognize the possibility of real accidents. After some preliminary remarks, Descartes writes:

> Lastly, my saying that modes are not intelligible apart from some substance for them to inhere in should not be taken to imply any denial that they can be separated from a substance by the power of God; for I firmly insist and believe that many things can be brought about by God which we are incapable of understanding.[10]

Yet the explanation that Descartes offers of the nature of transubstantiation attempts not only to show that he is orthodox, but that it is the very subtleties of science that make the doctrine intelligible. Thus, he suggests, while the perception which we have is so entirely of the surface of the bread and wine, there is so much space in it that there exists the possibility of changing the substance without there being any perceptible impact upon the surface condition.

> Now the teaching of the Church in the Council of Trent session 13, canons 2 and 4 is that 'the whole substance of the bread is changed into the substance of the body of Our Lord Christ while the form of the bread remains unaltered'. Here I do not see what can be meant by the 'form' of the bread if not the surface that is common to the individual particles of the bread and the bodies which surround them.
> ...And everyone who believes that the bread is changed into the body of Christ also supposes that this body of Christ is precisely contained within the same surface that would contain the bread were it present. Christ's body, however, is not supposed to be present in a place strictly speaking, but to be present 'sacramentally and with that form of existence which we cannot express in words but nonetheless, when our thoughts are illuminated by faith, can understand to be possible with God, and in which we should most steadfastly believe'. All these matters are so neatly and correctly explained by means of my principles that I have no reason to fear that anything here will give the slightest offence to orthodox theologians; on the contrary I am confident that I will receive their hearty thanks for putting forward opinions in physics which are far more in accord with theology than those commonly accepted.[11]

To make plain matters plainer, however, Descartes affirms his rejection of real accidents and calls any continuing flirtation with the theory 'irrational, incomprehensible and hazardous for the faith'; he looks forward to the time when his 'theory will be accepted in its place as certain and indubitable'.[12] There may be those, he says, who having failed to refute him by rational argument, will fall back on holy scripture and revealed truth as if this will help. On the contrary, in a revealing remark, Descartes observes, 'To try to use the authority of the Church in order to subvert the truth in this way is surely the height of impiety.'[13]

Descartes sits comfortably with the outcomes of his reasoning because he believes that he has found good grounds to be certain of his own existence, and consequently of the existence of God. Moreover, because he holds a dualistic position over body and soul, but believes he has found a way consistent with physics to hold them together, he is able to 'explain' the nature of transubstantiation to his own satisfaction. However, one feels, if the authority of the Church's teaching on specific doctrines is to be believable, morally or intellectually, it will need to be supported by good reason based upon experience. The emerging questions of eighteenth-century empiricism challenge the very possibility of such support.

The Enlightenment

One might say that the philosophers of the Enlightenment both believed knowledge was dependent upon perception, and accepted the truth of Protagoras' dictum that 'man is the measure of all things'.[14] Hence we notice the critical importance for the British empiricists, and for Kant, of epistemological questions. On what can we securely ground the knowledge that we believe ourselves to be gaining of the world through experiment? What does this have to say about the limits of human knowledge? Are there implications for faith, for the role and nature of the church and for the possibility of knowledge and experience of God? The questions concern the nature of experience, the role of reason and the basis of authority.

Locke devoutly believed that humankind lived in a God-given world and had some expectation of an afterlife in another. He wanted to know what sort of things God had put within reach of human enquiry, and was of the opinion that they were all the product of sense experience: he denied the existence of innate ideas. So, beyond the reporting of the clear and distinct simple idea associated with a sense datum, there was nothing of which Locke believed the human mind could be certain. Attention, therefore, to the foundation of human understanding was essential since, 'All men are liable to error; and most men are, in many points, by passion or interest, under temptation to it.'[15] The possibility of error led Locke to develop the epistemological doctrine of degrees of assent in respect of every proposition that one was invited to believe or which one proposed to oneself. Indeed, a person's love of truth – which was a necessary condition of making progress towards knowledge – would be judged by the extent to which in each case he proportioned his assent to the strength of the evidence.[16]

Locke remains faithful to his position when it comes to the matter of revelation. He distinguishes carefully between reason and faith and is insistent on the importance of the distinction. A statement based upon reason will be held with a conviction related to the strength of the evidence that can be adduced in its support.

> Faith, on the other side, is the assent to any proposition, not thus made out by the deductions of reason, but upon the credit of the proposer, as coming from God, in some extraordinary way of communication. This way of discovering truths to men we call *revelation*.[17]

Locke is quite clear that this reference to 'some extraordinary way of communication', and to the proposer as God, does not open the possibility of the
revelation of anything that is contrary to intuitive sense. 'Nothing that is contrary
to, and inconsistent with, the clear and self-evident dictates of reason, has a right to
be urged or assented to as a matter of faith, wherein reason hath nothing to do.'[18]
Moreover, even where he admits that the authority of God, who cannot err, must
be acknowledged in respect of revelation that it is beyond the power of the human
mind to discover for itself, it is necessary both that reason judge whether the
revelation be *divine* revelation, and what it means.

> But yet, it still belongs to reason to judge of the truth of its being revelation, and of the
> signification of the words wherein it is delivered. Indeed, if anything shall be thought
> revelation which is contrary to the plain principles of reason, and the evident
> knowledge the mind has of its own clear and distinct ideas; there reason must be
> hearkened to, as to a matter within its province. [19]

Hence, of course, quite apart from the moral argument in favour of religious
toleration, Locke has an equally important and critical epistemological argument.
If we cannot put any proposition, whether revealed or not, beyond the
peradventure of doubt, we shall be unjustified in requiring others to assent to a
revealed proposition on the authority of personal testimony. Such authority is
specious.[20] Knowledge, which every person desires, depends for its growth on the
reasonableness of *all* belief: this is no less true in the case of revelation than it is of
empirical theories.

David Hume did not take to his enquiries the same assumptions that
underpinned Locke's thinking: he had no sense of a God or therefore of a world
which was in some sense or another God-given. Hume was of the clear opinion
that the human mind had nothing on which to rely other than the evidence of its
senses: thus his view of religion was that it had an entirely natural origin.[21] He
believed that the idea of God was the creation of the human mind in the light of
reflection upon the ordinary experience of the order in the world, its power and
truth. There was no independent a priori evidence for the existence of God which
could stand up to reasonable enquiry, though by the same token the existence of
God as some form of intelligence to account for the order found in the universe
could not be disproved. Were such a God to exist it added nothing to the power of
human understanding.

Since any God who might be said to exist is a natural development,[22] there is no
need of, indeed any room for or possibility of, supernatural revelation by some
mysterious means of divine self-communication. 'We have no idea of the Supreme
Being but what we learn from reflection on our own faculties.'[23] The implication
of this for the immateriality of the soul or miracles is clear: there is no evidence for
them, because in terms of ordinary sense impressions they simply make no sense.
Nevertheless, Hume asserts, given that there is no other way of accounting for it,
the truth of religion depends upon the illusory miraculous. He writes at the end of
his essay *Of Miracles* in pleasant scorn:

So that, upon the whole, we may conclude, that the *Christian Religion* not only was at first attended with miracles, but even to this day cannot be believed by any reasonable person without one. Mere reason is insufficient to convince us of its veracity: and whoever is moved by *faith* to assent to it, is conscious of a continued miracle in his own person, which subverts all the principles of his understanding, and gives him a determination to believe what is most contrary to custom and experience.[24]

In view of his approach to the idea of God, it is understandable that Hume should write of the *natural* history of religion.[25] In tracing its history he declared monotheism to be morally inferior to what he calls polytheism, which in Humean terms must be construed as a type of atheism. The point was that since no religion could be based upon anything other than irrational prejudice, unthinking enthusiasm or superstition, monotheism was almost certainly going to be intolerant and give rise to immorality and violence. Atheism, at least in the form of polytheism, was on the other hand likely to be open to new ideas and fresh insights, and moreover, focused upon the limits of human nature and its essential well-being. In the light of the current fanaticisms of some adherents of religion, there must be many in the world today who have reason to share this view.[26] One must keep in mind the fact that any good or worthwhile project can be perverted for false ends; religion is no exception.

For Hume, the only certainty is that there is no certainty. However, the world of the natural sciences offers the best evidence for the existence of the material world, even if it provides none for the existence of anything one may regard as the spirit, or most particularly the self. There is, however, with both Locke and Hume emerging a sense of a common story to be told regarding the nature of human life, which is based upon sense experience, the capacity of the mind to organize experience, and the capacity to test hypotheses in experience. The Enlightenment is in full swing, and Deism rampant; in so far as there was any room for religion in this scheme at all it was not mysterious. Hume may himself have been talking through his character Cleanthes when he said: 'The proper office of religion is to regulate the heart of men, humanize their conduct, infuse the spirit of temperance, order and obedience.'[27]

One might say therefore that for Hume, any worth in the Christian religion required that the church work to inspire the population of the country to behave well to one another and to respect the power and limits of reason. The truth of Christianity was essentially a moral matter, and therefore in principle empirically verifiable. The ethics of Christian community have not hitherto been sufficiently examined but are of the first importance. While the truth of the faith will not be demonstrated by the moral character and moral relevance of the church, without a church inspired by the desire to be morally relevant, most will actually *experience* the Christian religion to be irrelevant and unbelievable – even if, *per impossibile*, it turned out to be true on other grounds.

Kant thought religion could be true on other grounds, but it is a moot point whether he regarded them as certain, and if so what was certain about them. In his first Critique,[28] Kant rejected the idea that thought of itself could provide assurance of the existence of the highest being. Anything that existed must have some sensible presence to stimulate enquiry, and if so then the assertion that 'x existed' added nothing to the claim for sense experience. So any metaphysical statement was beyond the possibility of investigation by reason. On this basis Kant found creeds, metaphysical beliefs, doctrines and activities such as prayer associated with them, to be of no significance.

Kant, however, had a problem. Convinced as he was of the importance of the moral life, he needed to find grounds for his belief. His controversial answer is found in his second Critique, and the volume he published in 1792 and revised later in 1794.[29] Every reasonable person, he claimed, experienced an interior sense of obligation, which itself provided the substance and drive for his commitment to moral behaviour. There was an absolute imperative to do what was moral, which Kant understood to be whatever one willed to be done by every like person in similar circumstances. However, an obligation existed only when an individual had the power to fulfil it, and it seemed that much of what one felt an obligation to achieve and which one might think to be properly required of a reasonable person was nevertheless beyond one's capacity. But since there was no denying the reality of the obligation, Kant believed there could be no denying the possibility of its fulfilment. Clearly the obligation, for example, to repay a debt to one's parents, could not be fulfilled in this life after their death; there must therefore be an immortal life if one was to make sense of the obligation. Moreover, since the guaranteeing of an immortal life was not possible for a mere human, the requirement that obligation could only be fulfilled in an afterlife required a power to guarantee it, which could only be God. Thus Kant claimed he had on the basis of the undeniable and sensible interior experience of the categorical imperative, established by reason alone, the requirements of freedom, an afterlife and the existence of an Eternal Being. This is not, as Kant is careful to point out in the Preface to the *Critique of Practical Reason*, a proof based upon pure reason, but is the *subjective* requirement of the experience of the categorical imperative.[30]

The notion of certainty here is profoundly interior. It is an interiority which one becomes aware of for oneself in the experiencing of it and which one can only share with others after the event. Such certainties are always arguable, though they are in a significant sense real. An indication that Kant was well aware of this is suggested by the role in his system that he attributed to the church. Objective laws can be legislated for by the will of the people, and indeed can only be so legislated for. The demands of the categorical imperative, however, were not of obedience to the law of the state, but to the moral law. Hence the need for a moral community to bear witness to the moral law which is what he understood the church to be. The church was not, of course, a metaphysical body, nor could it be described in traditional Christian language, for example, as 'the Body of Christ'. Rather the church is an ethical community under the power of ethical laws that are directed to promote the morality of actions, which is something internal and incapable of being imposed by human law. Such an ethical community can only be the result of 'legislation' by an ethical ruler of which there is a class of one, namely 'God'.

The communal nature of the personal confidence which gives rise to the freedom of reason to enquire after moral truth and to do it, is striking. In Kant there is now expressed the fruitful combination of the three dimensions of the

Enlightenment in full flower. Sense experience provides the basis of all genuine knowledge; reason the means whereby sense experienced can be organized, argued about and put in a form to be confirmed, and the individual put in command of his or her own world so that responsibility can be fully accepted and acted upon. Their interaction brings about a common worldview, common human experience and the possibility built upon in nineteenth-century optimism of a world of universal peace.[31]

Bertrand Russell (1872–1970) took a new direction: he sought certainty by working to ground mathematics in what he fondly thought was the indubitable nature of logic. He was not confident that our knowledge of the external world was soundly based on empirical data. Indeed he seems to have believed that, as in the case of mathematics, we could only work back from the results to the necessary conditions for the results. Thus the truth of any developed scientific theory depended upon the logical constituents of reality, namely fundamental sense data such as 'red patch here'. In the case of both mathematics and knowledge of the external world he believed that the fundamental realities were logical. Hence he collaborated with Whitehead with the ambition of deducing mathematics from logic, and devoted himself to the development of 'logical atomism'.[32] Following Kant, therefore, Russell believed that we could have no knowledge of things in themselves, only of the conditions which provide for confidence in the conditions which make experience and knowledge about it reasonable and consistent.

The certainties of Enlightenment optimism had come to a pretty pass if all we could be sure of was the logical atomic material provided by a sense datum and the confidence which flowed from the security of mathematical argument deduced as it was from five axioms and simple rules of deduction. However, even this was brought into question by Kurt Gödel's work. He published in 1931 a proof that has been argued about ever since.[33] He showed that in any system of arithmetic such as Russell/Whitehead there is at least one well-formed formula that is unprovable within the system. Suppose we accept that this is the case, then the security of mathematics – even simple arithmetic – is shattered since proof can only be provided by the additional of the unprovable formula within the axiomatic set which thereby becomes infinitely expandable. If neither empirical data nor mathematics can provide for certainty, where was one to look? Where was the grand narrative now?

Revelation and the appeal to history

For the church the situation was critical. It appeared that there could be no external guarantee of the ground of faith on which it believed it was established. To what could the church refer as providing evidence of the truth of the Gospel? The Enlightenment had brought into question the truth of a faith based upon the assertion of miracle, or of revelation. Both required the intervention of something beyond into the here and now: a dimension that was simply not intelligible given the nature of the world as it had come to be known. But if there was no external evidence in the sense that it could be demonstrated 'scientifically', what of the nature of historical enquiry? Could the historical be understood as somehow including both the 'beyond' and 'the here and now' so that the question of intervention would be replaced by a search for common understanding? Could there be an inner personal and therefore communal and potentially public experience within the historical process of the reality that was God? In what sense could this be fleshed out in human experience, and shown to be consistent with the changing sense of the self as the Enlightenment considered it?[34]

It was William Temple who claimed that Christianity was the most materialist of religions. For him that meant that the creation was of such a kind that God could be incarnated in Christ, and that death could be triumphed over in the Resurrection. Moreover, the church as the material embodiment of this real understanding of history had a profound role not just in the spiritual but also in the material, especially political, world of everyday experience and public affairs. The two realms, in so far as the reference to two was appropriate at all, were so interdependent as to be inseparable. This did not imply external intervention but discernment, so that (for example) revelation for Temple was the result of the exercise of imaginative human reason upon events. The events were not themselves the revelation; the revelation arose through the interaction of the human mind and the event.[35] The most profound interaction had taken place in the person of Jesus Christ, to whom the church attributed its origin and on whose life it based its life.[36]

The certainty on which Temple grounded his faith was experiential in the sense that it was the continuing life of the church through its worship and public witness that encouraged faith. There was no short cut: work was required, theological, practical, political and moral if the truth of Christ were to be apprehended and the presence of God enjoyed.

Historical experience, historical enquiry and the nature of history itself were matters for serious intellectual concern. Simple belief in the historicity of the Old Testament had long since been reinterpreted in the light of the rediscovery of Jewish history and the history of the Middle East; historical enquiry about the first centuries AD and BC had also given rise to new approaches to the New Testament. Archaeological discoveries, reassessments of Roman history and new understandings of the early history of the Christian church had led to the undermining of any confidence that historical research *per se* could throw up reasons for believing that Jesus Christ was the Son of God or even that he had risen from the dead.

Derrida and Foucault: truth, politics and power

History was vital in the making of human traditions. Indeed, it could condition if not exactly determine the sense of themselves that human beings possessed. The contrasting approaches of Foucault and Derrida bring together reactions to the collapse of the Enlightenment ideal. If there is no overarching narrative, no human story which all humanity can aspire to understand and learn to share, what can be said about the human condition?

Jacques Derrida (1930–2004) draws attention to the fundamental distinction between language and philosophy.[37] Language, he asserts, says far more than philosophers realize; by the sheer fact of writing and formally recording their ideas on paper philosophers define and limit the range of language in a way which speech does not allow. The Truth, with a capital *T*, for which philosophers strive, is in fact merely the product of writing which is nothing more nor less than the means whereby power is asserted within a hierarchical structure. Hence we have the association of writing with law, with oppression, with definition, with limitation and essentially with the denial of freedom. The result is that Truth has withdrawn in the face of such aggression, leaving the human with the local enquiring that arises from personal statement and the many implications of the ambiguities, nice distinctions, indeterminacy and metaphor of ordinary speech.

The effect of Derrida's thesis is to disassociate the human individual from the truth that is expressed in the ambiguities of human speech because he regards what is said as the product of cultural forces and styles of communication that are beyond the immediate apprehension of the individual speaker. A consequence is that the individual may find the freedom of expression that belongs to him, which enables him to become conscious of his situation and to seek truth. This latter is most important to affirm because Derrida is too easily accused, and wrongly so, of having no interest in truth: on the contrary, he affirms the unknowability of The Truth, while retaining and indeed emphasizing the vital importance to human well-being of truth and the search for it.

Michel Foucault (1926–84) believed that the human being's sense of himself was a product of the cultural environment in which he was set but that he possessed a radical freedom to challenge the structures. The church, he argued, accepted what it believed to be the universal and necessary bases of human experience and established its authority on the confessional and a hierarchical power structure. What Foucault was concerned to identify within any such commanding cultural structure was the role of the contingent, the particular, the personal, the individual. It is intriguing for our present purpose to note his belief that while the style of theology is itself grounded in an appreciation of the role of the human being in the world, once one realizes the freedom open to the individual, theology is liberated to play a central role in history because it can be a medium of challenge to the structures, and a means whereby liberation can be achieved for the human being. Thus for Foucault, mysticism constitutes the first real challenge to the status quo. But whereas for many such an assertion would open up the question of other worlds or at least other dimensions, for Foucault, since the human experiences the mystical in human history, human spirituality must therefore be totally embodied in the historical and is essentially a *political* exercise; it is a means whereby use of language frees the individual to think and be himself. This explains in some part, for example, Foucault's intriguing interest in the revolution of Khomeini in Iran and his sensitivity to the person of Jesus Christ, while being critical of the domination of the church – as he saw it.[38] In both cases, as it were, it was the religious language and the theological claims that provided the framework for the apparently unreasonable challenge to the 'Western' wealth of the Shah and his backers and of the Christian church to the overwhelming power of Rome. The consequences were political, but the vision and the stimulus came via a dimension of thought that entertained the possibility of doing what was obviously humanly out of the question. In a sense, it is revolution that appropriately follows *Aufklärung* (Enlightenment). Kant might have recognized that the use of the term was justified intellectually, but not politically.[39]

The church: centralization, authority and truth

It may seem that we have come a long way from the search for the foundations of knowledge only to find ourselves in the midst of personal intrigue, political posturing and power-seeking. However, the impression is illusory. There has of course been a fundamental shift in the identification of the locus where the foundation should be located. Whereas it was the Enlightenment task to locate it in the firm knowledge of the material world, it is now more frequently sought in the person and the sense that, with others, he or she makes of the experience open to them. But of course one should not forget that Kant, the most significant philosopher of the Enlightenment, found the basis of his sense of self and the nature of the personal in the Categorical Imperative, which was the common experience, he believed, of every human person.

Parallel to the developments consequent upon the Enlightenment, the church has sought for loci of basic security in herself, her sense of identity and her mission. The mistaken notion of separation has been fundamental to this development, and is so still. The church instead of seeing herself as the expression of the truth about the nature of creation, embodying God's redemptive creativity in the celebration of her life in Christ, has become a political structure determined to maintain her difference and establish her power. The opportunity to do so has been enormously increased by the enhancement of communication, first via the railway system, then by air routes and now more sinisterly through the medium of the Internet which makes possible the instantaneous delivery of decisions or policy-statements to all parts of the world.[40]

The claim to know, and not to require 'other' evidence, even to claim revelations that are somehow communicated but in principle unverifiable or even discussable, once the mark of the sects, is now sadly all too easily associated with the mainstream churches. But statements which are not discussable are not simply implausible but incredible, because they are not capable of being embodied and taken into personal thinking; this is hardly surprising since it has been decided on the authority of the church after all, that they are not part of the public experience of ordinary human beings. And if not part of public experience they cannot be argued for, but only imposed. What we are now finding is that such unthought-out authority is no authority at all; it has no power beyond itself.

By contrast, a view of the church which holds it to be the public embodiment of the faith that the world is the world of God's creatively redemptive presence, means that the truth which it knows is coherent with the truth that we human beings know of the world and the expression of its essential nature. Hence far from being an independent body whose truth is itself independent of the truth about the world, it is the coherence of all truth of human experience. In fact this is the position of the Catholic Church, indeed part of what is meant by claiming that the Church is catholic. She is for all; she is the moral community; she celebrates the whole truth; and she makes room for the perspective of the divine – that is of love, within the culture of the public society of humanity-in-the-world. The Church as catholic, is open to all truth, all persons, all hope because it is open for God.

Does this mean that the truth that it knows is uncertain and tentative? Not at all! It means that the truth, which it expresses, is intelligible, capable of development and nourishingly life-giving.

A theory of everything or a search without end?

The claim of the Enlightenment, rightly or wrongly, has been taken to mean that there is in principle a story to be told which is the truth, the whole truth and nothing but the truth about the world. Such a claim is mistaken. We should see the Enlightenment as the period during which we came to understand that the truth about the world is not private but public, not idiosyncratic but universal, not segmented but whole. None of these mean that the truth about the world as we know it is not personal, that is the product of cooperative enterprise by people of goodwill. Indeed, the position of the Christian church is that the truth about the world is both publicly knowable and capable of being personally appropriated. The church precisely claims that this is what Jesus Christ both bore witness to and embodied.

Stephen Hawking once entertained the thought that it might be possible to discover 'a theory of everything' and indeed to prove it. He has decided, however, that this is impossible. Since the human mind that would create such a theory is itself a part of the world that needs to be explained, it would neither be possible to prove the theory, were one posited, nor even to state it correctly. The value and essential truth of what it is to be human is that we can continually pursue truth, become aware of the inadequacies of its present expression and devise means whereby further insight and discovery can take place.

Far from an engagement in an unending search being a refutation of Christian faith, it is an assertion of it and bears witness to the relational nature of all human being and the world of which it is an expression. Thus it is, as we intuitively recognize, the unknowability of the other person which gives rise to the possibility of greater knowledge of one's self, and that greater personal knowledge that in turn gives rise to further knowledge of the other. This is only true, of course, if one loves the other and commits oneself to loving the other for his or her own sake. And this is the essential insight of Christian faith asserted in the development of a theology that understands God to be committed as God's self to loving the world for its sake and not for the sake of the benefit that it brings to God, who as the acme of all perfection lacks nothing and can have nothing added to him.

Moore, Wittgenstein and Grice: sense-data, language games and implicature; Newman and certitude

The world really exists. As Moore said, one can have no doubt that when one holds one's hand up one knows that one has a hand and that it exists. Sense data are crucially significant in one's search for truth, as the Enlightenment delighted to say. But there is a wholeness and interdependence of the language which enables one to see that there is no independent language; not even the language of logic or of mathematics is independent of the experience which the human has of the world as a whole. Wittgenstein's image of language as a city with a centre and suburbs is illuminating, both in the fact that it bears witness to a coherent whole and that some parts are nevertheless more central to an understanding of it than others. The insight of Paul Grice that each statement, each proposition, inherently carries the whole framework of language and meaning is also important.

Perhaps Newman was right when he spoke of certitude rather than certainty. There may be no individual proposition the truth of which we can sensibly be confident of beyond a peradventure, but that there is sense in it all of which human beings are an integral part is something in which we can have reasonable confidence. At any rate we have the sort of confidence that gives us grounds to continue the search with the anticipation of success and enjoyment. I have always enjoyed W. V. Quine's remark, that even a mathematical tautology is simply the last thing he could envisage giving up believing. There are no certainties!

The Church: the life-giving community that embodies humility, intellectual, moral and spiritual

If, as I am claiming, the church has nothing to which it can point as the ground of certainty, it will do well to embody the humility of its Lord and refrain from making claims to certainties that are in principle beyond all possible human experience. There is no absolutely certain intellectual security, no moral certainty, and no spiritual certainty. What there is, is the possibility of confidence in God, a relationship with whom will transform one's willingness to engage in the unending search for meaning and purpose with the sort of love which offers enjoyment, satisfaction and hope. Of this we can have some understanding with the help of every fresh green leaf of human love in the here and now. Such experience is life-giving in the profoundest sense.

The church is the community of faith built upon such knowledge, embodying such hopes and committed, notwithstanding all evidence to the contrary, to transforming the world after the likeness of Christ.

Notes

1. Jonathan Barnes, *The Pre-Socratic Philosophers*, vol. 1, *Thales to Zeno* (London: Routledge & Kegan Paul, 1979), p. 3.
2. Richard Rorty, *Philosophy and the Mirror of Nature* (Oxford: Basil Blackwell, 1980). See also especially, Richard Rorty, *Truth and Progress* (Cambridge: Cambridge University Press, 1998), pp. 1ff.
3. The notion of *public* discussion is vital to the Christian faith at least, because it makes claims about the world that are of public significance for which the Church must be publicly accountable; they are not simply directed to the private comfort of believers.
4. *Independent*, 14 April 2004; letter from Roger Payne.
5. Thomas Aquinas, Exposition, *De Divinis Nominibus*, i, lect. 1.
6. John Jenkins, *Knowledge and Faith in Thomas Aquinas* (Cambridge: Cambridge University Press, 1997), pp. 51–98.
7. Josh. 10.12–13
8. The importance of careful observation can be seen in Romanesque art in both Germany and France as it moves from stylization to the portrayal of emotion. See, for example, the head of Christ from the crucifix in the collegiate church of Saint-Laurent, Auzon (Haute-Loire), the head of Christ in the crucifix from the cathedral of Sankt Peter und Gorgonius, Minden (Westphalia), or perhaps especially the wonderful donkey in the stained-glass window from the west façade of Chartres cathedral, c. 1150. For illustrations of these, see François Souchal, *Art of the Early Middle Ages* (New York: Abrams, 1968), pp. 83, 85, 140.
9. Descartes was educated by the Jesuits at La Flèche in Anjou.
10. René Descartes, *Objections and Replies*, Philosophical Writings of Descartes, vol. 11, trans. John Cottingham, Robert Stoothoff, Dugald Murdoch (Cambridge: Cambridge University Press, 1984), p. 173.
11. Descartes, *Objections and Replies*, p. 175.
12. Ibid., pp. 177–8.
13. Ibid., p. 178.
14. Plato, *Theaetetus*, 160d.
15. Locke, *An Essay Concerning Human Understanding*, Bk iv, ch. 20, §17.
16. Ibid., Bk iv, ch. 19, esp. §1, 17–22. 'On Enthusiasm'.
17. Ibid., Bk iv, ch. 18, §2.
18. Ibid., Bk iv, ch. 18, §8.
19. Ibid., Bk iv, ch. 18, §8.
20. Locke, *A Letter Concerning Toleration* (New York: Prometheus Books, 1990).
21. David Hume, *Dialogues Concerning Natural Religion*, repr. in Richard Wollheim (ed.), *Hume on Religion* (London: Collins, 1963), pp. 99–204.
22. On might say 'projection', though Hume nowhere uses the term.
23. David Hume, *An Enquiry Concerning Human Understanding*, §VII, Part 1, ed. E. Selby-Bigge (Oxford: Clarendon Press, 1902), p. 72.
24. David Hume, *Of Miracles: Essays, Moral, Political and Literary*, ed. Henry Frowde (London and New York: World's Classics, 1903), p. 544.
25. Hume, *The Natural History of Religion*, in Wollheim (ed.), *Hume on Religion*.
26. It is a mistake of course to think that fanaticism and fundamentalisms are the exclusive property of some monotheistic traditions; similar disastrous prejudices can be found in every religion.
27. Quoted in Roy Porter, *Enlightenment: Britain and the Creation of the Modern World* (London: Penguin, 2000), p. 127.
28. Immanuel Kant, *The Critique of Pure Reason*, trans. Paul Guyer and Allen W. Wood (Cambridge: Cambridge University Press, 1998). Cf. Div. 2, ch. III, 'The Ideal of Pure Reason'.

29. Immanuel Kant, *Critique of Practical Reason*, trans. T. K. Abbott (London: Longmans, 1909; 6th edn); Immanuel Kant, *Religion Within the Boundaries of Mere Reason*, trans. George di Gioyanni, in Immanuel Kant, *Religion and Rational Theology*, trans. Allen Wood and George di Gioyanni (Cambridge: Cambridge University Press, 1996).

30. Kant, *Critique of Practical Reason*, pp. 87–9.

31. Cf. Immanuel Kant, *Perpetual Peace*, trans. Lewis White Beck (New York: Liberal Arts Press, 1957).

32. Bertrand Russell and A. N. Whitehead, *Principia Mathematica*, 3 vols (Cambridge: Cambridge University Press, 1910–13; 2nd edn 1927–35); Bertrand Russell, *Our Knowledge of the External World* (London: Allen & Unwin, 1914; rev. edn 1929); *Human Knowedge: Its Scope and Limits* (London: Allen & Unwin, 1948). Russell's 1918 lectures on logical atomism and the article on logical atomism written for *Contemporary British Philosophy*, 1st Ser., 1924, are both reprinted in *Logic and Knowledge: Essays, 1901–1950*, ed. R. C. Marsh (London: Allen & Unwin, 1956).

33. Kurt Gödel, *On Formally Undecidable Propositions of Principia Mathematica and Related Systems*, trans. B. Meltzer, intro. R. B. Braithwaite (Edinburgh: Oliver & Boyd, 1962). For current discussion see S. Shanker (ed.), *Gödel's Theorem in Focus* (London: Routledge, 1990).

34. For the emergence in the English Enlightenment of questions about the nature of the self, soul, mind and body, see Roy Porter, *Flesh in the Age of Reason* (London: Penguin, 2004).

35. Temple's attention to the mind as having the essential role in human creating is striking. Cf. Porter who traces most interestingly the way in which the mind rather than the soul becomes the dominant focus of reflection as the new picture of what it was to be human in the English Enlightenment. See his *Flesh in the Age of Reason* and his *Enlightenment*.

36. William Temple, *Mens Creatrix* (London: Macmillan, 1917); *Christus Veritas* (London: Macmillan, 1924); *Nature, Man and God* (London: Macmillan, 1934); *Christianity and the Social Order* (London: Penguin, 1942).

37. Jacques Derrida, *Of Grammatology*, trans. Gayatri Spivak (Baltimore, MD: Johns Hopkins University Press, 1976); *Writing and Difference*, trans. Alan Bass (London: Routledge & Kegan Paul, 1978). Hugh Rayment-Pickard, *Impossible God: Derrida's Theology*, (Aldershot: Ashgate, 2003).

38. The primary text for understanding Foucault is *Les Mots et les choses* (Paris: Gallimard, 1966) (*The Order of Things* [London: Tavistock, 1970; Routledge, 1989]). For a discussion of the significance of Foucault in relation to the theme of this essay see James Bernauer and Jeremy Carrette (eds), *Michel Foucault and Theology* (Aldershot: Ashgate, 2004).

39. Bernauer and Carrette (eds), *Michel Foucault and Theology*, p. 102.

40. 'For state-of-the-art Catholic news there are some 663,381 different websites, so the searcher needs to choose carefully to avoid saturation' (Lavinia Byrne, *The Tablet* (8 May 2004): 45).

Chapter 4

HERMENEUTICAL INVESTIGATIONS: DISCERNING CONTEMPORARY CHRISTIAN COMMUNITY

Gerard Mannion

Introduction

In Umberto Eco's *The Name of the Rose*, we are given a glimpse into the late medieval world of theology, philosophy and the church. Against the backdrop of a monastic and local community where heinous crimes have been committed and where moral boundaries are traversed seemingly everywhere, we are introduced to the conflicting religious movements of an age where differing schools of thought, conceptions of ecclesiology and belief are all in great tension. Questions which run as an undercurrent to the goings-on at the unfortunate abbey include: Who or what is the church? Who are the true custodians of its 'truth'? Who are its enemies? Who are true 'members' of the faithful and who are the heretics? What is the true relation between the church and the world beyond its confines? Nothing is what it seems and certainty is the one aspect lacking from the situation, in any respect. But it becomes clear in the novel (as so well captured, also, in the film), that *hermeneutics* is a predominant theme of the work.

Everywhere there are persons, texts, symbols, signs and, indeed acts to be 'read', to have their meaning discerned. The nature and meaning of 'church' are predominant themes. The conflicts witnessed are really also ones of a hermeneutical nature as we see that uniformity is unachievable. The story reaches a crescendo when William of Baskerville, the hero, makes some impassioned speeches concerning the elusive nature of truth, making clear that orthodoxy and heresy are likewise terms which he believes are very much in the eye of the beholder or, we might say, of the *hermeuneut*.

Umberto Eco has gone on record as saying that he was really seeking to illustrate the contemporary *postmodern* world, as much as the late medieval age. An age that is very much one of flux and change. I believe his novel thus may serve as an excellent illustration, albeit allegorically, metaphorically and symbolically – as one would only expect from that wise and mischievous professor of semiotics – of the issues which need to be addressed today concerning the interrelation of hermeneutics, ecclesiology and ecumenism. We, too, no less than the learned Spiritual Franciscans, the Dominican Inquisitors and the scholarly Benedictine communitarians in Eco's novel, live in an age of competing and conflicting theological, ecclesiological and, indeed, moral priorities. And so many of our present difficulties are likewise a question of *interpretation*. This is not to dismiss them lightly, however. It is rather to show them for what they really are – no more and no less.

Here, for the sake of space, I shall assume that a common *basic* understanding of hermeneutics, namely, as the science, art or practice of interpretation and/or meaning may be taken for granted. The history and development of hermeneutics has been well documented. From its philological and theological roots, down to more scientifically methodological developments (Schleiermacher) and its entry into the heart of philosophical systems (Dilthey), further refinement in new schools of thought (Heidegger) and consolidations as *the* leading 'methodology' for fruitful human understanding (Gadamer), along with its politicization and recognition of its contemporary anthropological significance (Ricoeur),[1] down to its 'foundationalist' status as the bedrock of antifoundationalist thinking (e.g. Foucault, Derrida and the postmodern turn) – all have been widely charted elsewhere.[2] In this chapter I shall also largely take for granted that *ecclesial* hermeneutics is acknowledged as something *desirable* and so focus upon the differing proponents of such a view, for there are numerous differences amongst them as to how to go about engaging in such an undertaking.

Indeed, we might say that so many of the fundamental 'insights' which we see discussed at length in the works of the great hermeneutical pioneers might really be distilled to the common-sense awareness of contextuality, situation, historicity, the cultural-linguistic factors of human existence and the need to read the 'signs of the times', that is to say, the wider picture where we and the 'text' or the 'other' are respectively 'coming from' and where 'we' wish 'to go', together or otherwise. Hence a brief 'definition', of sorts.

Narrowing our focus, all interpretations of religion are, of course, hermeneutical exercises in themselves, bar none. There is no 'universal' and objective, truly value-free form of such, especially not those of, say, Feuerbach, Durkheim, Freud and, above all, Nietzsche. So, in attempting to draw the questions surrounding hermeneutics into our ecclesiological considerations, this may, surprisingly, give us much more cause for hope rather than despair. In the churches we have many contending ecclesiologies. Hermeneutics, I suggest, might help us better to understand this, along with why it is inevitable and why it is a *good thing* – both in terms of prospects for ecclesiology and for ecumenism.

David Tracy believes that hermeneutics, that is to say the question of interpretation, has been with us throughout history and, in particular, has been 'the central issue in times of cultural crisis'.[3] This was so, he continues, for Aristotle and the Greeks as Greek culture descended from its halcyon days, to the allegorical interpretative methods that emerged from Stoics, Jews and Christians in Hellenistic times. It was also thus for Augustine as antiquity turned towards the medieval age, or for Luther at a pivotal time for Western Christianity. In early modernity we see this typified in Descartes, Spinoza, Schleiermacher and Hegel. In later times, Tracy argues, we see how historical consciousness transformed the questions of interpretation once more, seen, for example, in very different forms in the likes of Troeltsch and Lonergan.

Of course, Tracy goes on to suggest that with the undoing of modernity and the various critiques offered by Freud, Marx, Nietzsche and feminism, we have seen how modernity and its legacy (as well as such critiques, themselves) have been radically reinterpreted in so many ways. Postmodernism represents many such attempts in its various guises.

> The emergence of a hermeneutical consciousness is clearly a part of this cultural shift. For hermeneutics lives or dies by its ability to take history and language seriously, to give the other (whether person, event or text) our attention as other, not as a projection of our present fears, hopes and desires. The deceptively simple hermeneutical model of dialogue is one attempt to be faithful to this shift from modern self to postmodern other. For however often the word is banded about, dialogue remains a rare phenomenon in anyone's experience. Dialogue demands the intellectual, moral, and, at the limit, religious ability to struggle to hear another and to respond critically, and even suspiciously when necessary, but only in dialogical relationship to a real, not a projected other.[4]

Hence, I believe that hermeneutics relates to every facet of Christian belief and life. Indeed, I think we can suggest the Christian understanding of God is a hermeneutic of being itself.

The ecclesial context of hermeneutics today

Sadly, a fundamental *refusal* to engage in probing and self-critical ecclesiological hermeneutics has been a marked feature of much ecclesiological thinking across numerous denominations in recent decades. It is a product of the rise of inward-looking and neo-exclusivistic ecclesiologies which are in the ascendancy throughout the Christian church in the West.

We shall also note that certain lessons concerning this situation may be learned by engaging with those thinkers who have resolutely emphasized the importance of allowing ethical concerns to shape ecclesiological hermeneutics. Duncan Forrester has suggested that 'the Church is . . . a kind of hermeneutic of the gospel', but we suggest there is a need for Christians, in each generation and especially in the present era, to ensure that the gospel is also allowed to provide a hermeneutic of the church.[5]

This chapter will engage, albeit briefly, with a variety of thinkers, focusing in particular upon those who have embraced the hermeneutical task in our present era, in order to recognize the need to embrace also the variety of pluralistic realities in which the church finds itself, intellectually, culturally, socially and, of course, religiously. Not least of all, the contemporary task and challenge of ecumenism will be addressed in relation to such hermeneutical debates. I make no claim for this to be a comprehensive survey of hermeneutical contributions to ecclesiology, rather just a sampling of some interesting and potentially fruitful voices in a much wider conversation.

Why hermeneutics? Brief methodological considerations

In a study in theological method, Gareth Jones argues that a theology that is critical in nature must therefore be hermeneutical in method and character also. Such a theology feeds into the critical theologian's approach to questions of revelation, church and context alike:

> Critical theology, therefore, is concerned with questioning of understanding and interpretation, and is hermeneutic in character, being centred upon the quest for meaning ... critical theology is hermeneutic in so far as it interprets not only the Bible, but also tradition, Church, faith and particularly society. The hermeneutic 'circle' thus relates the theologian not only to the Bible, as one source of authority, but also to Church in its broadest possible sense, and the world in which it lives.[6]

But it would appear that not every theology is sufficiently critical in nature, nor is every theology which engages in hermeneutics necessarily critical at all. A further question raised here concerns what *form* of hermeneutical theory the theology in question is engaging with. Indeed, even to get so far as to discern the nature of a critical hermeneutic theology, we must first explore a number of other factors.

Despite its continuous involvement in the development of hermeneutics throughout the history of interpretation itself, theology has recently been following in the wake of more particularly *philosophical* schools of hermeneutical method and practice.[7] This, in itself, has meant that, no less than in times past, differing philosophical influences will lead to differing theological priorities and method-ologies (and hence ecclesiologies). In one sense, then, we see that an absence of uniformity characterizes not simply theology (and ecclesiology), but so, too, hermeneutics. This, in itself, may be no bad thing. It could urge us towards the acceptance of the pluralistic reality in which we live – and this chapter will be concerned with commending approaches which serve such ends. But it can also lead to division and disagreements likewise. Thus, for example, in recent decades, the theological and subsequent ecclesiological divides between the 'postliberal' schools of theology and the 'revisionists' are, above all else, attributable to differences in *hermeneutical* priorities and methods. We shall explore why this might be so.[8]

In a historically and methodologically broader perspective, Jeanrond has identified 'three camps in Christian theology'. Although we must be ever mindful to remember key (hermeneutical) rules of engagement when dealing with such categorization, his summary is worth quoting here at length in order to aid our understanding of the recent and contemporary ecclesial hermeneutical horizons. First, he identifies those who embrace a wholehearted theologically-engaged form of hermeneutical endeavour,

> Christian thinkers like [David] Tracy, [Hans] Küng, and [Peter] Berger who favour an open-ended dialogue on method between Christian interpreters and other thinkers interested in hermeneutics. Generally speaking, they wish to assess the particular Christian vision for this world in the context of a great conversation with all other

group of human thinkers who care for the people of this world and for the universe in which we live.

The second camp offers only a most limited and textual (in the narrow sense) form of engagement,

> There are those Christian thinkers like [Peter] Stuhlmacher, [George] Lindbeck and the late Hans Frei who feel that they ought to determine the specifically Christian vision predominantly from inside the church and biblical theology. According to Lindbeck, a dialogue with other religions or secular intellectual forces can happen on the basis of comparing different religious stories and their grammars.[9]

The third group are marked by a refusal to participate in a broader hermeneutical exercise at all, rejecting such endeavours in favour of perceived dogmatic certainty.

> And finally ... there are those Christian thinkers who call again for an 'orthodox' approach to the Scriptures. Obviously, such a dogmatic approach to the texts of the Christian tradition is not in favour of contemplating the insights of philosophical hermeneutics for its own interpretive work. Instead it rejects this 'alien' interference and claims thus to protect the integrity of its sacred texts. Karl Barth is a representative of this approach as is the current Magisterium of the Roman Catholic Church. The underlying thesis is, of course, that divine revelation does not need human methods or philosophical sophistication to do its job successfully. Christian thinking is understood to confront the world on the basis of its particular reception of the Word of God or of divine knowledge, whereas the world has access only to ordinary language and natural reason, however philosophically purified.[10]

We shall work towards some reflections upon the 'interpretation' of the meaning of existence and community in the Christian context, in other words, upon the church as hermeneutical community and what this means. But, likewise, we also hope to offer some observations upon a few varieties of 'reading' the church itself. It is hoped that, by and large, the principle of the 'hermeneutics of suspicion' (take nothing for granted or at surface value) shall prevail throughout in the service of dialogue and ecumenism. Hermeneutics, therefore, is necessary, so unavoidable and it has practical consequences. Let us explore what the churches have recently been saying about such matters.

The churches' hermeneutical 'turn': refusal or engagement?

If one might be permitted a rhetorical question for the sake of illustration here, it is easy to see that some in certain quarters of the church might ask why should or would the churches become so concerned with contemporary developments in hermeneutics at all, when they have such a rich scriptural, theological and philosophical set of traditions on which to draw? Are not the 'interpretations' which Christians require, 'given' to them via revelation and, on the other hand, provided in these vast stores of reflective teaching, insight and judgement? Here we must answer in the negative, for I think such attitudes would betray a misunderstanding of the nature of revelation, doctrine, Christian ethical discourse and, indeed, of the church itself.

Jeanrond has argued that the hermeneutical engagement (to which we might here add the clarificatory word 'ecumenical') for Christian churches today is unavoidable if they are to flourish, for

> attitudes towards particular questions and problems in the different Christian Churches vary enormously as illustrated by the number of debates at present[11] ... In all these conflicts and debates 'tradition' has been used to protect the *status quo* of ecclesial positions as well as to question it.[12] Different appeals and interpretations clash with one another.[13]

Happily, of course, many in the churches are not blind to such matters. Indeed, so much of the World Council of Churches' work, both practical and theoretical, and the subsequent documents and initiatives which have emerged from this can all be seen, in some way, to be examples of the hermeneutical engagement with Christian living and community. In an analogous manner, the work of the many departments of the Vatican Curia, the Magisterium (teaching authority) of the Roman Catholic Church and, of course, the teaching of the Pope himself can also be viewed in a similar fashion. But obviously some documents issued by such global bodies are more explicitly hermeneutical in character than others.

Yet the tendency Jeanrond identifies is an ever-present and all too tempting threat across the churches. One very prominent and pertinent example of a document emerging from *within* one particular community is the Roman Catholic document, *Dominus Iesus*.[14] This purports to engage in ecclesiological hermeneutics, but many critics have perceived it rather to be an example of an actual *refusal* to engage in meaningful hermeneutics that take full account of the pluralistic world in which we live. Such critics believe it actually results in reversing positive steps taken earlier by that community in terms of dialogue with other Christian, religious and human communities. The language and tone of this document simply indicate that neither a true hermeneutical engagement, nor any charitable spirit of dialogue could be detected in the thinking that lies behind its absolutist and exclusivistic pronouncements. Indeed, this document has, in the opinion of its many critics, done a great disservice to ecclesial hermeneutics and religious dialogue in general.

However, an example of where Christian churches seek to engage in *positive* ecclesial hermeneutics is the study programme initiated by the Faith and Order Commission of the World Council of Churches (between 1994 and 1998) which culminated in the publication of the report, *A Treasure in Earthen Vessels*.[15] This explored, in the words of its preface, 'the complex, potentially conflictual but often creative field of hermeneutics, focused specifically on the hermeneutical task entailed in the ecumenical search for visible church unity'. It explored earlier studies of such questions, the place of the scriptures in such tasks and the importance of 'interpreting the interpreters', along with the notions of (and differences between) 'the tradition' and 'traditions'. It then turned to the challenges posed by Christianity's faith in one gospel, lived out in many diverse contexts. The concepts of both contexuality and catholicity alike were hence explored.

In its final quarter, the document explores the idea of 'ecclesial discernment' in relation to the 'truth' of the Gospel, before turning to explore questions of authority, apostolicity and shared accountability. It ends with an interesting reflection on the very notion of ecclesial reception. Each of these themes have increasingly been the subject of numerous studies across various Christian communities in recent decades. The document sets out why it believes such a study programme was necessary,

> The Church is called to be a *hermeneutical community*, that is, a community within which there is a commitment to explore and interpret anew the given texts, symbols and practices. The tasks of a hermeneutical community also include overcoming misunderstandings, controversies and divisions; identifying dangers; resolving conflicts; and preventing schisms predicated on divisive interpretations of the Christian faith. The needs of the people of God in ever-new circumstances of faithful life and witness are also integral to this task. As a hermeneutical community, the Church also submits itself to being interpreted by the ever-challenging Word of God.[16]

It then moves on to discuss the report from Fourth World Conference on Faith and Order (on 'Scripture, Tradition and traditions, Montreal, 1963), in order to highlight issues which remain outstanding from that ecumenical gathering (§15), most notably the understanding of 'tradition' itself,

> By the *Tradition* is meant the Gospel itself, transmitted from generation to generation in and by the Church, Christ Himself present in the life of the Church. By *tradition* is meant the traditionary process. The term *traditions* is used ... to indicate both the diversity of forms of expression and also what we call confessional traditions, for instance the Lutheran tradition or the Reformed tradition ... the word appears in a further sense, when we speak of cultural traditions. [Montreal] (Section II, para. 39)
>
> Our starting-point is that we as Christians are all living in a tradition which goes back to our Lord and has its roots in the Old Testament and are all indebted to that tradition inasmuch as we have received the revealed truth, the Gospel, through its being transmitted from one generation to another. Thus we can say that we exist as Christians by the Tradition of the Gospel (the *paradosis* of the *kerygma*) testified in Scripture, transmitted in and by the Church, through the power of the Holy Spirit. (Section II, para. 45)
>
> The traditions in Christian history are distinct from, and yet connected with, the Tradition. They are the expressions and manifestations in diverse historical terms of the one truth and reality which is Christ. This evaluation of the traditions poses serious problems ... How can we distinguish between traditions embodying the true Tradition and merely human traditions? (Section II, paras 47 and 48)[17]

What is crucial to the contemporary situation, the 1998 documents states, is that 'Montreal did not fully explain what it means that the one Tradition is embodied in concrete traditions and cultures',[18] and furthermore it also 'left open the vital question of how churches can discern the one Tradition. Therefore there is a danger that churches identify the one Tradition exclusively with their own tradition.'[19] In other words, questions of a fundamentally hermeneutical nature.

The second part of *A Treasure in Earthen Vessels*, on scriptural hermeneutics, echoes Roman Catholic debates, which received much stimulation from the Second Vatican Council Dogmatic Constitution on Divine Revelation, *Dei Verbum*.[20] The more constructive sections on the relationship between 'One Tradition and Many Traditions' follow in §§32–7, where questions of re-reception are raised, along with the idea of ecumenical hermeneutics as 'an ecclesial act led by the Spirit'.[21] It then moves into considerations of continuity and discontinuity (§34), as well as the importance for a hermeneutics of Christian *practices*.[22]

But, amongst the more significant sections of the document, is that where the hermeneutical task for the present age is laid out in the discussion on 'Interpreting the Interpreters', which not only appears to offer *some* recognition of the contemporary pluralistic reality, but also commends the methodological value of the hermeneutics of suspicion.

> Christians are to be conscious that interpretations come out of special historical circumstances and that new issues may come out of various contexts. In considering these circumstances and issues, Christians involved in the hermeneutical task do well to investigate the location from which the text is being interpreted; the choice of a specific text for interpretation; the involvement of power structures in the interpretation process; prejudices and presuppositions brought to bear on the interpretation process. It is in the light of this understanding that ecumenical hermeneutics needs to operate as a hermeneutics of coherence, showing the positive complementarity of traditions. It needs also to include a hermeneutics of suspicion. This does not mean the adoption of an attitude of mistrust but the application to oneself and one's dialogue partners of an approach which perceives how self-interest, power, national or ethnic or class or gender perspectives can affect the reading of texts and the understanding of symbols and practices.[23]

It is all the more a pity, then, that *A Treasure in Earthen Vessels* does not consistently act on such laudable principles throughout. It goes some way towards further commending such a methodology in its recognition that faith 'is not only a condition of dialogue, but a fruitful product of dialogue, that the partners come to appreciate and trust one another's sincerity and good intention. This means each is sincerely seeking to transmit that which God wishes to pass on through the Church.'[24] Furthermore, the difficult issue of 'authoritative interpretation' is not shirked,[25] when it affirms that

> Clarity about authority is a crucial element in that dimension of hermeneutics which concentrates on the faithful communication and reception of the meaning of texts, symbols and practices. Consequently, the relationship between Scripture, Tradition and traditions and Christian experience arising from liturgical and other practices needs to be dealt with again and again within the hermeneutical process.[26]

The third part, on 'One Gospel in Many Contexts', is another that promises much in its echoing of numerous debates concerning the pluralistic reality of life, but one gets the impression that this is a most *qualified* acceptance of such. The debate between Cardinals Kasper and Ratzinger concerning the respective primacy of the local or the universal church[27] are also brought to mind by the section on 'Contextuality and catholicty',[28] as typified by §44:

> In order to reflect theologically upon both the diversity of and the relationships among local Christian communities, the terms 'contextuality' and 'catholicity' are especially helpful. The dimension of contextuality refers to the interpretation and the proclamation of the gospel within the life and culture of a specific people and community. Such a proclamation of the gospel can seek to judge the cultural context, it can seek to separate itself from the culture in which the church is set and it can seek to transform culture.

However (no less than in the many writings and pronouncements of Joseph Ratzinger[29] here and the hermeneutical *refusal* epitomized in *Dominus Iesus*), if one reads between the lines of this section of the document, one may find a carefully guarded understanding of contextuality at work, and one which is still firmly between an insular and inclusivistic framework and ecclesiological worldview. And this, even if, like Kasper, the document affirms the primacy of the *local* over the universal church (§45, where Catholicity 'is ascribed, first of all, to each local community, inasmuch as each community expresses in its faith, life, and witness this fullness that is not yet fully realized').[30]

The most constructive part of the document of all comes at the end – 'The Church *as* Hermeneutical Community', which contains the discussions of many of the most important ecclesial concepts for our times (or indeed, for any), namely, ecclesial discernment, authority, apostolicity, shared accountability and the extremely important concept of ecclesial *reception*.[31] Here, we see it proclaimed that ecclesial *formation* is identified as a prime duty for the churches. We also see acknowledgment of the emergence (or, I would suggest, the *re*-emergence) of an *inter*-ecclesial magisterium, beyond denominational boundaries, 'An ecumenical exercise of teaching authority is already beginning to develop in some respects. It is hoped that ways of common decision making can be developed, even as there is allowance for certain decisions a church must take without or even against the opinion of others.'[32] Likewise, the *conciliar* tradition in Christianity is here celebrated, also, but anew in the hermeneutical context (§61).[33]

The document is offered as a resource, although much of it is rather more descriptive than exploratory.[34] Indeed, the tone of the document is, at times, contra the very spirit of hermeneutics, bordering, as it does, on the insular and, occasionally even *exclusivistic* in Christian terms. Indeed, it is most peculiar that *ethics* is mysteriously absent from much of the document. Strange, given the recent ethical turn in much philosophical and, subsequently, theological and ecclesiological hermeneutics. The document sought to present *coherence* as a fundamental aspiration for ecumenical hermeneutics but, as Simone Sinn suggests, this document, itself, is found wanting in this respect in many parts.[35]

Furthermore, the document seems to address ideal and perfectly functioning Christian communities and yet we know that any real acknowledgment of contextuality reveals a very different reality. Sinn – on a similar note – asks, particularly in relation to the ambivalence of the notion of 'formation' as employed in the document,

> Who is the 'church' when it is separated from 'its members'? Who is the subject of formation? What makes us faithful? Is faithfulness a precondition for hearing and interpreting? The concept of formation outlined [in the document] is obviously in danger of remaining a top-down model, as long as the traditioning of apostolic faith is seen as a prerequisite for being allowed to perform discernment.[36]

Thus one of the major difficulties with the interaction between theology, ecclesiology and hermeneutics (and hence ecumenism), is that particularist thinking and priorities all too often prevail over more crucial wider and general questions. Francis Schüssler Fiorenza has noted that philosophical hermeneutics since early modernity has shifted 'from a more specific or regional hermeneutics to a more genuine or universal hermeneutics' – that is to say, neither a *universalizing* hermeneutics, nor one specific to a single discipline (e.g. biblical or legal hermeneutics). He thus also suggests that a parallel may be drawn here because, for many theologians today, the 'crucial issues' also appear to be 'general problems of understanding and interpretation rather than issues specific to a particular discipline'.[37] As we shall see, all too many hermeneutical endeavours, including the World Council of Churches' own reflections upon hermeneutics, display a difficulty in breaking away from *specific* – namely, biblical, hermeneutics, in order to engage in genuine reflection upon wider questions of interpretation, meaning and understanding. *A Treasure in Earthen Vessels* is a very general and, admittedly, relatively short document. Yet, considering its subject matter, it works with many *assumptions* and aspects taken for granted.

Simone Sinn accords with such a view, and she suggests that the very definition of hermeneutics offered in the document[38] is problematic, by virtue of the fact that it stands alone and is not applied consistently throughout the remainder of the text:

> This definition goes along with current philosophical and theological thinking on hermeneutics. Yet, this definition stands quite isolated, as it is not taken up in the following reflections. A weakness is that what is meant by *interpretation* and *application* is not discussed; moreover, the relation of those two classical hermeneutical aspects to the triad *interpretation, communication and reception*, which is put forward in the same paragraph, is not clarified.[39]

Sinn goes on to discuss the context of modern and contemporary debates within philosophical hermeneutics, stating that they centre around three levels, namely, methodology, epistemology and ontology.[40] I believe that a further key problem with *A Treasure in Earthen Vessels*, and indeed for theology and the churches in general today, is that it is never clear which particular 'level' is being addressed, nor what the precise differences between the respective levels actually are. As Lewis Mudge has stated,[41] *A Treasure in Earthen Vessels* has failed to fulfil the promise which the conversations and studies that led to its formation had generated. It has yet to bear fruit. But can it do so given the criticisms thus far outlined? Perhaps some of these issues can be overcome if we explore what other recent work has been undertaken in the field of hermeneutics in relation to ecclesiology. This may allow us to appreciate better why the promise of *A Treasure in Earthen Vessels* has not been so forthcoming.

Hermeneutics, ethics and ecclesiology

Sinn's is just one of a number of recent studies that have suggested how important due attention to *hermeneutics* is to understanding the interrelation between ethics and ecclesiology, and so in taking the debates concerning them forward in a positive fashion.[42] Yet as Sinn herself has illustrated, key ecumenical discussions on the interrelation between ethics and ecclesiology, on the one hand, and ecumenical hermeneutics, on the other, have often been conducted as if in effective ignorance of or isolation from one another. Sinn's analysis and suggestive methodology point us in the direction of hermeneutical engagement in discerning the interrelation between ethics and ecclesiology.

Not least of all, this is because many of the insights which emerged from the World Council of Churches (WCC) Faith and Order discussions on ecclesiology and *ethics* were actually of a *hermeneutical* nature. Hence Sinn has expressed surprise that *A Treasure in Earthen Vessels* did not take into account the hermeneutical insights of the earlier ethics and ecclesiology discussions in any fulsome sense.

Sinn herself offers an assessment which builds upon the hermeneutical theories of Paul Ricoeur. She highlights the fact that the ethics and ecclesiology debates resulted in an emphasis upon the concept of *formation*, which combined elements of both liturgical and ethical concern. She links this to Ricoeur's hermeneutical process whereby distanciation and appropriation are properly related to allow semantic innovation and hence transformation. The path to understanding and meaning is thus illuminated and facilitated all the better.

Sinn herself offers the concept of *participation* as the key to interrelating the ethical, ecclesiological *and* hermeneutical elements of church life and mission: 'By understanding itself as a participatory community the church relates the hermeneutical character, the ethical structure and the ecclesial being of its existence.'[43] In other words, building upon the Ricoeurian hermeneutical method which seeks to explain the dynamic between interpretandum and the interpreter, and what results from this, Sinn extrapolates from such analysis a model by which the community called church can be analysed in its epistemological, ontological and hence ethical aspects. For crucial to Ricoeur's theory is 'the interpreter's existential participation in the interpretation process in which understanding is perceived of as a metamorphosis'.[44] Transferred to a communal scenario, Sinn perceives participation as the analogical ecclesiological correlate to hermeneutics whereby the church is not simply understood better, but is transformed into fuller ecclesial being with the missionary and so ethical empowerment which follows from such a process.[45]

For Sinn, ecumenical hermeneutics should therefore be understood as a 'transformative participatory event'.[46] What other thinking on the relationship between hermeneutics and ecclesiology has come to light in recent years?

Recent critical studies in hermeneutics and ecclesiology – some examples

As well as collective ventures, such as *A Treasure in Earthen Vessels*, there has been an upturn in the study of the ecclesiological significance of hermeneutics in recent years emanating from *individual* scholars as well. Some of these engage with contemporary philosophical debates in hermeneutics; some are reflections upon collective undertakings in the field; others are methodological and theoretical reflections. Some studies are primarily aimed at the *scriptural* relevance of hermeneutics; others at the liturgical and practical aspects; yet others at the implications of hermeneutics for fundamental, philosophical and systematic theology, including theological method. Many cross over into the consideration of the interrelation between hermeneutics and ethical questions – as one would expect, for hermeneutics has an especially social and communitarian relevance, and hence an obvious ecclesiological significance.

Scholars follow a range of hermeneutical schools and begin from a variety of starting-points, ranging from the Gademerian through the Ricouerian and the classical 'hermeneutics' of suspicion, to more recent postmodern and deconstructionist positions.

So, for example[47] (and I must stress that our list is by no means exhaustive)[48] amongst those scholars whose work may (to varying extents) be bracketed in this field are those such as the late evangelical theologian, Stanley Grenz, who died so unexpectedly and prematurely in March 2005. In numerous works Grenz attempted to develop a positive 'postmodern' ecclesiology and to offer a Christian theology which moves 'beyond foundationalism'.[49] More specifically, he made a plea for evangelicals to occupy the 'centre' in a postmodern world where Christians too often allow themselves to be polarized between conservatives and liberals and hence for divisions to matter more than communion. Grenz identified himself as a 'postconservative' evangelical and offered his studies as works in the genre of 'constructive theology'.

Grenz wished to move theology beyond divisive debates and stagnant waters towards a vibrant engagement with the contemporary world through a positive celebration of the fundamentals of the evangelical tradition. At the heart of this, for Grenz, was the spirituality fostered through the experience of *conversion*. In a Schleiermachian methodological turn, he asserted that doctrine follows from this as the articulation of the 'second language' of evangelical Christianity.[50] But, above all for Grenz, *community*, hence ecclesia, was *the* overall fundamental focal point of theology. His ecclesiological thinking thus moved from reflection upon the Trinitarian being of God and onto the implications of this for ecclesial and societal living today. His series, *The Matrix of Christian Theology*, remained unfinished at his death, although the second volume, *The Named God*, saw the light of day.

Dan Stiver has utilized the philosophy of religion and, in particular, studies in the philosophy of language in the service of the church. He both epitomizes and illustrates where the contemporary situation 'is at', with regard to competing schools of thought and practice in hermeneutics, theology and, more implicitly, ecclesiology. Yet he also acknowledges there is a need to transcend divisions in the service of the church. In a recent work,[51] he sets out to offer a

> particular framework for doing theology based on an unusual connection between 'postliberal theology,' also known as the Yale School, and a circumspect appeal to the hermeneutical philosophy identified particularly with the thought of Hans-Georg Gadamer and Paul Ricoeur. Usually, these two traditions have been seen as sharply opposed, but I suggest that they can mutually enhance one another, thereby illustrating one of the marks of postmodernism, namely, the weaving together of seemingly disparate threads. The significance of Gadamer and Ricoeur is that they are significant postmodern philosophers in their own right, whose ideas have been appropriated by many theologians, albeit usually in an unsystematic way.[52]

Stiver champions '*ad hoc*' as opposed to foundationalist connections with other disciplines, particularly philosophy. Stiver thinks we can gain from such an exercise the acceptance of the fact that 'conviction can be combined with a lack of strong objectivism'.[53] He embraces Gadamer's attack upon the Enlightenment 'prejudice against prejudice'[54] – we cannot escape from what we bring to a text and so a fusion of horizons is always going to lie at the heart of any act of understanding. For Stiver, the importance of our own horizon as a help and not a hindrance to understanding is crucial.[55]

Miroslav Volf (of Yale) has attempted to offer a more contemporary and Free Church-oriented take on the orthodox tradition of *trinitarian* ecclesiology.[56] For Volf, the church that embraces diversity is a healthy church. We should always perceive the 'other' in terms not of their distance from us, but rather in terms of their *approximation* to us.[57] Arne Rasmusson has attempted to explore ecumenical, ethical and ecclesiological divisions and conundrums in our times and one of his major works offers a hermeneutical assessment of what it means to conceive and speak of the church *as polis*.[58] Although such scholars focus, primarily, upon the relevance of hermeneutics in the service of their own community or particular Christian tradition, much of their work resonates with that discussed in the category described below as *comparative* approaches.[59] For example, although Volf describes his own ecclesiology as being a Free Church model, he nonetheless engages with ecclesiological studies in Roman Catholic and Orthodox traditions, in order to construct that model.

Amongst Roman Catholic studies, we see a wide variety of scholars engaged in work upon hermeneutics which addresses particular areas of concern relevant to that communion and, also, to its relation to the wider human family. For example, Charles Curran focuses upon the moral and ecclesiological debates and their interrelation in contemporary Catholicism.[60] Elisabeth Schüssler Fiorenza's work upon biblical and feminist hermeneutics[61] has moved from considerations of the theology and practice of women's ministries in the church, through the impact of patriarchal biblical hermeneutics for women in the church, and onto constructive suggestions. This all leads into ecclesiology for the future, most notably the development of the concept of 'woman-church' and its requisite 'ekklesialogy'. Leonardo Bŏff's well-known work has focused upon liberation, political, social, anthropological and ecclesiological concerns.[62] Rejecting the outdated and oppressive hierarchical model of church organization and authority, Boff draws upon social analysis to demonstrate how such ventures as the basic Christian communities allow much greater consultation, collaboration and lay participation in the church. Structures are transformed and new ministries are coming to the fore. Boff argues that the rigidity of current church structures can be overcome and decision-making processes can become more inclusive of the whole community, for the exclusion of the laity from participation in such decisions is a fundamental problem for the church in our times. Hence the base communities help to develop a new non-linear form of church structure where the roles of all, including priests and bishops, are transformed. The church is declericalized as the emphasis switches to the whole 'people of God', to whom collegiality now belongs. This offers not a 'global alternative' for the entire church, but instead a 'leaven of renewal' for the church.

Of course, the work of Joseph Ratzinger, now Pope Benedict XVI, could also be presented as engagement in ecclesial hermeneutics, albeit with a very different agenda in mind to, say, that of Boff, and reaching very different conclusions.[63] In particular, his call for tradition and church teaching to be interpreted in the light of a 'hermeneutics of unity'. Nonetheless, his influence upon documents such as *Communionis Notio* and *Dominus Iesus*, do suggest that his approach more often than not displays elements of a hermeneutical *refusal*, as opposed to genuine engagement.[64] Critics suggest that imposed uniformity, not true unity, is what follows from such pseudo-hermeneutical enterprises.

We mention David Tracy's work here, for in much of it he has explored the methodological, fundamental theological, revisionist and pluralistic questions which confront the Roman Catholic Church today, for which hermeneutics, he believes, is a key tool in the examination of such. However, as we shall see, Tracy's thinking goes well beyond the boundaries of his own Catholic tradition.

Aside from contributions from the representative bodies of global ecclesial communities, perhaps the most interesting and *promising* contributions in the field of hermeneutical engagement with ecclesiology, are what we might term *Comparative Studies*, which attempt to explore such issues from a more broad-ranging, cross- and intercommunitarian perspective. They might attempt to discern similar trends across ecclesiological and indeed religious divides; they may highlight different realities, concerns and approaches across differing communities. They may seek to offer some methodological reflections and systematic recommendations. Their remit may also be to contribute to a practical and moral positive 'way forward' for the future of such communities and the human family in general. In this, we thus see many parallels with the still developing discipline of 'comparative' theology, as witnessed in the works of those such as the US Jesuit scholar Francis Clooney and the British Anglican Keith Ward.

Pre-eminent amongst such scholars of this comparative type is American Presbyterian Lewis Mudge.[65] He has not only worked tirelessly for both the Faith and Order as well as the Life and Work Commissions of the World Council of Churches since the 1950s but he has also served on numerous interchurch bodies and bi-lateral forums across communions, contributing to a very large number of influential documents (including the WCC's Ethics and Ecclesiology studies). Always bringing a critical eye to such ventures, himself, one would expect nothing less from a former student of Paul Ricouer. Mudge has published a large number of articles and books in the fields of ecclesiology, hermeneutics and their interrelation. He suggests that a new and non-parochial concept of catholicity can be witnessed in the wider church in recent decades, and he has argued that churches are not just moral communities but also 'communities of interpretation'. But perhaps his most ambitious project to date, is his recent methodological analysis of the possibility of practising what he terms 'parallel hermeneutics' across differing world faiths and wider communities, so that the global challenges facing all human communities may be better addressed.[66]

The Roman Catholic Nicholas Healy, a student of both Barth and Balthasar, has also published recent work in the comparative field across Christian denominational and traditional divides, which is perhaps best represented in his attempt to construct a 'practical-prophetic ecclesiology'.[67] In this he considers a wide variety of ecclesiological methodologies and priorities concerned with the church-world relationship. He examines this, in particular, in the light of the pluralist reality today and he brings to bear the influence of Balthasar, MacIntyre, sociology and postmodern ethnography in his own methodological conclusions aimed at the construction of a less rigid, though no less real, ecclesiology that allows the church to fulfil its mission to and in the world. Hence, he purports to offer a 'practical prophetic ecclesiology' as opposed to one that is primarily 'speculative and systematic'. However, although he deems himself more truly 'pluralistic' in outlook than what traditionally passes for pluralistic approaches (which he heavily criticizes and deems to be inconsistent in the final analysis), Healy's position in this study appears to have much more in common with – at best – inclusivistic approaches and even with neo-exclusivistic ecclesiologies than he might perhaps realize or wish to acknowledge.[68]

Natalie Watson has offered valuable systematic, ethical, political and methodological reflections in her comparative study of a variety of *feminist* ecclesiologies. Influenced by Schüssler Fiorenza's work, she suggests that the time has come for a reinterpretation of church history in the light of feminist critique. Only thus can the 'invisibility' of women in the Church be countered.[69] Simone Sinn's work – as we have seen – shows much promise and in her aforementioned study of the interrelationship between ethics, ecclesiology and hermeneutics is of direct relevance to our topic in hand.

One interesting work which deserves to be bracketed in this company is a recent study into the contemporary context of Christian apologetics by the non-conformist scholar Alan Sell.[70] He offers a thoroughgoing and somewhat exhaustive study into the nature and possibility of the contemporary 'intellectual commendation of the Christian faith' (i.e., apologetics), which is informed by his previous studies of similar questions in relation to the Enlightenment and the English Idealists of the late nineteenth century.

Because of the intra-denominational nature of the study, it thus also makes a contribution to the field of comparative hermeneutical ecclesiology, even though it does not explicitly claim to do so. Sell believes that apologetics is neither a task addressed exclusively to an extra-ecclesial and hostile audience, nor a justification of the faith to those within the confines of the church. Apologetics addresses those both within and without the church. Sell understands apologetics as a task that involves both word and practice. It is philosophically informed and, being concerned with something more fundamentally basic to Christianity, differs from the construction of a systematic theology (which, he believes, is a fuller articulation of the faith which should normally take on a trinitarian shape and form). It is both a task for the Christian individual and an ecclesial task.

Sell states that apologetics is the church confessing the faith and commending it through faithful witness: 'in its broadest sense, confession includes commendation, while the intellectual task of apologetics is a variety of commendation'.[71] Sell neither harks back to the apologetical methods of old, nor dismisses the achievements and positive outcomes of the Enlightenment. Apologetics demands both humility and charity in method.

Apologetics, for Sell, involves shaping and defending a particular worldview, though always mindful of the implications of the fact that it is one amongst (and necessarily in dialogue with) many such worldviews.

Finally, the Jesuit Roger Haight has written extensively in the fields of systematic theology, liberation theology, Christology and, of course, ecclesiology itself. He excels in addressing where the churches and theology currently find themselves *at* in the contemporary world and in suggesting ways forward for the future in the engagement of the churches with those across the numerous churches, religions and beyond the confines of either. He champions the need for the church to embrace a *dialogical* mission. His latest work is a monumental three-volume study in *comparative* ecclesiology, itself.[72] An entire volume in this series, 'Ecclesiological Investigations' is devoted to exploring and discussing his work.

It is all the more disappointing, then, that a focus upon Haight's excellent and pioneering work in this area only serves to highlight further the 'hermeneutical refusal' of the Vatican's Congregation for the Doctrine of the Faith under the then Cardinal Ratzinger. Haight's work on christology was publicly condemned and, in February 2005, he was prohibited from teaching Catholic theology and so forced to leave his post in the Weston Jesuit School of Theology and to transfer to the long-standing 'Hermeneutical-Pluralist' haven of Union Theological Seminary in New York City. Not least of all, the Vatican condemnation make it clear that the Congregation for the Doctrine of the Faith (CDF) took issue with Haight's affirmation of the need for Catholics to take the contemporary pluralist reality seriously.

Again, the work of David Tracy serves as an excellent example of comparative hermeneutics and shall be further discussed, below. Naturally there are so many others besides whom we could also mention here, not least of all those who have influenced such figures and those whom they, in turn, have influenced.[73] Nor can we, alas, provide a more detailed account of specific works of each, but we will, at least, touch upon aspects of just a few of the more pertinent issues (for our purposes here) which preoccupy such works.

Hence, having considered some of the methodological issues and potential pitfalls, as well as the obvious 'factionism' at play here (as so often elsewhere in contemporary theology), we turn our attention to more specifically *ecclesiological* questions in relation to hermeneutics.[74]

Commending the hermeneutical imperative of contemporary ecumenism

Thus the differing theologies, the competing and sometimes conflicting ecclesiologies, often arise from or give rise to contending hermeneutics.[75] Hence an acceptance of the reality and *value* of pluralism would appear to be crucial for any positive way forward, and this must bear fruit in ecclesiological and ethical thinking alike. Hence Jeanrond concludes that,

> In such a state of confusion it must be the task of theologians to serve the Christian community by attempting to clarify the issues as far as possible and to develop an adequate method which will allow them to offer possible criteria for a critical and constructive examination of our common Christian heritage. The simple appeal to tradition in favour of or against a particular ecclesial or theological position can never replace critical and faithful argumentation. The Christian faith must be appropriated, and not just repeated, by all Christians and in every generation anew.[76]

Jeanrond, therefore, espouses the need for a *critical* theology today which not only would help us understand the Christian *message* in our contemporary world, but also would allow us better to 'understand the multi-dimensional context in which we are trying to grasp the heart of this Christian project ... If the Christian tradition is not to end soon altogether, a critical theology and a critical faith-praxis are urgently demanded.'[77]

Likewise, he calls for a critical *hermeneutics* where the theologian views appropriation not as the means by which texts are made to accord with one's own preconception but, rather, 'by adopting a critical and self-critical method of text interpretation theologians will always be prepared to challenge and transform their own preunderstandings and interpretive horizons'.[78] In this task, Jeanrond commends, in particular, the methodology of David Tracy.[79] Alas, space does not permit a fulsome discussion of Tracy's method here, but suffice to say this approach might best be summed up in Tracy's own words where he states that his own theology 'Has two principle foci: a hermeneutics in which the "other" and not the "self", is the dominant focus; and a theological insistence that only a prophetic-mystical form of theology for naming God can help us now.'[80] Jeanrond's brief account also helps readers to grasp the essence of Tracy's later approach, whereby 'plurality and ambiguity' are seen as being 'at the heart of the Christian message'.[81] As Tracy himself suggests:

As greater ecumenical self-exposure takes firmer hold on all Christian theologies, the present conflict of interpretations may yet become a genuine conversation. As all theologies – whether focused proximately upon manifestation, proclamation or prophetic action – focus ultimately upon the reality of the event of Jesus Christ, the full scope of the grace released by that event upon the world in its entirety will follow. What unites these conflicting understandings of world will prove none other than the singular clue which informs their different understandings of God and self. That clue remains the grace which is agapic love disclosed in and by the proleptic event of Jesus Christ. That love as healing gives and demands an opening of every Christian understanding of world to the full scope of the always-already presence of that grace, that love in the worlds of history and nature alike.[82]

However, whilst the likes of Jeanrond and Lewis Mudge demonstrate just how possible and necessary it is to make that shift from a more general *theological* to more specifically *ecclesiological* hermeneutical engagement, David Tracy would appear to wish to hold the two more closely in tandem – the hermeneutics of community wedded together with our attempts to 'name God' in the present – these two forming two further constant themes in his own thought.[83]

As *A Treasure in Earthen Vessels* states, quoting 1 Corinthians 10, all may well be lawful, but not all builds up [community].[84] In one sense, all ecclesiology is hermeneutics. Our aim should today be to build upon those who have fused the most valuable insights of those pioneering theorists such as Gadamer and Ricoeur in order to shape not one overall and overarching ecclesiology, but always to allow a healthy and developed hermeneutics of suspicion in the service of praxis-oriented pluralism and one which is always guided by true conversation.[85] But our pluralism must always be genuine and seek to avoid the pretence of pluralism or the varieties of pseudo-pluralism which mask exclusivistic strains in our churches still (and which we saw even in parts of *A Treasure in Earthen Vessels*). So, also, must it not shirk difficult and persisting issues and differences that remain. 'Woolly' pluralism is no real pluralism at all. The importance of sincerity, both intellectual and existential, is further borne out by Bradford Hinze's groundbreaking study focusing on the Roman Catholic Church, which illustrates how fruitful an appropriation of contemporary hermeneutics can be. Hinze makes a convincing case for the necessity of a dialogical ecclesiology, concluding that

> Ultimately, an alternative theology of the church that advocates dialogical discernment and decision-making will be based on a more comprehensive understanding of the communicative character of revelation, liturgy, and the church, and a revised understanding of all the baptized faithful, and the ministries and offices of the laity and ordained; and on a theology of the communion of the Catholic Church in relation to other Christian communions and a theology of the people of God that can illuminate the relations between all God's people in the world. Most importantly the identity and mission of the church draw their inspiration and justification from Christian convictions about the identity and mission of the Triune God. This has always been the case.[86]

Whether we are concerned with intra- and inter-Christian ecclesial and ecclesiological questions, questions of inter-faith dialogue or quests for global means of conversation, solidarity and community alike, our hermeneutical endeavours are geared towards reconciling the conflicts (or potential conflicts) between differing horizons – towards finding common ground in order to facilitate peaceful, meaningful and fruitful coexistence.[87] Perhaps, in relation to this, the passage in *A Treasure in Earthen Vessels* which contains most promise for both ecumenical hermeneutics and hermeneutical ecclesiology and ecumenism, in turn, is that which seems to embrace the need for humility,[88] and which contains what I have called the ecumenical *necessity* of acknowledging and embracing pluralism, albeit in pregnant form (though much less latent than in other sections of that document):

> no interpretation can claim to be absolute. All must be aware of the limitations of any perspective or position. The catholicity that binds communities together makes possible this awareness of limitation as well as a mutual acknowledgment of contribution to one another's interpretation. In this way, catholicity enables communities to free one another from one-sidedness or from over-emphasis on only one aspect of the Gospel. Catholicity enables communities to liberate one another from being blinded or bound by any one context and so to embody across and among diverse contexts the solidarity that is a special mark of Christian *koinonia*.[89]

Indeed, if we even allow ecumenical and intercultural hermeneutics to inform Christian *apologetics*, the service of communion can only be furthered. In this repect, Alan Sell offers hope for the validity and possibility of *extra*-ecclesial apologetics, by affirming the existence of basic common 'epistemological ground' between the apologists and their audience, as well as, in many instances, there being shared social and ethical goals. Sell, refreshingly given the neo-exclusivistic tones of much recent debate surrounding Christian 'orthodoxy' and the interrelation between faith and philosophy, acknowledges the cultural and contextual conditioning of our apologetics. Christian apologetics must, he argues give due attention to the pluralistic context in which Christianity finds itself alongside other religious and secular worldviews. The nature of truth is a question which must be explored with full honesty.[90]

The nature of both hermeneutics in general, but also of our own particular undertakings in hermeneutics, must be as subject to the hermeneutics of suspicion as anything – *A Treasure in Earthen Vessels* is a calling to engage in this, as much as all else to which it calls us. Hence we might we be able to approximate to what Jeanrond calls the 'ethics of reading'[91] in our attempts to engage in discerning not simply a hermeneutics of ecclesiology, but, also, an ethics *of* ecclesiology and *of* ecumenism. Although not explicitly addressing ecclesiology as such, Francis Schüssler Fiorenza echoes similar sentiments, in highlighting the importance of 'the ethics and practice of interpretation'. He goes on to offer some thoughts which might help build upon the tentative methodological sentiments of *A Treasure in Earthen Vessels*:

> Such an ethics and practice of interpretation should acknowledge that the plurality of criteria are in play and a broad reflective equilibrium among the very diverse, and sometimes opposing, criteria is sometimes necessary. Among these criteria is the

interpretation of tradition itself. However, tradition itself is diverse so that 'traditions' in the plural is the more appropriate term. These traditions often have diverse, if not at times conflicting values. They often represent what is and what is not paradigmatic, what is primary and what is secondary, what is an ideal and what is distortion or deformation of an ideal ... Consequently, it has been suggested that the point of interpretation is to work out the integrity of the traditions, of what is normative and paradigmatic within them, to use integrity as a critical evaluative principle.[92]

Here we see suggestions which could bear much hermeneutical fruit in future ecumenical discussions.

Dynamic tradition *is* nothing other than the acceptance of multiplicity and of the inevitability of differing horizons of meaning and interpretation emerging out of differing contexts – often even from within similar contexts. Hence the very concept of tradition itself and the sense of the development of doctrine both affirm the hermeneutical exercise. Remember Christ posed the ultimate hermeneutical question for Christians – 'Who do you say that I am?' And in Paul's letters we see a constant grappling with questions concerning the hermeneutics of the church.[93]

In all, then, and towards such ends, we should be aware of the fundamental importance and *value* of pluralism, dialogue and encounter. The methodological priority of such is again illustrated by Gareth Jones:

A hermeneutic theology ... seeks to go beyond the subject/object dichotomy and is not, therefore, concerned with the discovery of facts. Rather, it is concerned with being meaningful. One of the necessary implications of this position is *pluralism*, the acceptance of a variety of equally meaningful different theological viewpoints, each of which can be genuinely critical ... critical theology as *hermeneutic* theology explicitly recognizes the possibility of many different ways of speaking of God and God's relationship with the world. This is the most important quality of the *open* rhetoric of critical theology in terms of its methodological *character*: its effectiveness and applicability is determined by the establishment of its first principles in the process of naming mystery by reference to a specific event.[94]

In appropriating Jones's sentiments in a more explicitly ecclesiological context, I would change the emphasis here from a focus on 'being meaningful', to a concern with 'meaningful being'. Indeed, such would tie together aspects of systematic theology in general, the fundamental metaphysical importance of trinitarian doctrine of God,[95] and the ethical and practical priorities demanded in ecclesiology itself.

Here the promise of comparative theology and, in particular comparative *ecclesiology* is vital. The debates we have here discussed offer great scope, also, for dialogue beyond the churches and beyond the religious faiths altogether. In particular, they offer scope for how people of faith and/or goodwill may today, in unison, confront the most pressing ethical and social challenges, most notably globalization, which, as a universal, i.e. *ecumenical* problem, requires just such an answer. The work of Sinn, Mudge and Tracy are again most illuminating and useful here. But these are questions for another work![96] For each of these, *hermeneutical engagement* provides a crucial method and hence resource whereby the churches can fulfil their moral mission. Again, Fiorenza's general principles have a striking relevance to our particular ecclesiological and ecumenical concerns here:

> Any interpretation of a tradition takes place within communities of discourse and within the dialogue and discourse among the members of the community. The importance of conversation and dialogue as a hermeneutical principle underscores that the interpretive act is related to diversity of preunderstandings, background theories, and consequence brought into consideration. The integrity of the meaning of the tradition has to be brought into relation (equilibrium) with the experience of practice (retroductive warrants) and with various background theories of the communities of interpretation. The bringing of such diverse actors into play can be called a broad reflective equilibrium, and such integrity is as much a constructive as an interpretive endeavor.[97]

The nature and purpose of the church is to be an interpretive community and so, in its mission, the church performs a ministry of interpretation. In its ecumenical endeavours, the church offers great promise for the wider human family, for such ecumenism provides a very real example of what it means to be an 'interpretive community' and, therefore, offers something to the wider world that is redemptively created.[98]

Like Ricoeur, I believe we can and must learn from many methods of hermeneutical engagement, but be slaves to none. The same, indeed, might also be said for ecclesiology (and, indeed, ethics in its theoretical sense, or even theology in general). In *A Treasure in Earthen Vessels*, we see the *Trinitarian* aspect of Christian community celebrated:

> The Church is a communion of persons in relation; thus active participation and dialogue between communities, and within each community at all levels, is one expression of the Church's nature. The divine being of the Triune God is the source and the exemplar of communion.[99]

Here we may conclude that if, for Tracy, the life and work of Jesus Christ was *the* analogical 'classic' for Christians, i.e. the primary analog for our hermeneutical way of being human selves,[100] then, we may also conclude, that the Trinity is the primary analogue for the church and Christians seeking to discern their mode of societal and communitarian existence in general.[101] Hence it is so for our ecclesiological and ecumenical endeavours, also.[102]

Notes

1. Though Ricoeur's thought will be encountered again, so central has been his influence upon specifically *theological* hermeneutics – not least of all in methodological terms and, above all else, the famed principle of the hermeneutics of suspicion. One recent study of interest here is Mark I. Wallace, 'From Phenomenology to Scripture? Paul Ricoeur's Hermeneutical Philosophy of Religion', *Modern Theology*, 16.3 (July 2000): 301–13. See, also, Lewis Mudge's works, especially his introduction to Ricoeur's hermeneutics itself, *Paul Ricoeur: A*

Guide for the Perplexed (London: Continuum, 2005) and numerous sections of Werner Jeanrond, *Theological Hermeneutics* (London: SCM Press, 1994). Mudge's work is discussed, in its own right, below.

2. A very readable survey is Jeanrond, *Theological Hermeneutics*. Cf. also Martin G. Cartwright, 'Hermeneutics', in Nicholas Lossky, Jose Miguez Bonina, John Pobee, Tom Stransky, Goeffrey Wainwright and Pauline Webb, *Dictionary of the Ecumenical Movement* (Geneva: WCC Publications, 2002), pp. 513–18. A shorter survey and introduction, with particular relation to *biblical* hermeneutics is Raymond E. Brown and Sandra M. Schneiders, 'Hermeneutics', *The New Jerome Biblical Commentary* (London: Geoffrey Chapman, 1991), pp. 1146–65. A recent critical study is Jens Zimmerman, *Recovering Theological Hermeneutics* (Grand Rapids, MI: Baker, 2004).

3. David Tracy, 'God, Dialogue and Solidarity: A Theologian's Refrain', *The Christian Century*, 107 (10 October 1990): 902.

4. Tracy, 'God, Dialogue and Solidarity', p. 903. On this need to 'respect otherness and even radical otherness', see Jeanrond, *Theological Hermeneutics*, p. 174.

5. See ch. 6 of this volume which discusses ethics in relation to ecclesiology.

6. Gareth Jones, *Critical Theology* (Cambridge: Polity Press, 1993), p. 31.

7. And the rise in new schools of hermeneutical thought is, of course, very much an ongoing process. Cf. (e.g.), Giuseppe Zaccaria, 'Trends in Contemporary Hermeneutics and Analytical Philosophy', *Ratio Juris*, 12.3 (September 1999): 274–85, for a discussion of some of the more surprising developments of late.

8. One recent study of relevance here is Garrett Green, *Theology, Hermeneutics, and Imagination: The Crisis of Interpretation at the End of Modernity* (Cambridge: Cambridge University Press, 2000).

9. Here Jeanrond notes that the former are much more willing to engage 'radically' in methodological hermeneutical reflection, utilizing interpretation theory in a manner the latter only will do so only in a more limited sense and then in relation to specifically Christian texts (e.g., the Bible and Christian doctrines).

10. Jeanrond, *Theological Hermeneutics*, pp. 163–4. For an introductory discussion of the revisionist, liberal and postliberal schools of thought in contemporary theology, see the two chapters on these themes in David Ford (ed.), *The Modern Theologians* (Oxford: Basil Blackwell, 1997; 2nd edn); James J. Buckley, 'Revisionist and Liberals' (ch. 17) and William C. Placher, 'Postliberal Theology' (Ch. 18). See also Terence W. Tilley, (ed.), *Postmodern Theologies – The Challenge of Religious Diversity* (New York: Orbis, 1997), esp. ch. 3, 'Revisionist Theology and Reinterpreting Classics for Present Practice', and ch. 7, 'Intratextual Theology in a Postmodern World'. Note, however, that the intricacies of the Roman Catholic magisterium are far more complex than Jeanrond here suggests.

11. He lists lay participation, women in the Church, religious education and attitudes to homosexuals and lesbians in the Church and ministry as examples.

12. Here we see a parallel with concerns expressed in certain sections of *A Treasure in Earthen Vessels*, which is discussed below.

13. Jeanrond, *Theological Hermeneutics*, p. 166.

14. And, likewise, the more recent CDF document, 'Responses to Some Questions Concerning Certain Aspects of the Doctrine on the Church', issued July 2007. I discuss *Dominus Iesus*, and the wider issues it raises, in *Ecclesiology and Postmodernity: Questions for the Church in Our Times* (Collegeville, NY: Liturgical Press, 2007), ch. 4, pp. 75–101. See, also, Gerard Mannion (ed.), *Church and Religious Other: Essays on Truth, Unity and Diversity* (London: T&T Clark, 2008).

15. Faith and Order Commission, World Council of Churches, *A Treasure in Earthen Vessels: An Instrument for Reflection on Ecumenical Hermeneutics* (Geneva: WCC/Faith and Order Publications, Faith and Order paper 182, 1998). For a commentary, see Simone Sinn, *The Church as Participatory Community: On the Interrelationship between Hermeneutics, Ecclesiology and Ethics* (Dublin: Columba Press, 2002), pp. 23–33.

16. *A Treasure in Earthen Vessels*, §7. In relation to the final point made in this quotation, an interesting essay of relevance is Oswald Bayer, 'Hermeneutical Theology', *Scottish Journal of Theology*, 56.2, (2003): 131–47, which speaks of God, in the communication of Godself, being 'himself [*sic*] a *hermeneut*, an interpreter: he himself accomplishes the hard work of translation, from his heavenly language into our earthly human language', p. 131.

17. All references taken from the Montreal report. Such passages illustrate that the document often seems to offer *parallel* sentiments to those expressed elsewhere. For example, in speaking of the historical and contextual *variety* of hermeneutical engagement throughout Christian history, along with the hermeneutical task of discerning the *mystery* that is God (§10), we hear echoes of the work of David Tracy, amongst others. Whilst in the section on tradition and traditions, we obviously hear echoes of the 'father of Roman Catholic ecumenism', Yves Congar and his seminal studies of these very concepts, along with intimations of the ongoing debate concerning the Church particular and the Church universal. Following a meeting in Bristol, Faith and Order issued a further report, 'The Significance of the Hermeneutical Problem for the Ecumenical Movement', in 1967. Also of significance was the Faith and Order meeting at Santiago de Compostela, in 1993, where the commitment was given to move towards the definition of an 'ecumenical hermeneutic'.

18. §17.

19. §18. Indeed, it appears that Congar's shadow looms large across the Montreal discussions.

20. Cf. *Treasure in Earthen Vessels*, §21–7.

21. §32.

22. §35 Though, strangely, *ethics* does not figure prominently amongst these in the discussion here, as elsewhere in the document. Of related concern here, is Edward Farley's important suggestion that we perceive contemporary practical theology, itself, as *the hermeneutics of practice*, 'Interpreting Situations: An Inquiry into the Nature of Practical Theology', ch. 1 of Lewis S. Mudge and James N. Poling (eds), *Formation and Reflection: The Promise of Practical Theology* (Philadelphia, PA: Fortress Press, 1987).

23. §28.

24. §30, echoing David Tracy in general and, indeed, the critical work of Sinn in relation to this very document. I have offered an analogous argument concerning dialogue in my 'Ecclesiology and Postmodernity – A New Paradigm for the Church?' *New Blackfriars*, 85 (May 2004): 304–28.

25. Thus echoing the myriad of debates concerning authority in the churches in recent decades and, in particular, the work of Roger Haight.

26. §31.

27. Cf. Kilian McDonnell, 'The Ratzinger–Kasper Debate: The Universal and the Local Churches', *Theological Studies*, 63 (2002): 1–24, Robert Leicht, 'Cardinals in Conflict', *The Tablet* (28 April 2001); Walter Kasper, 'On the Church', in *Stimmen der Zeit* (December 2000), repr. *America*, 184 (April 2001) and *The Tablet* (21 June 2001).

28. As are Hans Küng's sentiments on the notion of true ecumenical catholicity, at both length and breadth, which relates, especially, to §45. Cf. Hans Küng, 'Why do I Remain a Catholic?', postscript to English edn of *The Church – Maintained in Truth* (London: SCM Press, 1980), pp. 80–87.

29. I.e., his writings, in the main, when prefect of the Congregation for the Doctrine of the Faith. His recent elevation to the Chair of Peter has, initially led to more ambiguity in the form and character of his statements on such issues – on the one hand continuing the neo-exclusivistic agenda from his CDF days, on the other stating that he wishes to reach out to other churches and faith groups. Yet documents such as the July 2007 CDF 'Responses to Some Questions Concerning Certain Aspects of the Doctrine on the Church' suggest continuity with earlier stances will be the norm.

30. Cf. also, §49:

This ongoing dialogue involving both catholicity and contextuality characterizes the

Church as a 'hermeneutical community'. The Church, whether embodied in a local congregation, episcopal diocese, or a Christian World Communion, is called to interpret texts, symbols and practices so as to discern the Word of God as a word of life amid ever-changing times and places.

Further discussions of these ecclesial concepts can be found in Christopher Duraisingh, 'Contextual and Catholic: Conditions for Cross-Cultural Hermeneutics', *Anglican Theological Review*, 82.4 (Autumn 2000); and Gerard Mannion, 'What's in a Name? Hermeneutical Questions on "Globalisation", Catholicity and Ecumenism', *New Blackfriars* (March 2005): 204–15.

31. For discussions of these themes, see Gerard Mannion, ' "A Haze of Fiction" – Legitimation, Accountability and Truthfulness', in Francis Oakley and Bruce Russet (eds), *Governance, Accountability and the Future of the Church*, (New York and London: Continuum, 2003), pp. 161–77; and 'What Do We Mean by Authority?' in Bernard Hoose (ed.), *Authority and Roman Catholicism – Theory and Practice* (Aldershot: Ashgate, 2002), pp. 19–36. A number of essays and debates concerning each of these concepts are also featured in Gerard Mannion, Richard Gaillardetz, Jan Kerkhofs, Kenneth Wilson (eds), *Readings in Church Authority – Gifts and Challenges for Contemporary Catholicism* (Aldershot: Ashgate, 2003). On reception, in particular, cf. the chapter by Richard Gaillardetz on this topic in Hoose (ed.), *Authority and Roman Catholicism*.

32. §59. Cf. the discussion of this, particularly in relation to Roger Haight's conception of 'many magisteria' in Mannion, *Ecclesiology and Postmodernity*, ch. 5, pp. 105–23 and ch. 7, pp. 151–74; also, Gerard Mannion (ed.), *Comparative Ecclesiology: Critical Investigations*, (London: T&T Clark, 2008), chs 1 and 9.

33. In the discussion of *reception* we once again hear echoes of similar themes from David Tracy's work, here most notably the notion of hermeneutics as engagement with and acceptance of the other, as discussed below.

34. In some parts where it is more assertive or suggestive, it is sometimes lacking sufficient argumentation or evidence in support.

35. Sinn, *The Church as Participatory Community*, p. 27.

36. Ibid., p. 31.

37. Francis Schüssler Fiorenza, 'The Conflict of Hermeneutical Traditions and Christian Theology', *Journal of Chinese Philosophy*, 27.1 (March 2003): 3–3 (3).

38. §5, 'In this text we take the term hermeneutics to mean both the art of interpretation and application of texts, symbols and practices in the present and from the past, and the theory about the methods of such interpretation and application'.

39. Sinn, *The Church as Participatory Community*, p. 27.

40. Ibid., p. 34.

41. In a conversation with the author of the present article at Union Theological Seminary, New York, July 2004.

42. In addition to Sinn, *The Church as Participatory Community*, which we discuss, cf. also Lewis Mudge, *Rethinking the Beloved Community: Ecclesiology, Hermeneutics, Social Theory* (Geneva: WCC Publications and University Press of America, 2001). The ongoing work of Bradford Hinze is a particularly promising example of the sort of constructive ecumenical ecclesiological employment of hermeneutics that this chapter seeks to commend: see, for example, Bradford Hinze, *Practices of Dialogue in the Roman Catholic Church: Aims and Obstacles, Lessons and Laments* (New York and London: Continuum, 2006).

43. Sinn, *The Church as Participatory Community*, p. 11.

44. Ibid., p. 55.

45. Cf. pp. 57–60.

46. Sinn, *The Church as Participatory Community*, p. 64. Chapter 3 of this work in its entirety, 'Developing the Idea of Church as Participatory Community', expands upon this notion at length. See also Sinn's excellent overview, 'Hermeneutics and Ecclesiology', ch. 34 of

Mannion and Mudge (eds), *The Routledge Companion to the Christian Church* (London: Routeledge, 2007).

47. Here we do not mean to suggest that these categories in any way conform to Jeanrond's 'three types'; on the contrary, they represent significant developments from the situation which he described in 1994.

48. One could not hope to cover the vast array of scholars whose work has focused upon or engaged with issues pertaining to the interrelation between hermeneutics and ecclesiology. Thus what follows is merely a discussion of representative samples of work in this field. Space alas, does not permit a proper study of numerous classic studies, nor of recent suggestive monographs.

49. Works of particular relevance, here, include *Created for Community: Connecting Christian Belief with Christian Living* (Grand Rapids, MI: Baker, 1998; 2nd edn): *Theology for the Community of God* (Grand Rapids, MI: Eerdmans, 2000); *Revisioning Evangelical) Theology: A Fresh Agenda for the 21st Century* (Downers Grove, IL: Intervarsity, 1993); *Renewing the Center: Evangelical Theology in a Post-Theological Era* (Grand Rapids, MI: Baker, 2000); *Theology for the Community of* God (Grand Rapids, MI: Eerdmans, 2000); and *The Social God and the Relational Self: Trinitarian Theology* (Louisville, KY: Westminster John Knox Press, 2001). A short representative example of his work is Stanley Grenz, 'Ecclesiology', Ch. 15 of *The Cambridge Companion to Postmodern Theology,* ed. Kevin Vanhoozer (Cambridge: Cambridge University Press, 2003).

50. Cf. *Revisioning Evangelical Theology.*

51. Dan R. Stiver, 'Theological Method', in Kevin J. Vanhoozer (ed.), *The Cambridge Companion to Postmodern Theology* (Cambridge: Cambridge University Press, 2003).

52. Dan R. Stiver, 'Theological Method', p. 171. In a very different fashion, we see similar and related themes explored in Francis Schüssler Fiorenza, 'The Conflict of Hermeneutical Traditions and Christian Theology', 3–31.

53. Stiver, 'Theological Method', p. 179.

54. Hans George Gadamer, *Truth and Method* (New York: Crossroad, 1991; 2nd edn), p. 270.

55. Stiver, 'Theological Method', p. 179.

56. Cf. Miroslav Volf, *After our Likeness: The Church as the Image of the Trinity* (Grand Rapids, MI: Eerdmanns, 1998).

57. Two other works of most relevance here are *Exclusion and Embrace: A Theological Exploration of Identity, Otherness, and Reconciliation* (Nashville, TN: Abingdon Press, 1996), and Miroslav Volf and William H. Katerberg (eds) *The Future of Hope: Christian Tradition amid Modernity and Postmodernity,*(Grand Rapids, MI: Eerdmans, 2004).

58. Arne Rasmusson, *The Church as Polis: From Political Theology to Theological Politics as Exemplified by Jürgen Moltmann and Stanley Hauerwas* (Lund: Lund University Press, 1994).

59. The hermeneutical and ecclesiological works of John Howard Yoder and Stanley Hauerwas resulted in profoundly ambivalent and therefore ultimately methodological sterility owing to the inward-looking and 'world-renouncing' ecclesial focus found running throughout the numerous volumes of both. Hauerwas's work is discussed in greater detail in Chapter 6 of this present study.

60. Curran's work is also further discussed in Chapter 6.

61. Cf., for example, her *Discipleship of Equals – A Critical Feminist Ekklesia-logy of Liberation* (London: SCM Press, 1993); *In Memory of Her* (London: SCM Press, 1983); and *Women Invisible in Theology and Church*, ed., with M. Collins (Edinburgh: Concilium T.& T. Clark, l985).

62. Cf., for example, *Church, Charism and Power* (London: SCM Press, 1985) and *Ecclesiogenesis – The Base Communities Reinvent the Church* (London: Collins Flame, 1986).

63. Cf., for example, *Church, Ecumenism and Politics* (Slough: St Paul's Press, 1988); *Called to Communion. Understanding the Church Today* (San Francisco, CA: Ignatius Press, 1996); *The Ratzinger Report: An Inclusive Interview on the State of the Church* (with Vitttorio Messori) (San Francisco, CA: Ignatius Press, 1986).

64. See Mannion, *Ecclesiology and Postmodernity*, esp. ch. 3, pp. 43–74 and ch. 4, pp. 75–101.

65. Cf. Lewis Mudge, 'Thinking in the Community of Faith: Toward an Ecclesial hermeneutic', ch. 6 of Lewis S. Mudge and James N. Poling (eds), *Formation and Reflection; The Sense of a People: Toward a Church for the Human Future* (Philadelphia, PA: Trinity Press International, 1992); *The Church as Moral Community: Ecclesiology and Ethics in Ecumenical Debate* (Geneva: WCC Publications, 1998); *Rethinking the Beloved Community;* Lewis Mudge, 'Ecclesiology and Ethics in Current Ecumenical Debate', *The Ecumenical Review*, 48 (January 1996): 11–27; and also his 'Towards a Hermeneutic of the Household: "Ecclesiology and Ethics" after Harare', *The Ecumenical Review*, 51 (July 1999): 243–55. See also his *The Gift of Responsibility: The Promise of Dialogue among Christians, Jews, and Muslims* (New York: Continuum, 2007).

66. See Mannion, 'What's in a Name?' for a discussion of Mudge's work, alongside other recent treatments of ecclesial hermeneutics, particularly in relation to the challenges posed to the Church by globalization. Also of relevance here are the works of Robert J. Schreiter, cf. *The New Catholicity: Theology Between the Global and the Local* (Maryknoll, NY: Orbis, 1997) and *Constructing Local Theologies* (Maryknoll, NY: Orbis, 1985). Cf. also Gregory Baum was addressing the issues pertaining to this chapter as early as the 1960s: cf. 'The Church as Hermeneutical Principle', part III of Gregory Baum, *Faith and Doctrine: A Contemporary View* (London: Newman Press, 1969), pp. 91–133.

67. Nicholas Healy, *Church, World and the Christian Life* (Cambridge: Cambridge University Press, 2000).

68. Of greatest concern is his somewhat 'straw-man' dismissal of pluralistic perspectives.

69. Natalie Watson, *Introducing Feminist Ecclesiology* (London: Continuum, 2002). Cf. also, her 'Feminist Ecclesiologies', ch. 25 of Mannion and Mudge (eds), *The Routledge Companion to the Christian Church*.

70. Alan P. F. Sell, *Confessing and Commending the Faith* (Cardiff: University of Wales Press, 2002).

71. Ibid., p. 15.

72. Cf., Roger Haight, *Christian Community in History*, 3 vols (London: Continuum, 2004 and 2008) (vol. 1, *Historical Ecclesiology;* vol. 2, *Comparative Ecclesiology;* vol. 3, *Ecclesial Existence*). Cf., also, his 'Comparative Ecclesiology', ch. 21 of *The Routledge Companion to the Christian Church*. For an outline and various discussions of Haight's ecclesiological work, see Mannion (ed.), *Comparative Ecclesiology: Critical Investigations*.

73. We have already mentioned Robert Schreiter and Gregory Baum, and other examples of leading figures here include Johan Baptist Metz, Rosemary Radford Ruether, Nicholas Lash, Gustavo Gutierrez, William Schweiker and, more recently, Lieven Boeve. Of course, structuralist and materialist hermeneutics have also been highly influential in the later decades of twentieth-century theology.

74. Cf. Hinze, *Practices of Dialogue;* Mannion, *Ecclesiology and Postmodernity;* Lieven Boeve, *Interrupting Tradition: An Essay on Christian Faith in a Postmodern Context* (Leuven: Peeters, 2003); and William Schweiker, *Mimetic Reflections: A Study in Hermeneutics, Theology and Ethics* (New York: Fordham University Press, 1990). For a very different take on methodological considerations in relation to theology (to, for example, Boeve's, Schweiker's and my own intimations thus far), see Donald Wood, 'The Place of Theology in Theological Hermeneutics', *International Journal of Systematic Theology*, 4.2 (July 2002): 156–71.

75. As, for example, attested to, in differing ways by Jeanrond, *Theological Hermeneutics*; in James Buckley, 'Revisionists and Liberals', ch. 17 of David Ford (ed.), *The Modern Theologians* (Oxford: Basil Blackwell, 1997); and Francis Schüssler Fiorenza, 'The Conflict of Hermeneutical Traditions and Christian Theology', 3–31. From a different angle, focusing upon 'practical' ecclesiologies, we have Nicholas Healy, 'Practices and the New Ecclesiology: Misplaced Concreteness?', *International Journal of Systematic Theology*, 5.3 (November 2003): 287–308.

76. Jeanrond, *Theological Hermeneutics*, p. 166.

77. Ibid., p. 173.

78. Ibid., p. 174.

79. Jeanrond's discussion of Tracy is contained in pp. 174–7. Tracy's primary works of relevance here include *Blessed Rage for Order: The New Pluralism in Theology* (New York: Crossroad, 1975); *The Analogical Imagination: Christian Theology and the Culture of Pluralism* (New York: Crossroad, 1981); *Dialogue with the Other: The Inter-Religious Dialogue* (Leuven: Peeters, 1990); *On Naming the Present, God, Hermeneutics, and Church* (Maryknoll, NY: Orbis Books, 1994). See, also, Werner G. Jeanrond and Jennifer L. Rike (eds), *Radical Pluralism and Truth, David Tracy and the Hermeneutics of Religion* (New York: Crossroad, 1991); and Gareth Jones, 'Tracy: Halting the Postmodernist Slide', ch. 5 of his *Critical Theology*, pp. 113–34.

80. David Tracy, 'God, Dialogue and Solidarity', p. 902. What Tracy means here is further explicated in a methodological sense in his 'The Uneasy Alliance Reconceived: Catholic Theological method, Modernity and Postmodernity', *Theological Studies*, 50 (1989): 548–70.

81. Jeanrond, *Theological Hermeneutics*, pp. 176–7.

82. Tracy, *The Analogical Imagination*, pp. 437–8.

83. None of this is to suggest that Tracy is without his critics – cf., for example, Gareth Jones's critque in his *Critical Theology*.

84. No. 38,

> In a context of what some call postmodern pluralism, where individual choice is so emphasized that common points of reference are obscured, an affirmation of commitment and of communion may become life-giving. This affirmation need not deny the value of personal freedom but rather recognizes the tension Paul addresses when he wrote to the Corinthians: 'All things are lawful', but not all things build up. Do not seek your own advantage, but that of the other' (1 Cor 10.23f.).

85. An interesting discussion of the nature of theological conversation is the contribution by Nicholas Lash, 'Conversation in Context', in Linda Hogan and Barbara Fitzgerald (eds), *Between Poetry and Politics: Essays in Honour of Enda MacDonagh* (Dublin: Columba, 2004), pp. 51–66.

86. Hinze, *Practices of Dialogue*, p. 266. Further discussion of the *necessity* of ecclesial dialogue and of the importance of trinitarian theological reflection for ecclesiology can be found in Mannion, *Ecclesiology and Postmodernity*, respectively chs 5–7 (pp. 105–74) and ch. 8 (pp. 175–91). Further recent and promising constructive essays on the promise of dialogue informed by hermeneutics can also be found in Paul Murray, *Catholic Learning: Explorations in Receptive Ecumenism* (London and New York: Oxford University Press, 2008).

87. Cf. Mannion, 'What's in a Name?'

88. Again, a theme explored throughout much of this present volume. Cf. also Mannion 'Ecclesiology and Postmodernity'.

89. §48.

90. Cf. Alan P. F. Sell, *Confessing and Commending the Faith*. Cf. also Christopher Duraisingh, 'Contextual and Catholic'.

91. Jeanrond, *Theological Hermeneutics*, pp. 116–18; i.e., an ethics of interpretation itself.

92. Francis Schüssler Fiorenza, 'The Conflict of Hermeneutical Traditions and Christian Theology', 23–4. See also Haight, *Christian Community in History*, vol. 3, *Ecclesial Existence*. and Mannion (ed.), *Comparative Ecclesiology: Critical Investigations*. I realize here that we have left many debates concerning the nature and method of hermeneutics itself untouched. Whilst such debates are of vital importance, our focus here has been upon aspects of what hermeneutical engagement can offer to ecclesiology and ecumenism, and so space does not permit a worthy treatment of these additional debates. Thankfully, the literature on such debates continues to grow. Fiorenza's own article addresses a number of them, as does Mudge's *Rethinking the Beloved Community*. Again, cf. also Christopher Duraisingh, 'Contextual and Catholic'.

93. Cf. Yves Congar's seminal study, *Tradition and Traditions – An Historical and Theological Essay* (London: Burns & Oates, 1966).

94. Jones, *Critical Theology*, pp. 31–2.
95. Cf. Joseph Bracken, 'Images of God within Systematic Theology', *Theological Studies*, 63 (2002): 362–73. Here he argues for our images and models of God to go beyond 'mere' metaphor and to bear some relation, in a wider metaphysical explanatory framework, to the reality with which Christian theology is concerned – the being of God. Bracken's preference here then is for the methodological primacy of 'social ontology' in a systematic exploration of the Christian God – i.e. focusing upon an understanding of God as a community of divine persons. Cf. also his *Society and Spirit: A Trinitarian Cosmology* (Cranbury, NJ: Associated University Press, 1991) and also *The One in the Many: a Contemporary Reconstruction of the God–World Relationship* (Grand Rapids, MI: Eerdmans, 2001).
96. See, e.g., Sinn, *The Church as Participatory Community*, pp. 64-70; 'Towards a Hermeneutic of the Household: "Ecclesiology and Ethics" after Harare'. Cf. also Mannion, 'What's in a Name?', 204–15.
97. Fiorenza, 'The Conflict of Hermeneutical Traditions and Christian Theology', p. 25.
98. I am indebted to Kenneth Wilson for suggestions concerning these elements of church and ecumenical life. On the wider implications of Christian ecumenism, see, also, Mannion, 'What's in a Name?'
99. §64.
100. See especially, David Tracy, *The Analogical Imagination*. Of particular ecclesiological and hermeneutical relevance here are the methodological discussions: pp. 21–79, 99–135, 339–64, 372–98 and 405–35.
101. But not in a hierarchical sense that we see in some more conservative ecclesiologies based upon trinitarian thinking. Anton Houtepen suggests the churches require *two* differing ecumenical endeavours. The one, a hermeneutics of tradition; the other, of communion. (i.e., hermeneutics of the faith in relation to the former and of the Church in the latter). (See Anton Houtepen 'The Faith of the Church Through the Ages: Ecumenism and Hermeneutics', *Bulletin: Centro Pro Unione*, 44 [1993] 3–15). On trinitarian ecclesiologies cf. again Mannion, *Ecclesiology and Postmodernity*, ch. 8.
102. Cf. *A Treasure in Earthen Vessels*, §68:

> In and through diverse historical and contemporary forms of inculturation and contextualization the bread of life, which is to be broken and distributed, remains one bread. Although the Word enters history, this historicity does not limit it to any single historical form or formulation. Yet this insight leads neither to limitless diversity nor to ecumenical complacency. Rather, as a hermeneutical community, the Church is called to grow into full koinonia by Spirit-guided discernment of the living Tradition. The Church should not be imprisoned by holding on to inadequate answers from the past, nor should it silence the Word of God by endlessly putting off a clear recognition of the way this Word continues to impart meaning and orientation for human life. Under the guidance of the Holy Spirit, in faithfulness to the living Tradition, and through genuine ecumenical forms of conciliar deliberation and reception, the Church is called to 'interpret the signs of the times' (Mt. 16.3) by looking to the One who is both in and beyond time, to the One 'who is the same, yesterday, today and forever' (Heb. 13.8).

Chapter 5

JOY IN THE PRESENCE OF THE CRUCIFIED

Kenneth Wilson

Never has it been more important to talk of joy when so much of our world, it seems, knows nothing of it. Surely, however, it is outrageous, even obscene, to talk of joy, health, justice, peace and prosperity in a world busily beating its ploughshares into swords, which is ravaged by disease and apparently organized to satisfy the desires of the powerful and rich at the expense of the marginalized poor! Yet there is One Body, which is called to do just that, the church, the community of faith. It is the purpose of this essay to explore how and why this is true, why the world needs such celebration and why it can have confidence in it.

The church is a sacrament; in her very being she is a sign of God's presence with God's world and with all God's people. She knows why it is neither a perverse prejudice nor a naïve assertion but a simple human necessity to be joyful in the presence of the Crucified, the head of the Church, the incarnate presence of God. It is only possible, of course, in the light of the post-resurrection faith that calls the church to be the Body of Christ and to share with him the self-sacrificial giving which transforms God's redemptively creative vision of wholeness, into the real liveliness of affection, justice, truth and peace graciously promised by God to all creation. But what do we mean by *creation*? How are we to deal with the subtle ambiguities that arise from the complexity of holding together the divine and the human, the natural and the supernatural?

I

The approach one adopts in order to understand the relationship between nature and grace lies at the heart of Christian theology and gives rise, for example, to many of the divisions between (and within) the Roman Catholic, Orthodox and Protestant traditions.[1]

On the one hand there is the view that nature and grace are separate in the fundamental sense that there is such a dimension of experience for the human as *ungraced* nature. This would imply in its extreme Catholic form that there could be a divinely given end for human nature that was entirely natural and which could therefore be achieved apart from the gift of grace. Given that salvation is possible but that nature and grace are utterly distinct, salvation in this life would not involve knowledge of the actual experience of divine grace but rather the realization of a potential in human nature that by divine grace offers the possibility of encouraging glimpses of the supernatural.

On the other hand, a Protestant tradition in an extreme form holds that salvation is by grace alone, *sola gratia*, so that there is no need for – because properly understood there is no possibility of – any participation of the human will in the transformation of human nature. Even the exercise of the will, it is claimed, occurs only because of the actual promptings of divine grace.

Important work, especially amongst French theologians of the twentieth century, for example Chenu, Rahner, and especially de Lubac, has introduced us to a clearer perspective from which to grasp the relationship of nature and grace.[2] They are separate in the sense that they must never be confused, but each implies a mutuality, an appreciation of which is necessary to the other. So it is that grace is only grace in so far as it supposes nature; there would after all be no point in grace being grace apart from nature. Without nature there would be – could be – no grace. And as for human nature, while it is indeed other than God, it is open to God's grace and cannot be what it is unless it is so. It is the mutual openness of this love and desire, divine and human, which is explored in the ways in which the life and work of the Christ is carefully expressed and contrasted in the many evolving themes included within christology. There is, as has been wisely said by Rahner amongst others, no such thing as *ungraced* nature – a fact for which we can be utterly thankful.

The matter can be taken further. For not only is it the case that human nature knows no such thing as *ungraced* nature, nature in itself is nothing if not graced. Indeed it might be argued that it is this very point that is a dimension of what is meant when one claims that the world is a creation and not a happenstance: that is, whatever else may be included within our understanding of creation, 'creation' *means* that the world – nature – will only be understood for what it really is when it is seen to be the context of God's creating presence.[3] The way in which, for example, the traditions express it that are gathered in the books of Genesis, Deutero-Isaiah, and later by the Evangelist in the Gospel of St John, suggests that they all share this understanding. All the primary relationships of God and the world expressed in Genesis are active; they emanate from God, they include the world and they are of course stated in verbs.

> In the beginning God *created* the heavens and the earth.
> The earth was without form and void, and darkness
> was upon the face of the deep; and the Spirit of God
> *was moving* over the face of the waters.[4]

The world of nature is defined as creation by the fact of God's relationship with it. Moreover it is a relationship that grows through the mutuality of conversation. 'And God said . . .' In a profound sense that we lose sight of at our peril, there is nothing more active, engaging, complete or demanding, than conversation. Even our language takes account of this; to be human is to *be* in conversation.

As the creation stories unfold we see that the world is affirmed as a habitable place fit for the responsible life of human being.[5] Deutero-Isaiah emphasizes this perspective:

> For thus says the LORD,
> who created the heavens
> (he is God!)
> who formed the earth and made it
> (he established it;
> he did not create it in chaos,
> he formed it to be inhabited!):
> I am the LORD, and there is no other.[6]

Considered in this way, the world as creation must be understood as graced, that is open to the possibilities which flow from the fact of shared conversation between Creator and creature, God and humankind. And, it seems to me, we are now helped to appreciate this by the very fact that we know beyond any doubt that the creation stories are not uniquely Israelite, and therefore not uniquely Jewish or Christian. On the contrary, they emerge from centuries of reflection and conversation amongst fellow human beings in the many related traditions of the Middle East – and more widely – where the puzzling experience of 'being human', is unpacked, expressed and lived out.[7] It was, therefore, in this pre-Israelite, pre-Jewish, pre-Christian world that the real nature of the world and of human experience within it began to dawn upon emerging humanity. The Spirit of God was indeed moving upon the face of the waters. Light was beginning to dawn in darkness, and the regular order (law) of a habitable world to emerge. The conversation of God with the world precedes the mythical formulations that we find in the Old Testament: the 'story-telling' implicit within the whole matter of conversation had already begun. In some circles the existence of similar stories predating the Jewish and Christian has been and is still regarded as a threat; the truth is the contrary. The discovery that they were the outcome of centuries of hard work lends them verisimilitude. The graced world of creation was always open to meaningful questioning through 'conversation' and vigorous debate about the relation of the divine with the human.[8] Moreover, subsequent reflection has shown these same stories to be capable of bearing the weight of continuous reinterpretation in the substantial continuing conversation that includes the new 'myths' arising from scientific enquiry, imaginative exploration and creative endeavour.

II

For Christians, of course, the nature of God as God's self, is expressed in God's living commitment of God's self to the world in Christ. God will not take 'no' for an answer; God's world can and will fulfil God's purpose in creating. No Christian interpretation of creation that is other than christological has been able to stand the test of time. Such a claim is based upon a firm understanding of nature as 'graced', for only such a nature can provide the substance for incarnation.

The Evangelist, St John, grasps the graced character of nature when he adapts
the hymn with which he begins his gospel to develop his own understanding of the
Incarnation:

> In the beginning was the Word;
> the Word was in God's presence,
> and the Word was God.
> He was present with God in the beginning.
>
> Through him all things came into being,
> And apart from him not a thing came to be.
> That which had come to be in him was life,
> And this life was the light of men.
> The light shines on in the darkness,
> For the darkness did not overcome it.
>
> He was in the world,
> And the world was made by him.
> To his own he came;
> Yet his own people did not recognize him.
> But all those who did accept him
> He empowered to become God's children.
>
> And the Word became flesh
> And made his dwelling among us.
> And we have seen his glory,
> The glory of an only Son coming from the Father,
> Filled with enduring love.
>
> And of his fullness
> We have all had a share –
> Love in place of love.[9]

The affirmation here is both dense so as to invite serious attention if one is to see
its profundity and astonishingly clear in its simplicity. The Evangelist intuits that
the gracing of the world by God is such that it can bear the full weight of God –
not simply the mark or sign of God, but God *really* – without threat to the
character of God or the nature of creation. Indeed, we can see here just what it
means to talk of nature and grace as mutually informative, as was discussed above.
There is nothing in God that militates against the fulfilment in the world of
human experience of everything that human beings want if they are to be
completely themselves. The Word which was with God from before the beginning,
which is therefore uncreated and uncontaminated in any way by nature itself, is the
same Word which was physically present in the world in the person of Jesus Christ.
There is no smidgeon of the created order that is outside or beyond God's creative
presence; the Word which was with God is incarnate in the world as a whole, there
is no bit of the world that is somehow open to God as opposed to the rest of the

world. The world is creation: if it were not so, there would be no incarnation of the Word.

The wholeness of the world which is asserted by the claim that it is created is affirmed now in human experience because of what we increasingly understand to be the balances, relationships – seen, half-seen and unseen – and the interrelatedness of the uncountable dimensions of the natural world. The very fact that everything is open, as far as we can see, to exploration by the human mind itself confirms that nature is graced and a real context for the developing conversation that God has established with the world. I used the term 'created *order*' above advisedly. The ordering of creation, its patterning and organization, owes everything to God. However, following the perception expressed in the creation myths of Genesis, the ordering of creation is what God does; it is not what God has done. Human beings who use their minds, feelings and imaginations in developing the conversation with God are not simply engaged in uncovering what the order of creation is, they are working with God to *order* creation. Moreover the creation so understood is not simply beginning with God, it also moves towards God, as its end.

This approach to God's creating requires us to see that an understanding of Jesus, whom Christians call the Christ, which looks only at his person will be incomplete; a more complete perspective will, as theologians have increasingly come to see, want to take into account 'the person *and work*' of Christ. The work of Christ was, and is, to make plain the 'gracedness' of nature, and to instantiate in intelligible, human experience the fact that the world is not 'abandoned' by God but is the place of God's absolute commitment of God's self to making a success of what God has begun.[10] What God has begun, God can and will finish.

At this point a serious problem arises, for notwithstanding the reasonableness of the position that the Evangelist advances, human anxiety is inclined to see things differently. So it is that while the light of the uncreated Word graces the world to illuminate its true nature, the world does not recognize it, and therefore loses sight of the true nature of things. While it seems to be true that every human being has a deep desire for love, truth, justice, peace – and joy, in the event that opportunities to enjoy them are present – the work necessary to make a reality of them is ignored, neglected or denied. A primary reason for this is the deepseated human suspicion that since there is only a limited supply of the things that matter to life, as we know it on a day-to-day basis, there may not be enough to go round. In order, therefore, to provide for oneself, one's family and friends, prudence dictates that one needs to secure a sufficiency not just for today, but for the long-term. This too is of course a reasonable position since it is obvious that not everything does exist in unlimited quantities.

But this fear is based upon treating 'nature' as ungraced, which is far from the truth. The Evangelist is not talking of the physical needs of food, health, education or transport, etc., he is talking of those affections, courtesies and relationships which arise from the fact that the world of nature is graced by the presence of God: it is a creation. The point is that the loving-kindness of the divine gift of the law by obedience to which the human world is beginning to express the *gracedness* of the natural world – something to be celebrated for itself and by no means despised – is vastly superseded out of the fullness (*pleroma*) of God, by the grace manifest in Jesus Christ.[11] If only the world understood the assurance of God that the things that matter for human flourishing – namely love, peace, truth and joy – are capable of being expressed because they are in conformity with the way creation is, then the life of human beings in society would be nourished in all the other important dimensions of the good human life: food, health, etc. A full life would be possible for human being, as for God, because the world is of such a kind as to make it always a possibility.

The work of Jesus Christ was, and is, to make plain this very fact. Thus without compromise, Christ's life of affectionate concern included his willing acceptance of the sacrifice of his own life if that was what was necessary for human society to understand that God was serious in God's commitment of God's self to making a success of God's world. The graced world of nature would not receive his dying as the end, any more than God would, so that resurrection is the ultimate judgement of God on the life of Christ, *and* of the world. By so living and dying, Christ affirmed for all to see once and for all that God's ordering of the world in creation was a temporally permanent feature of life.

Theologians ever since, and believers in their own experience, have worked at what this might mean. It has led them to draw the conclusion that since such a temporally permanent feature of human experience depended upon the character of God and the nature of the world's relationship with God, the claim for the world understood as creation could not be merely of temporal permanence; the ordering of the world implied an indelible relationship which it developed in Christological form in the doctrine of the Ascension. The uncreated Word which was with God before all things, through which the world's true nature is revealed, is the same Word which knows the intimacy of the Father now, and through whose work, continued in the Spirit, the world will be utterly transformed so as to enjoy God for ever. The joy that the world knows and seeks, it can know eternally.

III

The world did not recognize its own true nature, and as a consequence even his own people did not accept Jesus, the Christ, the uncreated Word. The usual interpretation of 'his own people',[12] is that it refers to the people of Israel since, for example, Yahweh says of Israel 'You shall be my possession among all the peoples.'[13] Since on many occasions in the Old Testament, the people of Israel can be said to stand for, even to embody in a significant sense, all peoples, the identification is unhelpful to the extent that it apparently privatizes the reference. It is Bultmann who suggests in his commentary that the reference was cosmological and there is sufficient truth in his position for us to want to hang on to it.[14] He may be wrong in his claim that the hymn was gnostic in origin, but surely we are right to follow Bultmann and see, given the tenor of St John's gospel as a whole, a certain inclusivity in the expression. The whole world of creation and the whole human race is God's possession in the sense that God has committed God's self to it. The lack of awareness of the real nature of creation as the place on which God had chosen to put God's name was common to all. The history of Israel was the type of experience in which the experience of the whole world was to be found.

However, there were those who were drawn into conversation with Jesus, and who grew to 'see' and accept him as a person with authority, so that they came to see themselves as, St John says, 'God's children' (Jn 1.12). They were not so much changed into God's children, but in the light of their understanding became aware of the fact that they were God's children and were free to live as God's family in the world. The reprise in the following verse sums it all up. The uncreated Word became flesh in order to show the habitable nature of the graced world in which humans lived. Seeing Christ's glory, that is his *doing* of God's work in the ordering of creation, all those who accept him, know not simply the grace of God in the world but the grace of God in their lives. They are able to live out thankfully in their lives what God has done, and be freed from the fear of failure and the disappointment which comes from the disillusionment of their deepest desires.

I need at this juncture in the argument to make three points about the development of Christian understanding of the Person of Christ, one negative, the other two positive. First, Jesus is not a hero, or a figurehead; the terms give totally the wrong impression. For one thing, a hero is admired rather than loved, an achiever rather than a visionary, a person who is inclined to demand more of others than they can reasonably be expected to give. Alexander the Great may be said to be a hero in this sense. Moreover, a hero often claims or is associated with superhuman power. None of these claims is true of the Jesus of Christian faith. Jesus was not endowed with superhuman power; he was a real human being.[15] Jesus never demanded of others a way of life which it was beyond them to achieve; Jesus was loved, not admired.

Above all Jesus was a visionary, not an achiever. Achievers are what is wanted of course in an entrepreneurial environment such as we have today. The signs are all around us – what is sought after and recommended in our culture is greater knowledge, greater disposable income, greater influence and greater power over others; if we can show any or preferably all of these consistently over time we shall be admired because we have 'achieved'. A successful person may not be liked, may become isolated, may even have little to celebrate in his personal life but that is of little significance in the public mind when put alongside the fact that he is seen to have achieved.

By contrast we are inclined at the present time to regard visionaries as persons who are likely to be self-deluded and seduced by illusion. Jesus was, on the contrary, a visionary in the sense that he saw clearly the nature of the life open to every human being in the world which God was ordering into being God's creation, the partnership open to every person to work with God in that ordering, and the likely demand for sacrifice if that partnership was to be established.

Secondly, Jesus, far from being a hero, was a victim. So great indeed was the threat it was believed he offered to the sly acceptance of powerlessness by the average believer of his time, that they were emboldened to take the limited power available to them and set about removing him. It is a thoroughly intelligible position. If one believes that there is nothing that one can do to make a worthwhile life out of one's deepest desires, which one nevertheless intuits in one's heart to be true and life-enhancing, nothing will be more important than removing the person who is intent upon showing that there is hope. The guilt that follows the failure of belief and consequent weakness of will, will be unbearable, with the consequence that one will seek every means to assuage it, even to the extent of denying life to the person who threatens one by affirming the truth of what one cannot bring one's self to accept. Paradoxically, of course, by removing the victim and confirming one's falsehood, one bears witness to the irrevocability of the truth embodied by the victim in his or her life and death. So it is with Jesus. This victim is Lord.

Interestingly, when the opportunity begins to take shape in our mind, our tendency to allow the present to be determined by the past is challenged. As a matter of fact, as Tsvetan Todorov says, 'Broadly speaking, we do not believe the past should rule the present'; it is just that we are worn down by the inertia that comes from a combination of lack of vision and ignorance of the graced nature that we share.[16] Jesus shows that the present is not determined by the past because the past, present and future are characterized by the presence of God.

Thus, thirdly, when the victim Jesus by his incarnation bears witness to the God who has graced nature with the inexpungable potential to be ordered in creation, he offers a present and therefore a future which is quite unlike the past. By his coming to birth in the powerlessness of human form he gives shape to the dynamic process both underlying and involved in the ordering of creation. It is a process which invites participation, which gives rise to puzzlement and the worthwhileness of curiosity; it asks to be opened up, unpacked, explored, spoken and shared in conversation; it suggests that the conversation of human being is open to and capable of being informed by the Word of God.

Jesus embodies the uncreated Word in his birth, life, death, resurrection and ascension, which are the dimensions that stimulate the enquiring by which Christian theology and the ordinary experience of the Christian believer make a reality of faith. What does it mean? How can one say it? What can one do about it? And the answer is that all those who want what God wants, namely the faithful ordering of creation, will find themselves incorporated into that longing which is fulfilled in Christ. The victim is Lord of life, Lord of the world, and Lord of the church: he fulfils the longing of the world in his person, and invites all his people to share in the work of ordering the world after the pattern of God's creation. In the sharing there comes growth in understanding and the deepening of one's curiosity; in the sharing also there comes the increased awareness that 'The world is charged with the grandeur of God.'[17] And that 'nature is never spent; There lives the dearest freshness deep down things'.[18] To appreciate 'all this juice and all this joy', [19] it is necessary to see things wholly from the right perspective, and to be able to do that one requires to be in the right place, and that 'place', Christians believe, is the church which is the Body of Christ.

IV

Lumen Gentium declares that 'the Church is in Christ as a sacrament or instrumental sign of intimate union with God and of the unity of all humanity'.[20] To be 'in Christ', is much more than being in partnership with Christ, as if there was a contract between the two – 'church and Christ plc', as it were: the two are not well understood if we think of them on the model of being in business together. When the church affirms that it is 'in Christ', it accepts the life that Christ lived and lives as its life, in the sense that God's world can be ordered creatively after the pattern of Christ, given that nature is graced. However, the Church as sacrament is not merely the sign of the union of itself with God in Christ but is also an anticipation of the unity of all things with God, and of all people with one another and with God. The tension between what is, what could be and what will be is profoundly important and cannot be wished away or pretended that it does not exist. Indeed the tension is all the more real for those who are the community of faith that is the Body of Christ, because they know that what they are celebrating is a real possibility. Hence the importance of recognizing that the church in its life celebrates the one essential fact of God's gracious presence in the world with God's people, and at the same time, experiences the hollow emptiness of an actual life lived only in the shadow of this reality.

Above all, it is important to see that the church is not a body that is superhuman or in some way introduced into the world from outside; the church is the most natural society of all. It is not an institution separated off from all other human institutions, but the life-giving witness to all other human institutions of the real nature of life together in society. It is not therefore so much organized to get every one else to *join* it; rather it sets out to be and to behave in such a way that other people will see that their deepest desires for peace, affection, truth and justice can be enjoyed. In the light of that realization and the attempt to live out the life of faith, people will recognize that since experience may question its truth they will want to be in conversation with one another to confirm and develop their faith.

The sacramental act of associating with others to celebrate the grounds of faith is not a remembering of a past event, least of all is it a matter of recalling to mind the exploits of a family hero. It is a sharing in the eternally present happening that is the presence of God with his world in Christ; to share in this celebration is to be encouraged to know that life can begin all over again. The church is the body whose nature it is always to bear witness in its life to the fact that since God is with all people, all things are possible for those who believe. Could there be any greater reason for joy?

Joy is however, a by-product. If one focuses upon being happy rather than on getting on with the job of making the world a happier place, then one is likely to miss the experience of what it is to be a happy person. So with joy, if one sets out with the intention of being joyful, one will miss all those opportunities for doing things the product of which will be the joy one seeks.

Moreover, as one knows, nothing worthwhile will be achieved without hard work to which there are at least four dimensions. First, there is the intellectual and imaginative challenge of trying to come to terms with the natural world as we experience it. The graced nature of the world means that it is open to intelligent enquiry, but it will need a great deal of cooperation with others, within disciplines and across disciplines if satisfactory progress is to be made. In other words, any chance that knowledge will produce wisdom will depend upon the extent to which the human enquirers are gracious in their approach to their experience and to one another. But the conversation that is initiated develops over time and includes God, with the real prospect that knowledge will grow into wisdom and be put to the proper purpose of enhancing human life and contributing to human flourishing. That human beings can individually and together share the sheer excitement of discovery is itself a matter for joy.

It is worth pausing to recall just how astonishing it is that the human mind has developed so that it can uncover the processes by which the human brain functions, explore the genetic code, plan and execute successfully the exploration of Mars, the landing of instruments on Saturn's moon, Titan, devise experiments which will help us to understand the origin of matter, and build the World Wide Web. Let's enjoy the fact 'That one small head could carry all he knew'.[21]

Secondly, by means of intellect and imagination, we can appreciate history, the way in which we have come to be as we are in society. While history and science may seem to offer two utterly different perspectives on the human experience, they are in fact complementary. History, of course, both very briefly and in huge aeons is the temporal dimension of science too. What history as we know it adds, is the story of the many human societies with all the individual perspectives generated by freedom of choice and the direction of policy. Perhaps the human animal is the only one which has a sense of its past, whether individually or as a race. Certainly it seems that the human being is the only animal that has a sense of a personal history with all that that offers for the appreciation of relationship and the opportunity for change and growth. There is an implicit sense of direction which, however, must not of itself be confused with anything one might call progress, especially if that includes the third perspective, the moral. Participation in this sense of time, of perspective, of movement is something else that can give rise to sheer joy.

Thirdly, experience of time and movement provokes the possibility of comparison, and in particular of preference, hence the emergence of the world of moral choice. While there are those who accept the total relativity of moral values, it is hard to see that this forms the basis of most lives. One motive for embracing moral relativity is to escape from the totalitarianism which stems from the belief by one party or church that right is knowable, that they know it, and that it has an absolute obligation to impose it. Morality is not expressed by means of the exercise of power. Actually some of the delight of sharing in the moral enterprise stems from the self-conscious debate in human society about the better way to behave. There are practices that are not excused on the grounds of historical context or religious belief; these would include, for example, genocide, torture and human experiment. On the other hand, given that a choice has to be made, it will not be possible often to say what is best; rather it will be necessary to discern the better way rather than the worse. What is more, having discerned the better way, as the subject believes, he or she will still have to find the will to do it. The sensitivity to be found in the moral teaching of Jesus is an inspiration, and the fact that he developed it in stories which we can read and by actions in which we can sympathetically share just gets us started on our own enquiring which will require us to do something as well as to think things out. For what we choose to do in the light of reflection we shall of course be held accountable: there is no escape, even if the person who holds me accountable is in the last resort myself. These dimensions of moral choice are implicit in an understanding of nature as graced and by the fact of the church as a sacrament which provides the place for debate, reflection, discernment and the 'courage to be'.[22]

Fourthly, the world of the creative arts offers a stimulus to satisfying the basic human need to learn to 'give attention' in such a way as to take one out of one's self. Each of the dimensions alluded to above has the potential to do this, because there can reasonably be said to be beauty in science, technical application, historical enquiry and moral endeavour. However, the arts, whether music, painting, sculpture, architecture or drama, or whatever, allow one to be freely critical of the creation of another and to enter into worlds where meanings are explored and judged. In order to learn how to do this one has work to do. The object has to be put into context, the techniques have to be understood at any rate to some degree, the tradition and style have to be interpreted and the historical traditions of creativity which led to this point engaged with: it is never enough to say, 'I like it', though that is not a worthless beginning! The history of interpretation together with the analysis lead one into the conversation, participation in which helps one to make sense of one's own relationship with it.

No artist can do other than tempt one to give attention to his or her work; no artist can force a meaning or an interpretation of a work on to the reader or the observer, for in so doing he or she is bound to sidetrack the reader's attention from the object or the performance to the artist, which frustrates the purpose of creating. Yet the exploration, usually involving conversation with others, always implies something beyond itself, so that a feeling of a depth, even a possible osmotic aspect of human experience with something beyond itself is suggested. One should not make too much of this sense of osmosis, but it is another way of drawing attention to what is meant in Christian theology when one talks of nature being graced. By learning what it is to give attention to something, one senses what it is to be taken out of oneself, so that one shares with the artist in the creating.

Each of these four perspectives of human intellect, imagination and feeling, has an objective world to which it is drawn to give attention. But the sense in which the term 'objective' is used is different in each case. The objective world of scientific enquiry is the material world; the objective world of the historian is 'what happened'; the objective world of the moral teacher is the one that is characterized by the Good; the objective world of the artist shares in the Beautiful. If this was an essay in technical philosophy it would be necessary to tease out the dimensions of these diverse 'objectivities'; sufficient here perhaps to say that in each case there is affirmed that we are talking of something which is more than the invention of a human mind or even the product of the conversation of human minds. There *is* an objective world upon which the scientist is focused; there *is* a world of events, processes and causes of which what the historian writes is more or less a good interpretation; there is a world of moral justice which tests the justice of the actual judgements we make in particular cases: a moral judgement does not become just because someone thinks it is. And perhaps above all, there is beauty, the appreciation of which in advance attracts the artist and the 'reader' to want to pay attention to a particular work of art and continue the process of creation.

That is the point; possibly it is the only point that actually matters for our humanity. The graced world in which we are set is always there to be explored and enjoyed. As Christians are inclined to say, it is a given, by which they mean it is given by God. But in giving the world God gives God's self because Christians understand that given what it is for God to be God, God cannot give something 'objectively', as if able to separate God's self from what God is doing. The world which is open to scientific enquiry, to historical exploration, to moral endeavour and to human creativity is one to which God has given God's self. Thus in exploring the world in any of these ways human being is engaged with a world in which God can be discerned and worked with in the ordering of creation. That is completely expressed in the world in the person of Jesus Christ, the Word incarnate. And it is also expressed really if imperfectly in the church, called to be the Body of Christ, the sacrament of God's presence with God's world. And it is the world of God's creation that the church points to witnesses to in its life and celebrates in its being.

Since the church shares the life of Christ, and therefore also the work of Christ, it cannot hope to escape the life that goes with that sharing: creating is not simply hard, it is a personally demanding business. In political terms, Daniel M. Bell has it right when he says that in following Christ, the church can never be herself and refuse to suffer.[23] Sadly in the course of history the church has all too frequently been tempted to look for the way of power as if by force one could demonstrate faith and bring order in creation. Nothing could be further from the truth and false to the tradition. It is of course not the *purpose* of the church to suffer, rather is it that as the Body of Christ it cannot still be church and refuse to suffer when called upon to do so. But it can truly be joyful in the work of ordering creation in the presence of the Crucified because, paradoxically one might think, it is the willingness of God to suffer as victim in Christ which proves that nature is graced and which demonstrates the powerlessness of the world to overcome the creative ordering of the world in truth, love and justice. Isaac Watts' carol is rightly sung at Christmas:

> Joy to the world! The Lord is come:
>   Let earth receive her King!
> Let ev'ry heart prepare him room
>   And heav'n and nature sing![24]

V

In order to carry on applying oneself with enthusiasm to a difficult task one needs encouragement. This is what the church understands to be the work of the Holy Spirit, which fills it with love, and faith to get on with the work of creation. The root of that encouragement comes from retelling together in worship the story of God's creating, so that the church can continue the telling of the story in its own life for the world's sake. I say 'telling', though it would be a mistake to think that to tell the story of God's creating is not doing something. It is very important to see that the church's worship of God in Christ through the Holy Spirit is an activity and a way of life, not something that can be done and finished with. God's 'saying' is not merely a 'stating' that something is the case, it is a 'doing': i.e. a making-something-to-be-the-case, as is clear even in the Hebrew *dbr*, which means both 'to say' and 'to do'. Actually we know that perfectly well in many contexts where to have said something is 'to have done something', which often implies taking on responsibilities or one will be taken to have acted with bad faith. The example of 'promising' is a case in point.[25]

The central act and focus of all Christian worship is the eucharist, the thanksgiving that those in Christ offer, not just for their own salvation but also for the promise of salvation for the whole world. Christian worship is not the private activity of a separated body, it is the public worship of the people of God on behalf of all people, and which in principle includes all people and all things. This is marked in the celebration both by the fact that the celebrant is God, and that the celebration of Christ's death and resurrection is not a repeat of anything but an actual sharing in principle in the ordering of creation that it represents. So in the eucharist there is affirmed the 'gracedness' of the natural world, its intelligibility and adaptability in the shared ordering of creation by God in Christ, with the church and for the world. The fear of failure is overcome by the fact that just as there could be no hope of creation but for the gracious presence of God, there could be no possibility of confession apart from the prior realization of God's presence. Forgiveness is implicit in the very nature of things, but needs to be stated as a fact, if the story to be told in the readings is to be listened to with attention, taken up and responded to.

As a first personal response to the Word the story is taken up by the preacher in the sermon the intention of which is to involve the congregation in developing their own stories in the light of the Gospel, and through them to engage others in the conversation of God with God's world. Hence the sermon is followed by the universal greeting one of another in the sharing of the Peace, the rehearsal of the outline of the Christian story in the creed and the association of the world through intercessory prayer in the offering of bread and wine, representatives of all God's creatures.

The offering of the bread and the wine, which the church makes, is accepted and blessed by the celebrant who represents Christ. Christ cannot give a blessing except that it involves the giving of his very self, so that, as Christians say, the bread and wine become the body and blood of Christ. This presents the reality of the gracedness of nature in its fullness, and as such it is received. The dismissal, the sending out into the world, is thus of a people who are confirmed in the grace of God to work for the ordering of creation by love, justice and peace.

This requires an attentive openness in conversation so that the inclusiveness that has been celebrated in worship comes increasingly to characterize not only our life together as church, but our intelligent, affectionate life together in the diversity of the human race in a world of nature graced by the presence of God, Father, Son and Holy Spirit.

Notes

1. The radical distinction between the Protestant and Catholic positions arose in the sixteenth century and was confirmed in the Council of Trent. However, subsequent study has shown that the views, for example those of Catholic Scholasticism and of Luther in particular, were more nuanced than was perceived at the time, and the contrast of the two positions, while still significant, is now true only of *some* of the more conservative Catholic and Protestant traditions. It remains to be seen what the fall out will be from the pontificate of John Paul II and the election of Cardinal Ratzinger as Benedict XVI.
2. While the work of Chenu, Rahner, and especially de Lubac, is most important, other names should be added, for example, Schillerbeeckx, Lonergan and even von Balthasar, from their slightly differing perspectives, who have pursued similar ideas.
3. See esp. W. Brueggemann, *Theology of the Old Testament* (Minneapolis, MN: Fortress Press, 1997), pp. 145–64.
4. Gen. 1.1–2.
5. It is interesting that *condo*, the word used in the Vulgate to translate *ba'ra'*, the word used in Hebrew uniquely of God's creative relationship with the world, means 'to found', as for example in founding a colony, and 'to make habitable'. See above, 'World as creation'.
6. Isa. 45.18.
7. On might say 'of human nature', except that the philosophical concept of human nature is foreign to the forms of life known to those who talked the mythological language of the Old Testament, let alone the contributory perspectives of neighbouring traditions.
8. One of the delights of the Old Testament, as of the later Jewish writing in Midrash and Talmud, is its argumentative character: there may be no final solution to the questions, but real questions can always be reasonably discussed with the possibility of new insight.
9. Jn 1.1–2, 3–5, 10–12, 14, 16. I follow the suggestion of Raymond Brown and others (Käsemann, Bernard and Guchter for example) that the prologue of the gospel incorporates an early Christian hymn perhaps emanating from Johannine circles. The translation is also taken from Raymond E. Brown, *The Gospel According to St. John*, Anchor Bible, vol. 1 (London: Geoffrey Chapman, 1966), pp. 3–4.
10. The concept of place is receiving welcome attention in contemporary theological writing, and not simply within theology. Thus while there is the need for specific religious symbols and institutions, it is important to see that they are not isolated from all experience. Their holiness and vitality depend upon the fact that all nature is graced. For an interesting discussion of the importance of 'place' for Christian theology, see John Inge, *A Christian Theology of Place* (Aldershot: Ashgate, 2004).
11. Jn 1.16. *Pleroma*, a favourite word of St Paul, is used here uniquely in the whole of the Johannine literature. This suggests a special significance that is perhaps properly interpreted as the means whereby St John underlines the utter completeness of the graciousness of God's loving presence with God's world. Absolutely nothing is held back; there is nothing left for which we have to wait – a significant way of putting it perhaps in view of the Jewish messianic hope.

12. Jn 1.11.
13. Ex. 19.5.
14. Rudolf Bultmann, *Das Evangelium des Johannes* (Göttingen: Vandenhoeck und Ruprecht, 1959), p. 35.
15. I realize that this raises many questions in some minds about the veracity of the gospel narratives because they appear to bear witness to Jesus's performance of miracles. The topic is too large to be dealt with here; suffice it to say that I prefer to see the miracle stories as demonstrating the presence of God in the graced nature of God's creation. It is simply wrong to regard miracles as things that Jesus did because he possessed superhuman powers. Indeed, such views have led to gross misunderstanding of such activities as praying, and the proper role of scientific enquiry and its technological application.
16. Tsvetan Todorov, *Hope and Memory* (London: Atlantic Books, 2003), p. 173. Tsvetan Todorov is a literary critic and cultural commentator who was born in Bulgaria under the communist regime; he is now Director of Research at the Centre national de la recherche scientifique, in Paris. He writes particularly about the literature of twentieth-century totalitarianism where he finds in the lives of some individual witnesses, reasons to be hopeful for the future of the human race.
17. G.M . Hopkins, 'God's Grandeur', in W. H. Gardner, *Gerard Manley Hopkins – A Selection of his Poems and Prose* (Harmondsworth: Penguin, 1953), p. 27.
18. Hopkins, 'God's Grandeur'.
19. Ibid.
20. *Lumen Gentium* 1.1.; Norman P. Tanner (ed.), *Decrees of the Ecumenical Councils*, vol. II (London and Georgetown: Sheed & Ward and Georgetown University Press, 1990), p. *849.
21. Oliver Goldsmith, 'The Deserted Village', l. 216, *The Poems and Plays of Oliver Goldsmith* (London: Dent, Everyman's Library, 1910), p. 29.
22. Title of book of sermons by Paul Tillich (New Haven, CT: Yale University Press, 1952).
23. Daniel M. Bell Jr, *Liberation Theology after the End of History: The Refusal to Cease Suffering* (London: Routledge, 2001).
24. Isaac Watts (1674–1748) wrote this hymn as an adaptation of Psalm 98, beginning at verse 2. There is no reference to Christmas in the psalm, of course, but the fact that Watts can adapt the psalm and make of it such a celebratory Christmas carol is itself evidence of the way in which reflection on human experience of the world is continuously demonstrating that there is no ungraced nature. For the text see Hugh Keyte and Andrew Parrott (eds), *The New Oxford Book of Carols* (Oxford: Oxford University Press, 1992), p .270.
25. For further examples and a subtle outline of the case see J. L. Austin, *How to Do Things with Words*, ed. J. O. Urmson (Oxford: Clarendon Press, 1962).

PART III

LIVING IN THE SPIRIT

Chapter 6

ACT AND BEING IN THE CHURCH: COMPARATIVE EXPLORATIONS IN ECCLESIOLOGY AND ETHICS

Gerard Mannion

This chapter explores some comparative considerations on ecclesiology and ethics.[1] Firstly, we shall look at historical and recent attempts to explore the relation between the two within the ecumenical movement. We shall discuss important themes and issues to emerge from such processes, as well as criticisms and shortcomings of the same. Next we turn to debates within the Roman Catholic community and explore, in particular, those surrounding the interrelation between ethics and ecclesiology since Vatican II and down to the present day.

In both cases, and across various ecclesial traditions, we see contrasting approaches to ecclesiology and ethics. In particular, on the one hand, we will see an attempt to offer an ecclesiological account of ethics (or an ecclesial – or indeed ecclesiological – ethics). On the other, we will see an account of the ethics *of* ecclesiology (or an ethical ecclesiology). We shall offer some observations on which method of procedure, if either, best serves the attempt to harmonize ethics and ecclesiology in a fuller sense. The importance of hermeneutics and moral discernment to such an exercise will be highlighted.

As we shall see, many problems encountered by Christians engaging in discerning the interrelation between the ethics and ecclesiology today often stem from confusion or disagreement surrounding these very terms.[2] Some seek to remove the distinction altogether, others to demarcate in a most rigid fashion. Some give considerable priority to one over the other. Our two primary 'case-studies' – the discussions on ecclesiology and ethics undertaken by the World Council of Churches and analogous debates across the Roman Catholic Communion, will help illustrate such problems.

I wish to work towards affirming the interrelatedness between ethics and ecclesiology so that the two may, in some sense, be seen 'as one', *in an ecclesial setting*. However, I do not wish to merge the two in a Hauerwasian sense,[3] but rather acknowledge that the *distinctiveness* of ethics as a separate entity is here to stay. Herein lies a clue to determining which of the methods mentioned above may better take debates concerning ethics and ecclesiology forward today.[4]

Nonetheless, although the debates we engage with do involve numerous difficulties created by differences in definition and interpretation my own position will be one of *both – and*, with regards to ethics and ecclesiology in the church.

Moral discernment and ethical struggle can inform our understanding of the nature of the church, as well as its practice, as much as vice versa. But ethics undertaken from within a Christian context can never be seen as purely intra-ecclesial in scope or outcome, and nor even *should* it be viewed as such in method of procedure. Neither is such ethics, itself, uninformed by or isolated from ethical engagement undertaken in other contexts. But in particular this essay works towards the conclusion that *in the present era*, more attention needs to be given to the ethical implications of ecclesiology.

Ethics, therefore, is more than ecclesiology, though it can permeate all aspects of ecclesiology and embrace them within its scope. So too does ecclesiology involve much more than simply ethical questions, though each and every aspect of ecclesiology has a moral dimension to it.

Discerning the relations between ethics and ecclesiology[5]

Duncan Forrester has commented upon the biblical roots and development of the *Christian* tradition of uniting ethics and ecclesiology. He believes that 'ethics is essentially a relationship to God'.[6] The Bible 'interweaves' doctrinal and moral teaching, indicative and imperative in an inseparable fashion. He believes that, by the time the New Testament was formed, something of a 'seamless web' of 'doctrine, story, moral teaching and membership of the community' was already present.[7] In expounding the New Testament ecclesiological motif of the body, and in reflecting upon later forms of ecclesial life, Forrester further illustrates both how Christianity shuns moral individualism, and that the church itself makes moral statements in the very fact of its being and the way in which it exists and orders itself:[8] 'The behaviour of the community confirms or questions the truth of the gospel that its members proclaim ... The congregation, the Body, the Church is thus a kind of hermeneutic of the gospel. The message and the ethics are inseparable from the life of the Church.'[9]

But, of course, differing Christian communities and denominations will have different and sometimes diametrically opposed interpretations and understandings of how faith and morals are and should be interrelated. Thus there will be differences of a similar fashion concerning the relation and harmony between Christian act and being, between ethics and ecclesiology.

And it is not simply *across* different Christian traditions where differences in perceiving the relationship between ethics and ecclesiology are manifested. It is evident that different visions and models of being church are present even within the confines of the same denomination. These also lead to such differences in relation to ethical questions, too. As Forrester states:

> It is not only that different ecclesial traditions nourish differing ethical approaches, which are often seen as opposed rather than complementary; varying ways of being 'church' seem to predispose towards certain styles of ethical action, each of which on its own may seem to lack the ecclesial and ethical fullness which has become possible in a more ecumenical age.[10]

Forrester appears to indicate that this point was of greater significance in bygone ages than today. But I suggest that our considerations throughout this essay may help illustrate that it is as true now as it ever was in the church. Indeed, it may even be more the case today than it ever was in the past. So we turn to examine some attempts at discerning the link between what the church is and what the church does in the modern and contemporary eras.

Ethics, ecclesiology and ecumenism

The ethical task of ecumenism

Ecumenism involves dialogue aimed at creating, enhancing and consolidating koinonia, i.e. communion, hence unity.[11] Doctrinal explorations and discussions are obviously relevant – for many divisions centre around differing teachings and interpretations. But practice and thus, above all, ethics are also central to the pursuit of ecumenism itself. It is only natural that debates concerning the relation between ethics and ecclesiology should have formed the focus of attention in numerous ecumenical discussions.[12]

But the response of most Christian denominations to the challenges posed by the modern and now postmodern contexts to the perennial task of harmonizing ethics and ecclesiology has certainly been an emergent one. As Forrester has stated:

> From its beginnings the modern ecumenical movement has wrestled with the relation between ethics and the being and unity of the Church. There has been a steady conviction that there is a relationship, but spelling out what it is has proved hard and controversial and continues to be so today ... But the project of relating ecclesiology and ethics has been there from the beginning and is in practice unavoidable.[13]

I shall here largely take for granted the account of this shared journey towards the development of the ecumenical movement, with the many organizations which contributed to the formation of this, as well as those additional movements and organizations which subsequently grew out of it and its eventual umbrella organization, the World Council of Churches (WCC), which has come to represent 340 different churches in 120 countries.[14]

Although we deal with Roman Catholic debates in the later sections of this essay, here it is important to acknowledge that the Second Vatican Council also played a major role in the growth of *ecumenism*, marking, as it did, a transformation in the explicit self-understanding of the Roman Catholic Church's own relationship with other Christian denominations and indeed, those of other faiths and of none. Obviously the discussions on ethics of the joint working group of the World Council of Churches and the Roman Catholic Church is also of relevance here.[15] Ethical concerns, then, have never been far from ecumenical discussions.

From polarisation to ambiguity – and beyond?

So it is important to recognize the historical efforts of the ecumenical movement towards facilitating a new vision of how ethics and ecclesiology should be intertwined. The ecumenical movement helped to place social and communitarian ethics firmly on the moral, doctrinal and hence ecclesiological agendas. A glance at the names of some of the movements which helped to bring the WCC into being (Life and Work, Faith and Order), or of the names and themes of some of the major conferences of the ecumenical movement along the way (e.g. 'Doctrine Divides, Service Unites'),[16] demonstrates this intertwining of ethics and ecclesiology in the service of the both the Christian and wider communities.

Forrester, in his brief sketch of the history of ecumenical discussions focusing upon ethics and ecclesiology, expounds the nature of the polarization on these very issues in the past. On the one hand were those who thought that ethical issues were secondary to the ecumenical cause (and so greater diversity believed to be acceptable in ethical matters). For such people, once *doctrinal* differences were tackled, *then* agreement elsewhere would follow (he calls this the 'traditional Faith and Order' approach). On the other hand were the proponents of such phrases as 'doctrine divides, service unites', itself what he calls the 'Life and Work' or 'Church and Society' approach.[17] But Forrester rightly acknowledges that the simplicity of such a divide masks the true complexity of the real situation *vis-à-vis* the relation between ethics and ecclesiology. His sketch continues with the examples of the churches' struggle in Nazi Germany and the possibility of 'moral heresy' (Willem Visser't Hooft's phrase) 'that certain types of practice were radically incompatible with Christian confession and that certain ethical issues at least were necessarily church dividing'.[18] Eventually the churches came to realize that

> ... in ethical struggles alongside others there was often a real and profound new experience of what it is to be Church, that *ecclesiogenesis* (Leonardo Boff's phrase) often takes place in the struggle for justice and truth. The being and message of the Church are often at stake, it was realized, when it wrestles with great ethical issues.[19]

Forrester rightly traces the recent ecumenical 'concern' with the relation between ethics and ecclesiology back to the Justice, Peace and the Integrity of Creation (JPIC) process undertaken by the WCC which, following its 1983 Vancouver General Assembly, sought to engage its member churches in a 'covenant and conciliar process' on these three issues. By 1990, 'the JPIC World Convention in Korea had honed that intention towards combining 'confessional statements with practical commitments'.[20] But Forrester notes that this particular process did not result in any clarity on the issue of the nature of the relationship between ecclesiology and ethics.

The next stage of the WCC's involvement developed out of a consultation at Rønde, Denmark, which committed the WCC to work towards 'Costly Unity' (1993, echoing Bonhoeffer on costly as opposed to cheap grace) – unity that fully acknowledges the ethical implications of the church's life and mission. This, of course, meant that ecumenical ventures which ignored or played down divisions on ethical issues would only be a sign of 'cheap unity'. Further consultations would follow and we shall discuss one, in particular, in what follows. Suffice to say that, by the time of the Fifth World Conference on Faith and Order at Santiago de Compostella, as Forrester suggests, the commitment to the harmonization of ethics and ecclesiology on the part of the WCC was now becoming better articulated. It was, Forrester comments, 'clearly shown how ecclesiology and ethics mutually illumine, question and interpret one another'.[21] We turn to one example how of such ecumenical efforts fared.

'Costly commitment' – a successful and systematic exploration?

The Faith and Order commission of the WCC initiated a series of discussions[22] at the Tantur Ecumenical Institute, Israel, in 1994.[23] It offered much hope, but the outcome of such discussions was not without its critics, as we shall see. Two fundamental axioms emerged from these discussions. The first of these was that ethics is intertwined with the entire *raison d'être* and thrust of the ecumenical movement itself, 'the quest for unity and the struggle for justice are integral to the life of the church. They should not be separated'.[24] The second fundamental axiom stated that 'In the living Christian community there can be no ecclesiology without ethics and no ethics without ecclesiology.'[25]

In the light of these two fundamental axioms, the document outlines and explores three key priorities for the church, namely, *reconciliation, healing* and *transformation*. The church exists to bring these about in the human family. Ethics and ecclesiology are thus intertwined in each of these priorities and in the document's essential affirmation that human existence is *moral* existence: i.e. to be human is to be a moral agent.

A further priority for the church follows from such considerations. To enable human beings to live morally (so harmonizing their essence, their fundamental being with their actions, their agency), the church must build community wherever it can make a positive difference. The term which the document employs is 'koinonia-generating involvement'.[26] The Faith and Order commission goes on to outline key areas of focus which might help the church in its quest towards generating such enhanced koinonia. They are as follows:

Eucharist, covenant and ethical engagement The Gospel calls Christians to a love *without* limits. Such love can, often does and should transcend *all* barriers. The document explains the fundamental links between these themes and core aspects of the Christian way of life, that Gospel-inspired and praxis-oriented way of being,

> Thus on the basis of the Christian understanding, we may say that the eucharist and ethical engagement are both expressions of God's covenant. Put differently, using the language of our earlier discussion of koinonia, we may speak of a "continuum" between the koinonia given and experienced in the eucharist, and the koinonia given and experienced in ethical engagement.[27]

Both serve as an *anamnesis*, an 'active remembering', a 're-presenting' of the promise between God, humanity and creation'.[28] Both the celebration of the eucharist and the engagement in an ethical life by Christians aim towards the '*realization of life lived in full dignity*'.[29]

In seeking to offer a vision of ecclesiology and ethics as one – to enable community to be generated wherever people bear witness to the Gospel and seek to live out a Christian life – the document recognizes many of the challenges which our present era presents to the church. We turn, next, to one of the most important challenges to be met.

Challenging the fragmentation of moral foundations The Faith and Order commission naturally sought to discuss the challenges posed by postmodernity to *morality* itself, namely that fragmentation and disintegration of the moral fibre and traditions across numerous societies and communities today. They discussed and considered the notions of moral *struggle*, moral *discernment* and moral *formation*[30] and concluded that in each of these areas, today, challenges are presented to the various Christian traditions.[31] The task and aspiration of those involved in the discussions was to consider how the churches might go about 'reweaving the moral fibre' of society.[32] Naturally, this would call for much self-critical reflection for the church in general,[33] and self-critical reflection on the interrelation of the 'Being and Doing' of the church, in particular.[34]

In these discussions, then, we have thus encountered a series of noble visions, charged with much inspiring ecclesial, ethical and theological imagery. How fruitful have the efforts of those engaged in these discussions been or could they be?

Evaluations of the Faith and Order ethics and ecclesiology study[35]

The *themes* and *issues*, as well as the priorities, identified by the Tantur discussions[36] help illustrate the nature and scope of the overall discussions on how best to understand the interrelationship between ethics and ecclesiology. But they do not, in their present form at least, provide the practical vision necessary to ensure that the churches move towards a default disposition whereby steps are *always* taken to ensure that what the church is and aspires to be are in harmony with what the church does – with how it lives, orders and organizes itself. Let us consider possible reasons why this might be so.

Limited horizons One of the oft-suggested reasons relates to the *ecclesiological* thinking which underpinned the discussions themselves. Critics believe that the problem was due to the fact that amongst those who *influenced* aspects of the discussions, thinking and writing undertaken by the Faith and Order's commission on the relation between ecclesiology and ethics were individuals whose own ecclesiology proved too insular to provide the foundations to allow ethics and ecclesiology to be fully harmonized in a positive sense in order to meet today's challenges. These are the 'neo-exclusivistic' tendencies I have identified elsewhere. In this instance, they include the ideas of John Milbank and Stanley Hauerwas.[37]

Much of the debate subsequent to the publications of the three 'Costly' documents centres around this issue,[38] despite the fact that 'Costly Commitment' calls for such a mission to be carried out both within and *without* the Christian Church, itself. Margaret Farley, who shares this concern, has commented upon a further fault of the WCC initiative here, namely, 'the tendency of the study to cede discussion of church-dividing ethical issues to discussion of the church itself *as* a social ethic did not fulfil the hopes of WCC participants'.[39] In other words, the problems emerged when ethics was collapsed into ecclesiology, as opposed to being perceived as a mirror to hold up to our ecclesiological thought and practice.

Of further concern, Farley notes, is that 'For many Roman Catholic readers of the study, moreover, the integration of mission in the world, solidarity with the poor, and universal concerns for justice are not yet adequate.'[40] Thirdly, Farley also notes how the insights of feminist scholars were also overlooked. Hence an ethical dilemma emerged at the heart of the discussions themselves, namely questions of inclusivity, pluralism and a genuine debate concerning the contemporary nature of church-world relations. This, in addition to those questions concerning the prioritizing of ecclesial matters over ethical ones.

Indeed, Duncan Forrester himself, whilst commending the WCC initiatives on ecclesiology and ethics, also warned of the dangers of *reductionism* inherent in it – although he cautions against *both* ecclesiological *and* ethical reductionism. He feels that there should be no return to viewing theology as simply a 'vivid' form of moral discourse and neither should the church be viewed *simply* as a moral community, fellowship of the good, or community working *simply* for social justice with the gospel as their manifesto.[41]

To my mind, it appears that the major difficulty is simply a new form of the old problem of where the *emphasis* in such discussions is to lie. In other words, it would appear that the WCC discussions and the documents which emerged from them placed an overt emphasis upon the ecclesial and ecclesiological aspects *to the neglect* of areas of the ethical (in that the Church itself was perceived as the *deliverer* of social ethics, aside from the need for social ethics to scrutinize our ecclesial thought and practice). In the final analysis, questions concerning the ethics *of* ecclesiology were far from the forefront.

In addition to the ecclesiological influences behind the discussions, perhaps another of the reasons why such a situation emerged was the (nonetheless sincerely intended) emphasis in the document upon the concept of moral *formation*. As Werner Schwartz has demonstrated, this concept came increasingly to be the central focus of the discussions on ethics and ecclesiology.[42] The discussions sought to reflect upon what it means for the church to be a moral community and, in doing so, they again took on board many of the themes which permeate the works of those such as Hauerwas and Milbank – including the polemical critique of 'secular' ethics and the 'secular realm' in general. Thus what may have started as a positive undertaking led to an overt emphasis upon the concept of formation which, by its very nature, led the discussions more and more in an inward-looking direction and thus to emphasize ecclesial matters first and foremost and genuinely ethical factors second. Instead of blending faith and life together in harmony, the ethical was absorbed into the ecclesial to the point where the latter dictated and even in parts consumed the former.

And yet it is not simply the WCC discussions which have led in this direction. A similar pattern has emerged – at an official level – in the Roman Catholic Church in recent decades, where ecclesial priorities outweigh ethical realities *de facto* so that, as with the WCC documents, we see an *ecclesial ethics* championed, but less attention given to the ethics *of* ecclesiology. Indeed, in Roman Catholic affairs, we have witnessed a distinct hostility to such an undertaking as the ethical assessment of ecclesiological thinking and ecclesial practice, themselves. Before examining the Roman Catholic context, let us explore the *methodological* difficulties raised thus far in more detail.

Questions of difference, method and emphasis The difficulties and divisions witnessed throughout such efforts can be examined on a wider level, in the light of challenges put to such organizations as the World Council of Churches (e.g. from the late Ronald Preston) and to the institutional Roman Catholic Church (e.g. from the theologies of liberation and, more recently, by the many groups and scholars in the church concerned with examining anew themes such as the magisterium, authority, governance and accountability).[43]

Obviously echoing our earlier considerations, differing confessional, doctrinal, ecclesiological and moral emphases within Christianity itself have had a profound influence upon attempts to articulate the relationship between ethics and ecclesiology.[44] As the late Ronald Preston put it: 'If there are contending theologies there will be different approaches and emphases in ethics, whether personal or social (in so far as these can be conceptually separated)'.[45] Indeed Preston's study in its entirety is a reflection upon the difficulties of articulating a consistent and wide-reaching Christian *social* ethic (with, nonetheless, his own particular perspective reflected throughout the study). Of course, this must also entail the plethora of issues which we have thus far outlined concerning the interrelation between ethics and ecclesiology. If this be accepted, then one may also consider the applicability of Preston's statements – with regard to *social ethics* – to our own concerns. This is, I believe, not least of all because the relation between ethics and ecclesiology lies at the heart of any Christian attempt to define, develop and apply social ethics.

Preston, himself, believes that 'there is room for a variety of stresses', as long as both the biblical-doctrinal *and* the empirical data elements are 'brought together so that in reflecting on both they reciprocally influence one another'. For Preston, it does not matter too much in what order one's procedures move. For example, whether deductively from Bible or doctrine to contemporary issues, or inductively from 'contemporary data back to basic biblical and doctrinal affirmations'.[46]

But a note of caution must be sounded at this point, and other thinkers in Christian social ethics might here disagree with Preston.[47] Indeed, I believe that the reason why differences in approach and method, as well as emphasis, *are* important is because they in turn reflect and further influence 'prevailing' ecclesiologies, which in turn affect the *practice* of ethics (and not just social ethics) within church communities and across entire denominations on both an *ad intra* and *ad extra* basis. As we shall see, it is one thing to acknowledge the pluralistic context of such debates, it is another to ignore the fact that certain methods of procedure might actually be to the detriment of ecclesial life and ecumenical advancement alike.

Hence difficulties *continue* to emerge where, for example, on the one hand Christians subordinate ethics to ecclesial concerns, or, on the other hand, where the gospel is reduced to morality.

But Preston offers a strong argument in stating that ethical theologies should focus exclusively neither on the building-up of a *koinonia* ethic within congregations, nor on ways in which 'Christians can contribute to a common human flourishing in plural societies in a plural world'. Furthermore, neither should the radical prophetic witness of the church, nor an emphasis upon the church as a 'vital conserving influence' which supports social institutions against the 'fragmentary tendencies in civil society' prevail, one over the other. As Preston states, 'It must be both.'[48]

And yet Preston also recognizes that the main problem today lies in discerning 'what mix is appropriate in particular contexts'. This, of course, takes us to the very heart of the matter here. The challenging nature of this question futher underlines those issues we have already considered in relation to the difficulty of identifying the precise nature of the interrelation between ethics and ecclesiology and how one goes about discerning it. The challenges posed by differing schools of Church ethics and differing ecclesiologies are also brought into sharper focus.

Preston himself identifies a series of 'contending theologies'[49] engaged in the process of seeking to articulate a social ethics: namely Christian realism, 'biblicalism', liberation theology, orthodoxy and social trinitarianism, eschatological realism and recent debates in Roman Catholic moral theology.[50] And, although Preston's concern is chiefly with the 'social witness of the church in the Ecumenical Movement',[51] his critique of Christian social ethics may nonetheless be deemed to incorporate a critique of certain attempts to articulate a vision which embraces and unifies ethics and ecclesiology.

What further problems have such efforts been obliged to face? Firstly, the end of the twentieth century saw many setbacks in the ecumenical movement. Clashes, divisions and negative retrenchment have been witnessed on numerous occasions. And many of the disagreements which emerged were precisely concerned with differences in emphasis and lack of agreement concerning priorities in Christian social ethics, as well as in ethics in general. But so too have there been still greater problems which stem from the aforementioned differences in ecclesiologies – differing visions of what it is to be church.

And here, of course, it will be of no surprise to find that I believe the two problems are once again fundamentally linked. Problems in social ethics both within and without various Christian denominations, along with differing and competing ecclesiologies being in operation, are thus both part of the problem here. And (notwithstanding the sentiments concerning the church's own moral failings and the need for self-criticism expressed in *Costly Commitment*),[52] so too are wider failings in ensuring that the moral and ethical traditions of such churches are actually put into *practice*, again both *within* and in relations with those without their own confines.

Let us now turn to examine recent attempts to analyse the interrelation between ethics and ecclesiology in another Christian communion, which does as not yet enjoy full membership of the WCC, in order to explore further insights into this whole process.

In turning to debates concerning the interrelation between ethics and ecclesiology in the Roman Catholic Church we shall see, firstly, that certain parallels exist between the tensions throughout that communion in this area and those identified in the critique of the WCC discussions. However, secondly, we shall also note that certain lessons for the latter may be learned by engaging with Catholic thinkers who have resolutely emphasized the importance of allowing ethical concerns to shape ethical and ecclesiological hermeneutics.

Ethics and ecclesiology in the contemporary Roman Catholic Church

The parameters of the Roman Catholic debate

The Second Vatican Council witnessed a radical transformation in the *ecclesiological* thinking of the Roman Catholic Church. Firstly, I suggest that this was in part necessitated by *moral* challenges and problems pertaining to social ethics in the wider world of the decades preceding the 1960s (e.g. the depression, the rise of totalitarianism, the Holocaust, the Second World War and its aftermath, etc.). And this new ecclesiological situation in turn led to a radical transformation in Roman Catholic *ethical* thinking (moral theology, social ethics and social teaching, etc.). Furthermore, in recent years this utterly transformed moral theology has been at the forefront of the thinking of those providing a (moral) critique of the present ecclesiological thinking and thus ecclesial life of the Church (particularly in relation to the magisterium and structures of authority, governance and leadership in the Church). This has led to new thinking and new developments, once again, throughout every level of the Roman Catholic Church. Let us explore the interrelationship between Roman Catholic moral theology and Roman Catholic ecclesiology a little more.

From the transformation of ecclesiology to the transformation of moral theology – and back again! [53]

In a comprehensive yet succinct survey, the moral theologian, Richard A. McCormick identified and outlined ten 'significant developments' that have impacted upon Roman Catholic moral theology since 1940. [54] These range from the theology of Karl Rahner and the notion of 'fundamental freedom', to revisions in method and new ways of examining and articulating moral norms (i.e. the development of proportionalism and the transformation of natural law moral theology).

The ten also includes the papal birth control commission of the 1960s along with the subsequent encyclical, *Humanae Vitae* and its aftermath. The emergence of feminism and then the 'maturation of bioethics' come next, followed by the influence of liberation theology. McCormick then turns to the emergence of 'personalism' – 'The person as criterion of the morally right and wrong', before discussing – *vis-à-vis* public dissent from 'some authoritative but non-infallible [official church] teaching' – the controversy over his friend and fellow moral theologian Charles Curran, who was dismissed from his post at the Catholic University of America over his public opposition to *Humanae Vitae*.

McCormick's tenth and final 'significant development' describes the recent situation whereby there has been renewed and increasing centralization of the Church upon Rome, which has led to theologians – above all moral theologians – being policed anew by the Curia, most notably through the Congregation for the Doctrine of the Faith. McCormick uses the term 'restoration' (in quotes) to describe this re-emergence of an authoritarian form of conservative governance of theology (and indeed the Church in general). This 'significant development', I believe, is one of two amongst McCormick's ten which are of the greatest relevance to our own debates. The second (the very first item on McCormick's list of ten), is 'Vatican II and ecclesiology'.[55] To some this might prove a strange and less obvious choice. Yet to others, it is *the* most obvious development with which to begin his survey. McCormick himself explains:

> The Council said very little directly about moral theology. Yet what it said about other aspects of Catholic belief and practice had an enormous influence on moral theology. *These other aspects of Catholic belief and life are largely, though not exclusively, ecclesiological.* For Vatican II was, above all, an ecclesiological council.[56]

Each and every one of these developments likewise marked an ecclesiological development and/or influenced substantial changes in ecclesiological and ecclesial thinking alike. McCormick tells us as much, himself, in quoting approvingly Richard McBrien's account[57] of the six most important developments in Roman Catholic ecclesiology to emerge from Vatican II: (a) The Church as mystery or sacrament; (b) the Church as people of God; (c) the Church as servant; (d) the Church as collegial; (e) the Church as ecumenical; (f) the Church as eschatological. Thus, 'I believe McBrien is absolutely correct when he asserts that these ecclesial metaphors affect both the substance and method of moral inquiry in very profound ways'.[58] This has also been echoed by Margaret Farley,[59] who identifies further examples of how intertwined ethics and ecclesiology were and became in the aftermath of Vatican II, thus both supporting and supplementing McBrien's analysis:

> Issues such as the meaning of church as People of God, the role of the laity in the church, the church as a world church, religious liberty, the function of the local church in relation to the church universal, openness of the church to the world, ecumenism, development of doctrine, and the church as pilgrim church each yielded new questions about a theology of communion, cultural diversity, freedom of conscience, the core

and peripheral status of truths, the 'sense of the faithful' as source and confirmation of church teaching, the church's mission, corporate responsibility, and on and on. *All of these questions are questions not only for ecclesiology but for ethics.* They have been extended with an urgency pressed in political theologies, liberation theologies, and the many forms of feminist theology, where the line between systematic and moral theology has usefully been blurred for some time.[60]

And so, once again we see an illustration of how ethics and ecclesiology are shown to be intertwined, even interdependent in an ecclesial setting *and yet distinct*.

Farley's own excellent account of the relations between ethics and ecclesiology in the Roman Catholic Church of recent years enables us to illustrate further how this complex series of interaction, reaction and counteraction has occurred. She acknowledges that one might be forgiven for initially thinking there is *no* real relation between the two (echoing Forrester's account of the ambiguity and lack of clarity on the topic), beyond ethics and ecclesiology sharing the same context – i.e., the Church, though with little interaction between the two. But she believes this would be to overlook the significance of Catholicism's 'century of ecclesiology', of which the *final* third also became known as the 'age of ethics'. Thus 'it was inevitable that theological paths would cross – that ethical assessments would be made of the church itself, as well as of theologies of the church, and that interpretations of the nature and function of the church would play a role in ethical debates'.[61]

Here we thus see a clear parallel with the undertakings of the WCC on ethics and ecclesiology.

Farley notes how, both for Roman Catholic ecclesiologists and moral theologians alike, their dealings with church leaders have often been 'adversarial' and that issues of church authority, as opposed to issues of morality, have been the focal point of such encounters (though I am sure Farley would acknowledge that the issue of church authority itself is also a moral one). But Farley thinks the main clashes are between church leaders and *moral* theologians, with ecclesiology only providing the main lines of a 'no longer surprising plot' (indeed, this entire situation itself is perhaps best perceived as only a subplot).[62] In articulating the 'major story', she thinks that the most important questions in this area should address the issue of why the church's moral teaching is so often divisive and/or ineffective or, indeed, frequently ignored by so many members of the church itself. In other words, Farley is concerned with the impact of this 'subplot' upon those many Catholics who, whilst only observers of it, are drawn into it 'with their lives at stake'.[63]

In line with the common subject of the Festschrift in which it appeared, Farley's essay discusses the work in this field of Charles Curran.[64] The primary aim of much of his work was to examine the impact of current ecclesiological failings upon moral theology. Whilst I believe such an approach is valid, called for, necessary and has been enormously illuminating towards demonstrably construct-ive ends, my own emphasis here would be to complement Curran's inspirational work by proceeding somewhat the other way around. I would wish to suggest that a key focal point should be the failure to apply fully the principles of moral theology *within* Roman Catholic ecclesiology. In other words, to examine the consequences of church leaders (and, for that matter, theologians) *not* integrating ethics and ecclesiology sufficiently or correctly, if at all (and here we see, yet again, further evidence to support the contention that ethics and ecclesiology, whilst fundamentally interrelated, are nonetheless distinct).[65] Of course, none of this is to suggest Curran had somehow overlooked such issues: indeed so much of his later work moved explicitly in such a direction and sought to examine many wider ecclesiological questions.[66]

But I also believe that both approaches are entirely compatible, and indeed complementary, in relation to the task of building an ethics *of* ecclesiology. As Farley echoed in a talk of 2003, the current 'crisis' of ecclesiology and ethics, need be neither institutionally nor personally tragic.[67] And it is Farley's analysis, itself, which helps bring both approaches into sharp relief, just as it offers concrete suggestions for how things might be otherwise in a positive sense.

It is furthermore significant to see how observers from outside the boundaries of Roman Catholicism have perceived the present situation within that communion. Duncan Forrester's account of how the two have been related in the Roman Catholic Church – most perceptively for a non-Roman Catholic – also turns to identify some of the key issues for Roman Catholics in this area. Echoing our earlier sketch, he correctly notes that Roman Catholic moral theology was (here citing Jack Mahoney) transformed into something approaching an 'ethics of *koinonia*' by Vatican II.[68] Again, he follows Mahoney (and again concurs with our earlier historical sketch) in noting that, after Vatican II, moral theology became more of an *ecclesial* theology (although, as we shall see, the picture here is again far from simple).

Above all, I would thoroughly endorse Forrester's concerns with regard to the *self-understanding* of the 'official' Roman Catholic Church in relation to moral theology. Forrester discerns a 'tension' with regard to whether moral teaching is supposed to flow from the hierarchy of the Church down to the faithful, whose only role is reception, or whether it does or should emerge from a *consensus fidelium*. Furthermore, Forrester is correct to state that this problem lay at the heart of the disputes between the Roman Curia and liberation theologians, as well as with the US bishops (concerning their pastoral letters on war and economics). And Forrester is most astute in noting that 'the increasing centralisation of the Roman Catholic Church's moral magisterium lies ill at ease with that same church's teaching on subsidiarity'.[69] He likewise correctly identifies a tension between such and the WCC's own pronouncements on hearing the voice of the powerless and oppressed along with its emphasis upon the notion of ecclesial *participation*.

Again, we see that these concerns are every bit as much of an *ecclesiological* nature as they are of an ethical nature. What they point to, I believe, is a serious disjunction between ethics and ecclesiology currently prevalent in the Roman Catholic Church which mirrors the situation which emerged from the WCC discussion – namely that, today, Christian churches are prone to subordinate ethical practice (and, indeed, theoretical discernment) to ecclesial priorities and hence to ecclesiology. In the Roman Catholic context, the backdrop to much of this (as Farley also acknowledges) is provided by the aforementioned and ongoing debates within Roman Catholicism concerning authority, governance, account-ability and the nature of magisterium.[70]

Are there insights to be learned here which may help those engaged in future debates in this area to avoid some of the pitfalls identified in relation to the WCC debates and their aftermath?

3 The ecclesial importance of moral discernment

Margaret Farley's assessment of the magnitude of Curran's work in relation to all such issues is itself telling.[71] Curran's distinctive contribution has been to oppose 'hierachology' in the Church particularly those instances when the teaching *office* is equated with the teaching *function* of the Church. Curran believes the latter is much broader than the former for the teaching *function* involves *all* church members and entails a mutual learning process.[72] It is no surprise, Farley indicates, that Curran's ecclesiology – a post-Vatican II, 'people of God' sacramental, communal and inclusive ecclesiology as opposed to an institutional, juridical and 'top-down' ecclesiology – informs such thinking. The issues of *participation* and *co-responsibility* in the Church loom large in that ecclesiology,[73] and (as we have seen) one encounters these topics again and again in analysing the interrelation between ethics and ecclesiology in the broader Christian church today, no less than the Roman Catholic Communion.[74]

Farley identifies the underlying theme throughout Curran's work here as being 'moral discernment in the church'[75] – in other words how the church functions as a moral community in the wider world. This is of especial importance to all contemporary discussions concerning ethics and ecclesiology. For Curran, as for Farley, the key issue in all this is the *nature* of moral knowledge and, above all, of moral insight. The Roman Catholic moral tradition is characterized neither by a divine command nor a church-absolutist form of ethics. Curran summarizes his own approach thus:

> With regard to morality, catholicity means that the moral aspect of the Christian life touches all realities in our world and is open to both human and uniquely Christian sources of moral wisdom and knowledge. The challenge for any church catholic is to live out its catholicity and to maintain the tension between unity and diversity. On the more general aspects of morality, such as general principles (respect for life) or virtues (hope, justice), the whole church universal can and should find agreement. But on complex and specific concrete issues, there will be legitimate diversity precisely because no one can claim certainty on these issues.[76]

Hence this entails that moral insight is not about blind obedience but rather attained as a result of the genuine discernment of moral obligation. This necessarily means that there are *limits* to all moral insight. Farley helps remind us that God clearly has not revealed everything to humanity and so moral insight is subject to error and is not conducive to certitude. As Aquinas said, the closer moral knowledge gets to particulars, the more subject it is to contingencies, and Farley reiterates his sentiments,[77]

Hence, whatever infallible powers the teaching church may have, they do not reach to the problems of particular ethical norms. Processes of discernment and deliberation inevitably include disagreement, mistakes, reversals, new insights, and conversions of both heart and mind. Moral certainty, therefore, comes in degrees, and dissent against noninfallible official church teaching can not only be justifiable but beneficial for the process as a whole.[78]

As Farley continues, the Holy Spirit gives assistance to this process which is real, but it does not 'magically' take over our fallible human capacities. The truth each generation shares with all others in the church community is not the totality of truth possessed once and for all. It is a truth that is always being searched for and in a search which is subject to the flux and change of differing eras and circumstances. Thus the teaching function of the Church itself should always be understood as a *participative* one. Just as tradition, itself, is not *self*-interpretative – we require processes of discernment to enable us to interpret and use tradition – so with moral teaching (just as with human experience).[79]

And here we can see further support for those arguments which suggest that any process aimed towards greater integration of ethics and ecclesiology, will require a third element: i.e. the *hermeneutical* endeavour.[80]

For Curran, the laity have a major role to play here in this process of discernment.[81] It is the duty of church leaders to facilitate a *collaborative* moral discourse and yet all too often we see failings amongst those leaders in doing so. Hence, as Farley suggests, 'Curran laments the inattention given to the moral formation of the church community, or even to theological reflection on the "ecclesial context" of the moral life of believers.'[82] But Curran does not intend to advocate that attention to such themes would lead in the same direction in which the WCC discussions proceeded. And here we come to an area of vital importance to any attempt to discern the relation between ethics and ecclesiology.

For too long, I believe, we have seen aspects of the ethical tradition of the Roman Catholic Church overlooked or even ignored by those within its membership, and particularly amongst some of its leaders, most notably in the Curia. Any examination of ethics and ecclesiology should seek to challenge this. We must consider possible ways in which we might promote more positive models of ecclesial authority and communitarian forms of governance, in order to facilitate the dialogue necessary for the enhancement of community (both in theory *and* practice) today. In the Roman Catholic communion, as in so many other churches, too often certain sectors are ecclesiologically 'privileged' (be they church leaders or even, indeed, theologians, in the case of the WCC discussions). But privilege dulls ethical attentiveness.

Indeed, Curran's own analysis of the interrelation between (and efforts towards the integration of) ethics and ecclesiology embraces an ecumenical focus in a manner which perhaps is still more open and fruitful than the WCC discussions. Curran believes we must attend to an analysis of the three areas of church life where ethics is paramount: (1) the moral identity of the Church in general; (2) the moral *actuality* of ethics in the life, thought and deeds within the Church; and (3) how the Church relates to the fact of moral pluralism in the wider society.[83] The

Church must be a moral community of *conviction* as much as of moral discourse and discernment.

Curran believes that whilst the essentials of faith require unity, a Church which seeks to shun exclusivity and embrace inclusivity should both acknowledge and allow greater diversity in less essential matters.[84] Indeed, here he moves on from his earlier focus upon the impact of current trends in ecclesial governance upon moral theology, towards articulating a form of what we might call ethical-ecclesiological hermeneutics. Curran believes that the acceptance of historical consciousness within Roman Catholic theology means that we must acknowledge and embrace the pluralism that exists in theology in general, as well as in moral theology and ecclesiology in particular.[85] As he states: 'The church must always live with many tensions, including the tensions between theology and official church teachings.'[86] And it is in the formation of such hermeneutics, I believe, wherein lies the foundations for a contemporary ethics *of* ecclesiology.[87]

So, with regard to the relation between ethics and ecclesiology, we have here encountered much debate and many criticisms, along with much disillusionment and disappointment, not to mention frustration with the lack of real progress across the divisions of Christianity. What tentative steps may be suggested to take the quest forward? Well, even when the primary goal is practical, there is nonetheless a necessity for theoretical thinking and reflection. Let us engage in a little of this.

Ethical-ecclesiological hermeneutics in the Church

The 'grace of self-doubt'

Recall that 'Costly Commitment' from the WCC sought to tackle the problems of moral struggle, moral discernment and moral formation in order to 'reweave' the moral fibre of society. Well, to the benefit of both church and wider society alike, Margaret Farley offers an insightful proposal with regards to how the church may embrace an ecclesiology more suited to a 'morally discerning and acting church'.[88] Again, she follows Curran in urging the church to nurture the virtue of 'epistemic humility'. In other words, following upon her arguments as discussed earlier, the church should abandon any pretence to certitude[89] and also, whilst nonetheless recognizing core common values and obligations, acknowledge the limitations of moral insight, accept the legitimacy of moral disagreement and dissent and recognize that the church can be a 'community of moral doubt'.[90] The church should develop the structures and modes of governance to facilitate such a strategy. And here we wish to emphasize the *ecclesiological* implications of this, for such a strategy might help overcome the aforementioned divisions and enable a healthy transcendence of differences in method and emphasis, as opposed to allowing tensions leading to a breakdown in community and to schism.

Farley offers a way in which this might be developed further still. She commends to the church the 'grace of self-doubt'. This is not an unhealthy kind of doubt that needs to be overcome but rather a *grace* that is necessary for those in positions of ecclesial power in order to counter self-righteousness and the grasping after certitude. This grace allows for that epistemic humility which Curran urged the Church to develop. Indeed, it is also a necessary grace for *all* in the Church.

Farley turns the focus towards the reception of church teaching: i.e. the 'acceptance and internalization of church teachings by faithful members of the church'.[91] One voice cannot speak for all in a divided church. Instead all must have their voices listened to. Church leaders have the responsibility to 'hear all voices, mediate them, and finally speak with humility, even – on some questions – provisionally if necessary'.[92] Farley believes that moral insight comes about when persons recognize a moral *truth*. The process involves one experiencing a claim upon one's freedom which is experienced as 'unconditional, perceived to be *justifiable* and experienced as both a *liberating appeal and an obligating demand*'.[93] Catholic Christians 'make sense' of such experiences of reality in the light of both reason and revelation.

But, because such recognition of a moral truth involves assent, then coercion can never lead to moral insight or even to moral obligation of a genuine kind – 'it is not possible for persons (especially persons in a tradition that affirms this approach to moral matters) to experience moral obligation simply because they are told that they ought to'.[94] Thus differences amongst, for example, Catholics on birth control, Farley contends, provide an instance of 'profoundly divergent experiences of moral obligation'.[95] We must recognize this, along with the limitations of moral insight.

Farley, like Curran, brings into sharp focus an issue of vital importance for any discernment of the interrelation between ethics and ecclesiology. It is the fact that today there exists within Roman Catholicism (and, I would add, across Christianity in general), a moral pluralism, just as much as a theological pluralism, indeed, just as much as there is an ecclesiological pluralism.[96] I believe we must acknowledge that it was ever thus. The problem here is not the actuality of the pluralist situation itself but rather any pretence that it can or should be shunned or eradicated.[97]

Thus Farley urges us to recognize that grace of self-doubt, which

> is what allows for epistemic humility, the basic condition for communal as well as individual moral discernment ... It is a grace that is accessible to those who struggle for understanding, those who have come to see things differently from what was once seen, those who have experienced the complexity of translating convictions into action.[98]

This grace does not question all our fundamental shared moral convictions, but rather recognizes the 'contingencies of moral knowledge when we stretch towards the particular and the concrete'. This grace allows us to listen to others and their experiences, to acknowledge differing viewpoints and experiences to our own. 'It assumes a shared search for moral insight.'[99] None of this would water-down the church's commitment to its most central moral values and to tackling the most pressing moral challenges. Instead, Farley offers a vision which truly is both ethics and ecclesiology 'as one'. But I suggest that we ought to perceive of 'one' here in the sense of 'in perfect harmony' or 'fully reconciled', rather than in the sense of fused into a single entity where distinctiveness disappears.[100]

Thus we see a further key element to forming an ethical-ecclesiological hermeneutic which would allow a contemporary ethics of ecclesiology to be pursued for the good of the various local and denominational Christian communities, as well as the church as a whole. This grace of self-doubt can inspire processes for ecclesial transformation: 'It can forge cross-cultural discourse and sustain a mission of justice in the world. The unanimity that emerges from diversity is powerful and will not be broken by the best efforts at moral discernment.'[101]

We earlier cited Forrester's contention that 'the Church is … a kind of hermeneutic of the gospel',[102] but we have now seen the case put that there is a need for Christians in each generation, and especially in the present era, to ensure also that the Gospel is allowed to provide a hermeneutic of the church. The 'grace of self-doubt' represents a major step towards a positive ethical-ecclesiological 'hermeneutic of suspicion'. Where have our many deliberations thus led us?

Unity through relational distinctions: embracing the inseparability of ecclesiology and ethics

None of the foregoing is to suggest that we embrace either moral relativism or an 'anything goes' approach to ecclesiology. Nothing here should lead one to deduce that we must succumb to any reductivistic and deconstructionist postmodern agenda. But if the church universal and each of the churches particular are to face the challenges of this era and to come through it with their Christian visions of community and the moral life intact, then the 'signs of these times' must be pondered anew and the voices of others must be heard. Here the 'inward-looking' focus of the underlying ecclesiology which informed the WCC discussions is found to be wanting, as is much recent curial and episcopal hierarchical thinking in the Roman Catholic Church.

So we have been seeking to suggest that the church must also engage in sustained reflection upon the ethics of ecclesiology, the moral dimension of being church and the moral implications of how the church lives, orders and governs its being. The WCC conversations were found wanting because they sought more to offer an ecclesial ethics or as ecclesiology of ethics – i.e. an account of ethics ecclesiologically shaped and formed – without balancing this out with a reciprocal examination of the ethical implications and aspects of that ecclesiology itself. We have also suggested that much recent curial Roman Catholic thinking appears to make the same mistake.

The WCC conversations, as we noted, were further led astray by their choosing to emphasise moral *formation* and, again, this is something which has also become a focus of attention across the institutional Roman Catholic Church. In both the WCC conversations and the Roman Catholic Church, this has been at the expense of due attention being given both to moral *discernment* and to the ecclesiological and moral facets of ecclesial *participation*.

We should strive to avoid anything which collapses ethics and ecclesiology into a single entity, but at the same also strive to ensure they are in harmony as much as possible. This is where *hermeneutics* finds its most significant role. Such an undertaking can aid our attempts to address the prevailing *moral* ecclesial dilemmas concerning our conceptions of church-world relations, inclusivity and pluralism.

Further reflection upon and dialogue concerning the very nature of hermeneutics and its ecclesiological implications[103] would also be of great value, for the myriad of factors of moral relevance which lie 'hidden' beneath the surface of our ecclesiologies and ecclesiological intentions and actions might be better brought to the surface. In our becoming aware of ecclesiological pluralities, we might better be enabled to acknowledge our living in the midst of a variety of ethical pluralities, as well. In Chapter 4 we observed that many of the present difficulties in the churches stem from what Jeanrond calls a 'hermeneutical refusal',[104] i.e. a refusal to engage. Neo-exclusivism, in many of its forms, appears to make such a refusal a defining methodological principle, in certain contexts.[105]

How can all this be taken forward in a positive sense? We mentioned earlier the fact of moral pluralism in the Roman Catholic Church, and if this fact can be acknowledged as non-threatening to the moral life of that Church, then valuable lessons can also be learnt for ecclesiology and its relation to ethics. In widening such considerations beyond the Roman Catholic Church and, indeed beyond the Church altogether, Ronald Preston echoes Farley's viewpoint that moral pluralism is not a cause for despair:

> The fact of moral pluralism in the modern world does not necessarily mean moral chaos. Different societies have different codes by which such virtues as justice, courage and honesty are expressed, but that does not mean that there is a complete mutual incomprehension between different societies when referring to them.[106]

Notwithstanding the fact that some official documents issued by the Roman Catholic Church appear to imply the opposite, we can echo Preston's words here with regard to ecclesiology, because if ethics and ecclesiology are as intertwined as we have suggested, then the analysis applied to one can equally be employed to the other. And in this instance we can say that *the fact of ecclesiological Pluralism* – that differing visions, models and paradigms of what it is to be church exist across denominations and even within particular communions (perhaps, even, especially the Roman Catholic Church) – is no cause for despair either. Differing communities of Christians have different ways and means of living out their life in faithfulness to the Gospel. Such faithfulness, as opposed to its exact and precise form and articulation, is the important thing.[109]

To stress this, once again, there is no reason why such may not be as true *within* particular communions as it is *between* communions, for ecumenism is simply that striving to be one – for that unity which transcends boundaries and divisions of any nature. Charity can guide our ethical-ecclesiological-hermeneutical endeavours.[108] Christian love can function as something of a key to our discerning the inseparability of ethics and ecclesiology in the Christian life.[109]

The churches have embarked upon a fresh quest for our time to discern how best to bear a living witness to the Christian God between whose act and being there is no disjunction. If the church can renew the harmony between what it is and what it does, then it may all the more credibly allow Christian hope to inform the pluralistic efforts towards meeting the many.

Notes

1. I wish to express my deep gratitude to Dr Bernard Hoose of Heythrop College, University of London, for taking the time to read earlier drafts of this chapter and for offering many helpful comments.
2. Throughout, we shall be working with an understanding of *ethics* as referring to the ethos, values and norms of particular communities, as well as being the technical term for how human beings go about shaping, debating, understanding and employing such values, norms, etc. Additionally, ethics also refers to how people come to understand the relation of truth to good and evil, right and wrong. It is acknowledged that different communities and scholars employ the term in widely differing senses, but some common ground may be discerned across most, if not all, of the various uses of the concept itself.

   Ecclesiology is a term understood here to embrace the attempts at self-understanding and self-determination (though neither undertaken, at least in principle, aside from the effects of God's gracious self-communication!) by the church universal and the various churches particular alike. It embraces questions of history, doctrine, mission, ministry, liturgy, worship, structure, governance, communication and participation.
3. Stanley Hauerwas's works of relevance here are almost legion. A recent study of his ecclesiology is John B. Thomson, *The Ecclesiology of Stanley Hauerwas: A Christian Theology of Liberation* (Aldershot: Ashgate, 2003). Hauerwas wishes to see ecclesiology functioning as ethics; I believe the problem is that we insufficiently see ethics impaling upon ecclesiology.
4. I believe Hauerwas often merges ethics and ecclesiology both too simplistically and polemically, to the detriment of both.
5. So numerous are the studies pertaining to this topic in recent years, here we can only touch upon certain representative or particularly informative examples. One excellent overview is Lewis Mudge, 'Ethics and Ecclesiology in the Western Church', ch. 36 of Gerard Mannion and Lewis Mudge (eds), *The Routledge Companion to the Christian Church*, (London: Routledge, 2007).
6. Duncan Forrester, *Truthful Action – Explorations in Practical Theology* (Edinburgh: T&T Clark, 2000), p. 190. Forrester examines this subject at greater length in his *The True Church and Morality* (Geneva: WCC, 1997). A further good summary of the key issues pertaining to any consideration of the relations between ecclesiology and ethics is provided by Lewis Mudge, *The Church as Moral Community* (Geneva: WCC Publications, 1998), pp. 19–24.
7. Forrester, *Truthful Action*, p. 189.
8. Echoing aspects of Yves Congar's ecclesiology here, perhaps unconsciously.
9. Forrester, *Truthful Action*, pp. 190, 191.
10. Ibid., p. 198.
11. One of the earliest pronouncements made by Pope Benedict XVI concerned the unity of the churches which, the new pope said, was a fundamental priority for him. In which case, the debates which we consider throughout this chapter are the very same ones which this papacy will need to address.
12. Cf. P. Lodberg, 'The History of Ecumenical Work on Ecclesiology and Ethics', *The Ecumenical Review*, 47.2 (1995): 128–39, (repr. in Thomas Best and Martin Robra, *Ecclesiology and Ethics: Costly Commitment*. [Geneva: WWC, 1995], pp. 1–12). Thus such

efforts can be traced to the earlier phases of the ecumenical movement and attempts to relate the respective ecumenical efforts of the then more disparate organizations, namely, Life and Work, Faith and Order and the International Missionary Society.

13. Forrester, *Truthful Action*, pp. 186, 188.

14. Another excellent overview of the ecumenical movement is provided by Thomas Best, recently retired head of the Faith and Order commission of the WCC, 'Ecclesiology and Ecumenism', ch. 21 of Mannion and Mudge (eds.) *The Routledge Companion to the Christian Church*.

15. On the latter, cf. Anna Marie Aagaard, 'Ethics on the Joint Working Group Agenda – Does Ethics Divide or Unite? Some Orthodox Visions of Ecumenism', *The Ecumenical Review* 48 (April 1996).

16. Later to be reflected in the joint Anglican–Roman Catholic International Commission (i.e. ARCIC) discussions as 'Communion in Mission'.

17. The noted ecumenist Lewis Mudge has stated (in a conversation with the present author at Union Theological Seminary, August 2004) that it is an ongoing travesty that the relationship between these two wings of the ecumenical movement has never been satisfactory.

18. Forester, *Truthful Action*, p. 187.

19. Ibid. Such a view relates to our earlier contention with regards to Hauerwas's occasionally simplistic fusion of ethics and ecclesiology – here we see that church can sometimes emerge *from* moral struggle (as opposed to ethics simply following from Christians 'being church').

20. Ibid., pp. 185–6.

21. Ibid., p. 188.

22. The overall process of engaging in exploratory discussions concerning ethics and ecclesiology involved both the Faith and Order and Life and Work Commissions of the WCC, between 1992 and 1996.

23. Published in Thomas S. Best and Martin Robra (eds), *Ecclesiology and Ethics: Ecumenical Ethical Engagement, Moral Formation and the Nature of the Church* (Geneva: WCC Publications, 1997). For the sake of space, I have here chosen to focus upon that part of the WCC ethics and ecclesiology initiative which offers the most pertinent analysis of the questions with which this essay is concerned. Additionally, it is also the document which contains some of the more positive suggestions for the future that emerged from the discussions.

24. 'Costly Commitment', in Best and Robra, *Ecclesiology and Ethics*, 24–9 no. 18 at p. 29.

25. Best and Robra, *Ecclesiology and Ethics*, no. 22 at p. 30.

26. 'This refers to the possible ecclesial significance of experiences (both within and outside the traditional boundaries of the church) of community arising through work for justice, peace or the stewardship of creation', §35, p. 33.

27. §49.

28. Best and Robra, *Ecclesiology and Ethics*, no. 28 at p. 32.

29. Ibid., (my italics).

30. 'Moral formation indicates the shaping of human character and conduct from a moral point of view; it involves both 'being' and 'doing'. Moral discernment indicates how we decide what we are to be and to do, that is, how character should be nurtured and what decisions and actions we take on particular moral issues. Of course all human interaction plays a role in forming character, and shaping decisions and actions; the process is, in this sense, 'worldly', and continual. But this only emphasizes the need for the churches *as churches* to offer both nurture and discriminating judgment, (§61, pp. 1–2).

31. 'The categories of moral formation and discernment follow from the nature of the church and its life as church in the world. The churches are expected to provide important moral resources both for their own members and for the wider world. This involves, as part of the churches' overall task of spiritual formation, the moral formation of the faithful. An important part of this is training in discernment, helping church members to analyse ethical issues from the perspective of the gospel and preparing them

to judge "how best to participate in the light of their faith in the moral struggles, complexities and challenges" of the present day. More broadly the churches are expected to contribute to the moral well-being of the societies in which they live, for example through informed participation in public debate on specific ethical issues. The fraying of the "moral fibre" in many societies makes this role all the more urgent today.' (§52, pp. 39–40)

32.   'A further implication is that the boundary between moral formation in the church and moral formation in the world is fluid. We noted in paragraph 16 above some important results of the churches' common struggle with ethical issues (for example, the affirmation of the fundamental equality of women and men, and the need to exercise a responsible stewardship of the environment). Yet these results have also come as the churches interacted with moral struggles in society, struggles in which the church has learned as much as it has taught. In this sense the efforts for moral formation in society have had an ecclesial significance: through these efforts the church has learned how better to be church.' (§72, p. 47)

33.   'This process will sometimes call the church to *self-criticism*, reminding it how these same worldly forces and structures affect its own life as an historical institution. Sometimes the church will need to confess that, wittingly or unwittingly, it condones attitudes which allow injustice to continue or which obscure the root causes of injustice. Sometimes the church will discover that its own processes of ethical judgment, and of moral formation, have become distorted by such factors.' (§60, p. 41)

34.   'These reflections on moral formation have important implications for our understanding of the church. While affirming the transcendent reality of the church we recognize that the church is not yet, in its empirical historical manifestation, fully what it is in God. In this sense we can say that the church as historic institution is itself undergoing a process of 'moral formation' guided by God, a process which will continue until the full reign of God dawns. Thus the tasks of spiritual and moral formation and discernment will always be part of the Church's life and mission. This is to say yet again: in the Church's own struggles for justice, peace and the integrity of creation, the *esse* of the church is at stake.' (§71, p. 47)

35. Numerous studies of these discussions and their outcome have appeared, as well as subsequent studies of related themes and our overall theme in general. For example, cf. Forrester, *The True Church and Morality*; Mudge, *The Church as Moral Community* and also his *Rethinking the Beloved Community: Ecclesiology, Hermeneutics, Social Theory* (Geneva: WCC Publications and University Press of America, 2001); Lewis Mudge, 'Ecclesiology and Ethics in Current Ecumenical Debate', *The Ecumenical Review*, 48 (January 1996): 11–27 and also his 'Towards a Hermeneutic of the Household: "Ecclesiology and Ethics" after Harare', *The Ecumenical Review*, 51 (July 1999): 243–55 and the aforementioned 'Ethics and Ecclesiology in the Western Church'; Arne Rasmusson, 'Ecclesiology and Ethics: The Difficulties of Ecclesial Moral Reflection', *The Ecumenical Review*, 52 (April 2000): 180–94; Simone Sinn, *The Church as Participatory Community: On the Interrelationship between Hermeneutics, Ecclesiology and Ethics* (Dublin: Columba Press, 2002) and, for a particular *theo*logical approach to ethics (though differing to that offered in this present volume), cf. Bernd Wannenwetsch, 'Ecclesiology and Ethics', Ch. 4 of Gibert Meilaender and Werner Werpehowski, *The Oxford Handbook of Theological Ethics*, (Oxford: Oxford University Press, 2005), pp. 57–73. Also of relevance here is Charles Curran, *The Church and Morality: An Ecumenical and Catholic Approach* (Minneapolis, MN: Fortress Press, 1993).

36. As well as those expressed in the other documents contained in the Best and Robra volume which emerged from similar processes – *Costly Unity* and *Costly Obedience* – the latter document being the result of discussions held in Johannesburg in 1996.

37. On the ecclesiological phenomenon of 'neo-exclusivism', see Gerard Mannion, 'Ecclesiology and Postmodernity – A New Paradigm for the Church?', *New Blackfriars*, 85 (May, 2004), esp. pp. 313–17.

38. See, especially, the above quoted works of Lewis Mudge in relation to this and Arne Rasmusson's partial rejoinders.

39. Margaret Farley, 'Ethics, Ecclesiology and the Grace of Self-Doubt', in James J. Walter, Timoth E. O'Connell and Thomas A. Shannon (eds), *A Call to Fidelity on the Moral Theology of Charles E. Curran* (Georgetown, Washington: Georgetown University Press, 2002), p. 64 (recalling Hauerwas's famous phrase).

40. Farley, 'Ethics, Ecclesiology and the Grace of Self-Doubt', p. 64.

41. Forrester, *Truthful Action*, p. 188.

42. Werner Schwartz, 'Church and Ethical Orientation: Moral Formation in the People of God', *The Ecumenical Review*, 51 (July 1999) 256–65.

43. Cf. initiatives and organizations such as the more radical 'We are Church', to the more the mainstream US group Voice of the Faithful, and the many research projects and ecclesiological conversations initiated in the UK by the Queen's Foundation Working Party on Authority and Governance in the Roman Catholic Church.

44. Thus returning our focus to aspects of Forrester's aforementioned arguments.

45. Ronald H. Preston, *Confusions in Christian Social Ethics – Problems for Geneva and Rome* (London: SCM Press, 1994), p. 146.

46. Ibid.

47. For example, Charles Curran, 'The Changing Anthropological Bases of Catholic Social Ethics', in *Directions in Catholic Social Ethics* (Notre Dame, IN: University of Notre Dame Press, 1985) (of whose work more is said below).

48. Preston, *Confusions in Christian Social Ethics*, p. 146. One finds similar arguments in Curran, *The Church and Morality, passim*.

49. Preston, *Confusions in Christian Social Ethics*, ch. 8, 'Where are we Today?, pp. 124–45.

50. Cf. also the more general 'five basic models of contemporary theology' discussed in David Tracy's *Blessed Rage for Order: The New Pluralism in Theology* (Minneapolis, MN: Seabury, 1975), ch. 2, pp. 22–42. He discusses orthodox theology, liberal theology, neo-orthodox theology, radical theology and, finally, the 'revisionist model'. To both lists one might add recent and somewhat hybrid 'movements' such as 'radical orthodoxy' as well as the ecclesiological outlook of Stanley Hauerwas itself, each of which have been referred to as examples of the 'theology of difference' by Frank Kirkpatrick in *The Ethics of Community*, (Oxford: Basil Blackwell, 2001), ch. 6 pp. 103–33.

51. Preston, *Confusions in Christian Social Ethics*, p. 159.

52. And, indeed, in certain official statements issued by the Roman Catholic Church in recent years.

53. A further and more wide-ranging survey can be found across recent essays exploring various aspects of the changes and developments within modern and contemporary Roman Catholic moral theology, including *vis-à-vis* ecclesiology, in the collection celebrating the life and work of one of the foremost pastor-theologians of the second half of the twentieth century, *Moral Theology for the 21ˢᵗ Century: Essays in Celebration of Kevin Kelly*, eds Julie Clague, Bernard Hoose and Gerard Mannion (London: T&T Clark, 2008).

54. Richard A. McCormick, 'Moral Theology 1940–1989: An Overview', *Theological Studies*, 50 (1989): 3–24

55. It is easy to identify parallels in other churches, with regards to both areas.

56. McCormick, 'Moral Theology 1940–1989', (my italics), p. 7.

57. Given to a gathering of moral theologians at the University of Notre Dame in June 1988.

58. McCormick, 'Moral Theology 1940–1989', p. 8.

59. Indeed, Farley virtually paraphrases McCormick on this very point: 'The [Second Vatican] council said very little explicitly about ethics, but what it said about the church – its life and practices – had great influence on developments in the method and substance of ethical thought', ('Ethics, Ecclesiology' and the Grace of Self-Doubt, p. 62 [my italics]).

60. Farley, 'Ethics, Ecclesiology and the Grace of Self-Doubt', p.62

61. Ibid., p. 55.

62. Ibid., p. 56. This is something I am inclined to disagree with. Ecclesiology should still be considered as very much being to the forefront of such debates. But this does not detract from the analysis which Farley subsequently offers.

63. Ibid., p. 56.

64. Here being a prime example of an account which offers a distinct alternative to the more inward-looking ecclesial vision of Stanley Hauerwas.

65. Space does not permit a full discussion, here, of the numerous church documents nor actual episodes of such failings. Here cf. Gerard Mannion, *Ecclesiology and Postmodernity – Questions for the Church in our Times* (Collegeville, MA: Liturgical Press, 2007), where I expand upon and flesh out this critique. For various other treatments of particular themes and documents pertaining to the criticisms in operation here, cf. Gerard Mannion, Richard Gaillardetz, Jan Kerkhofs, Kenneth Wilson (eds), *Readings in Church Authority – Gifts and Challenges for Contemporary Catholicism* (Aldershot: Ashgate Press, 2003). Cf. also Mannion, 'A Haze of Fiction'.

66. See Curran's own wonderfully honest and moving account of the development of his own thought in Charles E. Curran, *Loyal Dissent* (Washington, DC: Georgetown University Press, 2006).

67. At a conference on Governance, Accountability and the Future of the Church, organized by the Saint Thomas More Center, Yale University, March 2003. Cf. p. 70 in the original.

68. Forrester, *Truthful Action*, p. 194. Cf. John Mahoney, *The Making of Moral Theology: A Study of the Roman Catholic Tradition* (Oxford: Clarendon Press, 1987), p. 346. But note, also, that the ethical traditions of Roman Catholicism are more complex than Forrester here suggests, lest one overlook the long and complex history of the interrelationship between ethics and ecclesiology in the story of Roman Catholicism.

69. Forrester, *Truthful Action*, p. 195.

70. Cf. Francis Oakley and Bruce Russet (eds), *Governance, Accountability and the Future of the Church* (London and New York: Continuum, 2003) and Bernard Hoose (ed.) *Authority and Roman Catholicism – Theory and Practice* (Aldershot: Ashgate Press, 2002).

71. It is ironic, given that Curran, an esteemed moral theologian himself, was treated shamefully by church authorities because he 'dared' to exercise the office of theologian in a manner whereby his learning, expertise and conscience led him publicly to 'dissent' from 'official' church teaching on artificial contraception. Of nearly three dozen books which Curran authored, along with 18 edited and coedited, Farley highlights the very significant fact that 'only four do not address some aspect of the relationship between ecclesiology and ethics' (Farley, 'Ethics, Ecclesiology and the Grace of Self Doubt', p. 56). See the various essays in 'The Curran Case and Its Aftermath', part 5 of Charles Curran and Richard A. McCormick (eds), *Dissent in the Church*, vol. 6 of 'Readings in Moral Theology' (New York: Paulist Press, 1988).

72. Farley, 'Ethics, Ecclesiology and the Grace of Self Doubt', pp. 57–8. Cf. Charles Curran, *Moral Theology: A Continuing Journey* (Notre Dame, IN: University of Notre Dame Press, 1982); *The Catholic Moral Tradition Today: A Synthesis* (Washington, DC: Georgetown University Press, 1999).

73. Cf. Curran, *The Church and Morality*, esp.Chs 2 and 4; *Toward an American Catholic Moral Theology* (Notre Dame, IN: University of Notre Dame Press, 1987), pp. 18–19 and ch. 7. In relation to similar concerns, Margaret Farley cites *Critical Concerns in Moral Theology* (Notre Dame, IN: University of Notre Dame Press, 1981), ch. 1; *The Living Tradition of Catholic Moral Theology* (Notre Dame, IN: University of Notre Dame Press, 1992) and *The Catholic Moral Tradition Today*, ch. 1, pp. 1–29.

74. Cf. the various perspectives offered in Jan Kerkhofs (ed.), 'Synodality and Collegiality – The Dynamics of Authority' and 'The Sensus Fidelium and Reception of Teaching', Parts 3 and 5 of G. Mannion, R. Gaillardetz, J. Kerkhofs and K. Wilson (eds), *Readings in Church Authority*.

75. Farley, 'Ethics, Ecclesiology and the Grace of Self Doubt', p. 57.

76. Curran, *Loyal Dissent*, p. 182.

77. Cf. Curran, *Directions in Catholic Social Ethics*.
78. Farley, 'Ethics, Ecclesiology and the Grace of Self-Doubt', p. 59.
79. Curran summarizes the specific methodological principles of his moral theology, including articulating a visionary understanding of the role of the institutional teaching Church (magisterium) in moral theology in ch. 8, 'My Moral Theology', of *Loyal Dissent*, pp. 187–208.
80. Sinn, *Church as Participatory Community* is most instructive here, and I am indebted to her insight. Likewise, Sinn also highlights the importance of the notion of ecclesial *participation*. See ch. 4 this volume.
81. Again, a common theme throughout Curran's works but cf., for example, *The Church and Morality*, ch. 2; *The Living Tradition of Moral Theology*, pp. 120–2; *The Catholic Moral Tradition Today*, ch. 7, *passim*; and 'Kevin T. Kelly and the Role of the Pastoral Moral Theologian', ch. 27 in Clague *et al.* (eds), *Moral Theology for the 21st Century*, pp. 270–7.
82. Farley, 'Ethics, Ecclesiology and the Grace of Self-Doubt', p. 61. Cf. Curran, *The Catholic Moral Tradition Today*, pp. 2–3.
83. Cf. Curran, *The Church and Morality* – such issues corresponding to the topics with which its respective chapters are concerned. See also *Loyal Dissent*, pp. 187–207.
84. Curran, *Toward an American Catholic Moral Theology*, pp. 18–19; see also, *The Church and Morality*, *passim* and *Loyal Dissent*, pp. 182, 204–6, 246.
85. Curran, *Toward an American Catholic Moral Theology*, pp. 42–8. This includes what Curran calls 'the Dialogical Character of Contemporary Moral Theology' (p. 15).
86. Ibid., p. 47.
87. Though, admittedly, some have argued that Curran's work addresses the modern context more directly than the postmodern: hence the work of those such as David Tracy may supplement such efforts. For example, Bryan N. Massingdale's overview of the significance of Curran's work and ecclesial life, especially his 'creative fidelity' to the official Church and its living tradition ends with Massingdale suggesting that younger moral theologians face a very different interpretive context today, both globally and ecclesially. He calls for a strategy of 'faithful reconstruction' in method which (following David Tracy) acknowledges the deep ambiguity of the Catholic tradition and of postconciliar Catholic ethics, in particular. Curran's project, he contends, is modern: hence the new generation of ethicists face a new era with differing challenges. Massingdale writes from his specific 'social location' as an African American and thus calls for this reconstruction to free Catholic ethics from some of its white and privileged bias, as well as from 'patriarchy and other systemic evils': 'Beyond Revision: A Younger Moralist Looks at Charles E. Curran', in Walter et al., *A Call to Fidelity*, pp. 253–72.
88. Farley, 'Ethics, Ecclesiology and the Grace of Self-Doubt', p. 66.
89. Cf. Curran:

> Ecclesiologically, the total teaching function of the church is not exhausted by the hierarchical teaching office and function. Theologically, these specific moral questions are not core and central to the faith, so that in disagreeing with them one is not denying faith. Epistemologically, on such complex specific questions one can never achieve a certitude that excludes the possibility of error. (*Toward an American Catholic Moral Theology*, pp. 18–19).

90. Farley, 'Ethics, Ecclesiology and the Grace of Self-Doubt', p. 60.
91. Ibid., p. 66. For a selection of readings in relation to the notion of reception, see Jan Kerkhofs (ed.), 'The Sensus Fidelium and the Reception of Teaching', in Mannion et al., *Readings in Church Authority*. On the value of reception in this respect, see, also, Faith and Order Commission, World Council of Churches, *A Treasure in Earthen Vessels: An Instrument for Reflection on Ecumenical Hermeneutics* (Geneva: WCC/Faith and Order Publications, Faith and Order paper no. 182, 1998).
92. Ibid., p. 69.
93. Ibid., p. 67.

94. Ibid., p. 67.
95. Ibid., p. 68.
96. Again, David Tracy's work is instructive here, in particular, *Blessed Rage for Order*; *The Analogical Imagination: Christian Theology and the Culture of Pluralism* (New York: Crossroad, 1981); *On Naming the Present, God, Hermeneutics, and Church* (Maryknoll, NY: Orbis Books, 1994). Again, Tracy's work is discussed in ch. 4 in this volume. There, also, we discuss the pluralistic reality in which we now live.
97. Cf. the concluding words of Ian Markham's *Plurality and Christian Ethics* (Cambridge: Cambridge University Press,1994, p. 195), where he speaks of the need to view pluralism not as a threat, but as the way in which God wishes us to live in the world.
98. Farley, 'Ethics, Ecclesiology and the Grace of Self-Doubt', p. 69.
99. Ibid., p. 69.
100. And here hermeneutics can be added as a third aspect of this 'trinitarian' ecclesial analysis.
101. Farley, 'Ethics, Ecclesiology and the Grace of Self-Doubt', p. 70.
102. Forrester, *Truthful Action*, p. 191. See also Forrester's reflections on the WCC Ecclesiology and Ethics studying Best and Robra, *Ecclesiology and Ethics*, pp. 92–104.
103. Taking up, therefore, where *A Treasure in Earthen Vessels* left off.
104. Jeanrond, *Theoligical Hermeneutics* p. 164
105. Thus in ch. 4, we commend pluralism in a more general sense; here we address moral and ecclesiological pluralism.
106. Ronald H. Preston, *Confusions in Christian Social Ethics*, p. 156.
107. Forrester goes on to provide these further wise words:

> It is one of the glories of the modern ecumenical movement that churches with very different historical self-understandings and conflicting views of their ethical respon-sibilities now engage with one another in the common search for fuller ways of being the Church which does not have, but is, a social ethic. The modern ecumenical discussion of ecclesiology and ethics emerges from this remarkable convergence, conversation and conversion'. (Forrester, *Truthful Action*, p. 202).

108. As Richard A McCormick states:

> A Catholic moral theology that is not centered on Christ had better change its name. By 'centered on Christ' ... I mean ... the fundamental concepts of such a theology (e.g. vocation, telos, conversion, virtue, sin, obligation, etc.) should be shaped by the fact – and implications thereof – that Jesus is God's incarnate self-gift. The very gift of God in Jesus shapes our response – which means that *the central and organizing vitality of the Christian moral life and moral theology is the self-gift we call charity*. This must function, far more than it has, in the very notion of the moral life, in the discernment of moral rightfulness and wrongfulness of conduct, and in the pastoral education of the community of believers'. ('Moral Theology 1940–1989: An Overview', p. 24 [my italics]).

109. Pope Paul VI called for charity to inform all our dealings with one another within and without the Church. In recent times there has been a distinct lack of charity in how Christians of many denominations have behaved towards one another (be they, for example, Roman Catholics arguing over authority or Anglicans over the Bible and sexuality) and towards those of other faiths and of none. Yet charity, love, as said, is the most enduring Christian virtue. For a thought-provoking discussion of the concept, cf., David Tracy, 'Charity in the Catholic Tradition', in Tracy, *On Naming the Present*.

Chapter 7

ECCLESIOLOGY: CONTEXT AND COMMUNITY

Paul M. Collins

Introduction

There is a growing recognition that the subsection of systematic theology known in contemporary writing as ecclesiology would benefit from or indeed might require some connection with practice. This recognition is often articulated in terms of the inadequacies of 'blue-print ecclesiologies'. The writings of Dulles, Tillard, Volf and Zizioulas have each been subjected to such a critique. Nicholas Healy[1] has pointed to the need to earth the task of reflecting upon understandings of the church in practice. This of course resonates with what pastoral theologians have been seeking to do for some time. One of the difficulties of incorporating reflection upon practice into systematic theology has been a lack of consensus about a frame of reference by which to make this possible.

In this essay I shall analyse how the methods of contextual theology and pastoral theology may influence and change the way in which systematic theologians approach the task of reflecting upon what the church is and what it is for. For example, both Leonardo Boff and Gustavo Gutierrez[2] in their contemporary writings have set out a method for theology, which insists on the necessity to incorporate reflection upon experience and practice into the theological endeavour. To a certain extent this is echoed in developments in western pastoral theology. This is not surprising, as various strands of liberation theology have played a considerable role in the formation of present-day approaches to pastoral theology. In seeking a frame of reference whereby to facilitate an exchange between ecclesiology and contextual theologies, it is possible that Elaine Graham in her appeal to Habermas's understanding of the interplay between language and community provides at least one such frame of reference by which to incorporate practice-based reflection into systematic theology.

In pursuit of a frame of reference to facilitate the designated exchange, we will need to analyse key developments in pastoral theology, as well as the core methods of contextual theologians. In undertaking this analysis four key concepts will be borne in mind. (1) There is a general concern to reconsider and challenge the dominant status of Enlightenment paradigms of theory and practice. (2) Alongside this questioning of the primacy of rationality, experience, practice and the non-/ pre-cognitive are to be treated as fundamental components of the doing of theology. (3) There is now a recognition that these first two factors need to be pursued with greater rigour. Thus reflection upon experience, practice and the non-/pre-cognitive needs to be done in ways that are self-aware and self-critical, which means that other sources are required to enable and resource such critical self-awareness. The cumulative effect of these three is expressed in the value placed in factor 4: context, i.e. the historical, cultural and linguistic boundaries of all of our experience and knowledge. To these four key concepts a fifth will be added in the form of a question: How is it possible to hold together the primacy of context with understandings of the cosmological implications of the church within the divine economy of salvation?

1 The appeal to context

The appeal to context, which typifies contextual theologies, is of necessity also an appeal to community. The community and its context is the locus where the raw data for theological reflection arises, as well as being the fundamental instrument for undertaking that reflection. One of the crucial concerns, which arises from such context-based reflection is the need for rigour, as well as the need to be rooted in tradition. Contextual and pastoral theologians have sought to address these twin concerns and we shall examine these attempts below. Nonetheless, questions emerge concerning a community's awareness of its own rigour and relatedness to tradition. It is out of this paradoxical situation that the quest for a framework in which contextual and systematic theology can offer critique of each other's endeavour emerges.

We begin with a short analysis of recent developments in Western pastoral theology, particularly as they relate to the tasks of ecclesiology. The first development to be considered relates to the change of emphasis in both theory and practice from an individualistic, one-to-one, model of pastoral care, based upon various schools of counselling, to a more communal approach. This development is mainly associated with the work of Clinebell.[3] This shift in emphasis in practice is mirrored in pastoral theology by a clearer recognition of the community as a locus for 'care'. This in turn leads to a broader understanding of 'care' and a greater valuing of the community which provides the context and means for, as well as sustaining the endeavour to provide pastoral care. Stephen Pattison's work builds upon this change of emphasis to offer a clear challenge to older models of pastoral care and theology, as well as to traditional understandings of the church.[4]

> Contextually and situationally sensitive pastoral theologies will be modest in their claims and assertions. This is a welcome feature amidst the past grandiosity of many theological enterprises which have sought to control and order the world rather than to understand it and set particular individuals and communities free.[5]

Pattison's prescription for the theological enterprise, or at least a part of it, elicits different responses. However such a vision of pastoral theology in combination with the notion that all theological endeavour needs to take into account experience, practice and the communal places a clear challenge before any who would seek to craft an understanding of the church. Pattison is clear that 'theology-producing communities' have a crucial role to play: 'it is in communities and between communities that these [contextually and situationally sensitive] theologies will best be criticised, modified and expanded'.[6]

So we can see that these developments in pastoral theology set up a dialectical tension between the community of the church as a place of localized experience-based reflection and a place where resources are also to be found which can provide a critique of that reflection. A question that emerges is, How might one hold together Pattison's vision of contextual theology with understandings of the cosmological implications of the church within the economy of salvation?

In relation to the focus upon community, the influence of Alasdair MacIntyre is also noteworthy. MacIntyre presents theologians with a community-based vision of ethics in his work *After Virtue*.[7] A vision of the church as ethical community, is neither new, nor indeed ignored by other writers.[8] However, what is particular to MacIntyre's vision for the community is his appeal to a premodern paradigm. MacIntyre explicitly rejects the appeal to rationality inherent in philosophical, ethical and theological thought since the Enlightenment. This vision of community, put forward by MacIntyre, has been utilized by pastoral and systematic theologians.[9] Some see his description of 'dislocation' as a necessary pre-requisite to the process of relativizing the hegemonic status of Enlightenment paradigms of theory and practice. MacIntyre has certainly contributed to the movement to place community firmly at the centre of pastoral and ethical concerns, but his rejection of rationality puts him in a similar place alongside those postmodern thinkers who also seek to relativize the appeal to rationality. MacIntyre's vision to reconstruct community based on premodern conceptualities has stimulated a broad discussion and analysis of concepts of community. However, is it possible that such a vision be realized in relation to an appeal to contemporary experience and practice. It may be argued that the context to which MacIntyre appeals is paralleled in the contemporary situation of the West. But it is uncertain whether there could be practical outcomes from such an analysis. Indeed, pastoral theologians seem to have adopted few tools to make any such analytical comparison possible.[10]

A further development in pastoral theology has been the explicit adoption of methods of theological reflection as core elements in this discipline. Laurie Green, in *Let's Do Theology* [11] made significant inroads into rational/cognitive theology. This method has been extended and refined in the work of Emmanuel Lartey.[12] Lartey has sought to make the processes of reflection more rigorous. He and Pattison have recognized that experience and practice and the non-/pre-cognitive[13] need to be fundamental components of *doing* theology. However, both see the need for reflection to be self-aware and self-critical. Such self-awareness needs to be incorporated into the method(s) of reflection. This in turn requires the recognition that other sources are required to enable and resource such critical self-awareness. The methods of Green and Lartey provide a comprehensive possibility for encompassing and using the widely disparate and often conflicting sources and influences which pastoral and systematic theologians need to recognize and use.

However, the sources still call for a framework in order to be structured or brought into a meaningful exchange. The question to which we alluded above must now be posed more sharply. Where are the resources held and whose responsibility is it to bring them to bear upon the local, community-based theological reflection? A dialectic emerges between the polarities of local and universal, contextual and cosmological. These polarities begin to suggest the parameters for any framework to facilitate an exchange between contextual and systematic theology.

In this section we attempt to explore the possibilities of a framework based upon these polarities in a worked example of a critique of a particular 'traditional' example of 'doing ecclesiology'. We will bring this tradition into an exchange with theological reflection suggested by pastoral theologians we have discussed above. We shall attempt this by means of a critique of the work of Avery Dulles, which focuses on the method of examining models. This will be made in relation to the four factors of contextual theology outlined in the introduction to this essay, especially factors 2, relating to experience, practice and the non-/pre-cognitive and factor 4, relating to context.

I shall focus my response to Dulles's *Models of the Church*[14] around five combinations drawn out of and synthesized from his work.[15] These will be: (a) the political society model; (b) the Body of Christ model; (c) the Sacramental model; (d) the pilgrim people model; and (e) the church as Servant.

(a) The political society model: The analysis of the church as an institution and community, which parallels the political state and/or civil society is rooted in the understanding that a human community has 'visible characteristics'. This aspect of the model has an enduring contribution to make to the endeavour to craft a contemporary understanding of the church. However if we also accept that the church is more than a human social structure in the sense that it relates to the Transcendent, to *mysterium tremendum et fascinans*, then the usefulness of the model will be limited. It is precisely this qualification of the appeal to social structure, which connects with our present concerns to incorporate the pre-cognitive within contemporary ecclesiology. Also our concern to credit experience and context as theological resources alongside the appeal to the pre-cognitive, poses serious questions for the appropriateness of contemporary ecclesial structures.

(b) The Body of Christ model: The metaphor of the Body of Christ became the predominant model in ecclesiology during the twentieth century. The identification of the visible human community with Christ appeared to resolve the potential for a dualism between the invisible and visible church by situating the Transcendent in the 'now'. This 'solution' had a certain appeal in that it seemed to resolve some of the issues relating to a more institutional model through its apparent 'democracy'. However, the net effect of this model can be the 'divinization' of the earthly church, thus reinforcing institutionalism rather than relativizing it. This simplistic resolution of the transcendent into the mundane fails to do justice to the pre-cognitive, as well as frequently endowing the status quo

with a more enduring quality than a practice-based contextual theology of the Church would suggest.

(c) The sacramental model: While this model has roots which are distinctive from the 'Body of Christ' metaphor, the close identification between the community and Christ, often conceived in terms of a qualified 'extension of the Incarnation', results in an understanding of the church, which in net terms is hardly distinguishable from the 'Body of Christ'. This suggests that any model which conceives of the church community in too close an identification with the person of Christ is likely to be questionable when set against the twin criteria of an appeal to context and the pre-cognitive. In other words, the close identification of institution/community with the divine inevitably invests the status quo with an inherent value which vitiates against the ongoing reality of human community and its context.

(d) The pilgrim people model: The model of the church as the people of God, or pilgrim people apparently provides solutions to the issues, which we have identified in relation to the three models considered so far. Firstly it does not rest upon a close identification of the community with the person of Christ. Secondly it does not rest upon any understanding of the church which sees it as immune from the effects of time and place, i.e. context. However, because the connection with the person of Christ is less closely defined, it is also a matter of uncertainty as to how this model relates to the transcendent. Furthermore, if we accept that the church is (an essential) part of the divine economy of salvation, can this idea of a rather unstructured community effectively fulfil what is implied in traditional understandings of what the church is for? Possibly the best use of this model will be to reinterpret notions of institution so that models of community and institution can mutually inform and form one another to produce new understandings and practices. If these were to incorporate the contextual and pre-cognitive, then the model of the pilgrim people could provide a fruitful transitional model, or ongoing counterbalance to whichever model claims the favour of the moment.

(e) The church as servant: The final model, relating to servanthood, rests upon the Gospel claims that Christ came to serve rather than be served. It is parallel to the understandings of the church as the Body of Christ or of sacrament. This coincides with Pattison's prescription for pastoral theology in the sense that there is shared concern for the church to be alongside others, rather than dominating or controlling.[16] Nonetheless this understanding rests on a concept of the church being an extension of the functions of Christ's ministry and mission. This may be less 'triumphalistic' than claims to be an extension of the Incarnation *per se*, but it still rests upon an understanding of the close identification of the community with Christ. It may be that the characterization of this identification in terms of service can provide a reinterpretation of the mediation of the transcendent by and in the community. Thus as servant the church may be understood as an essential part of the divine economy of salvation without any attendant 'divinization'. The model

has been used by communities in the developing world and is a significant methodological feature in liberation theologies. A particular critique made of this model focuses upon the lack of clarity concerning the identification of change in the human context and the emergence of the divine Kingdom. In other words, does social progress inevitably equate with God's purposes and is the servant church called to facilitate this?

This worked example of a critique of Dulles's models of the church highlights a possible way in which the methods espoused by contextual and pastoral theologians might be applied to a 'standard Western' work of ecclesiology. It demonstrates considerable dependence upon the preconceptions of 'contextual theologies', which we set out in terms of four factors in the introduction to this essay. While there is general acknowledgement and acceptance of these, they are not without their critics and so it is to an analysis of these preconceptions that we shall now turn.

2. Contextual theologies

In setting out to examine the preconceptions which undergird the appeal to context and community, we shall be considering two related questions: (1) What do contextual theologies set out to achieve? and (2) What may contextual theologies be said to achieve? The critique on which we shall be focusing suggests two outcomes in particular. Firstly the understanding that the appeal to context seeks and expects to achieve the end of modernity; secondly (and by extension) how does this relate to what has come to be understood as postmodernity? I shall pursue these questions in relation to a critique of an article by D. Stephen Long, 'Fetishizing Feuerbach's God: Contextual Theologies as the End of Modernity'.[17] He sets out his thesis that rather than distancing themselves from the Eurocentrism of the Enlightenment, contextual theologians depend upon and repeat the very problem they seek to 'overcome'. He argues this in relation to two primary claims. First of all he appeals to the line of thought expressed by philosophers such as Gianni Vattimo[18] that the project of modernity envisaged from the Enlightenment onwards rests upon the understanding that the 'new' comes by the 'overcoming' of the old.[19] Secondly he appeals to Feuerbach's[20] understanding that theological predications are in effect predications about our own being.[21] Long argues that

> when it comes to the important questions of how theologians speak of God, these contextual theologies have not challenged but repeated key moments in European thought ... [Indeed] as presently constituted – 'contextual theologies' repeat that moment in European thought which has become known as 'the end of modernity'.[22]

This critique is based in particular on the notion that modernity was inexorably destined to continue the cycle of seeking the 'new' by sacrificing the 'old'. Long is especially committed to the view that those who espouse counter-politics among the contextual theologians repeat rather than resist the sacrificial economy of modernity. The ultimate outworking of this, both in the past and in the present, is found in Feuerbach's proscription of God's existence for the sake of our existence. Long argues that in many instances the methods of contextual theology collude with Feuerbach's proscription, particularly when politics is treated as the will to power. Long applies his critique in relation to three particular errors which he identifies in the method of contextual theologies. The first of these relates to what he understands to be the incorrect interpretation that Eurocentric thought claims to know reality as it actually is. The contextual theologies propose a limited, relative or contextual epistemology instead. This produces the second error. In producing a limited epistemology, contextual theologies make the assumption that the language to be used in relation to God and ourselves is a priori univocal. Finally the third error relates to the acceptance of politics as the will to power: in relation to theology, Long claims, this implies that all truth claims are to be understood 'a priori as disguised power plays'.[23] Thus in Long's view the attempt to deliver language about God from a Eurocentric bind into the hands of the local and contextual fails, because in restricting knowledge and language to the contextual, all other possibilities are sacrificed. And in seeking to overcome the Eurocentric, the contextual theologians repeat 'the end of modernity', rather than discovering a true alternative.

> By positing a collective 'European' subject who taught that he knew the truth of things-in-themselves with certainty, contextual theology mistakes the error that drives Eurocentrism. What is taught was that we cannot know the world as it is. All that we can know is our own linguistic or conceptual representations of that world, because all that was certain was the priority of our own subjectivity. By misidentifying the error of Eurocentrism and then reacting against this fictive subject, contextual theologies collude with the very object they seek to dismantle.[24]

Long's critique of the outcome of contextual theologies for epistemology and language requires further consideration, which I will offer below. The implications of his challenge for contextual theology, pastoral theology, and by extension ecclesiology, need to be examined and weighed carefully. If Long's critique were to be received even only in part, the use of the methods of contextual theology would need to be questioned and analysed thoroughly.

A major element in Long's critique relates to the work of Gianni Vattimo on the 'end of modernity'.[25] In particular, as we have identified above, for Long this relates to the emergence of the 'new' through the sacrifice of the 'old'. However, there are two aspects of Vattimo's understanding which Long chooses to downplay or ignore. These two aspects are closely related to each other and are crucial to Vattimo's advocacy of postmodernism. Firstly Vattimo is clear that although the 'new' emerges at the expense of the 'old', the new is also always interpreted as a recovery or (re-)appropriation of what is foundational or original. This in turn relates to the very notion of what can be said to be 'post'modern. In other words, for Vattimo 'postmodernism' is a taking leave of modernity. Thus he heralds the end of history or, more precisely, the end of historicity. These two central features of Vattimo's writing suggest at least a reassessment of Long's diagnosis. While Long's critique of the method of contextual theologies may hold in relation to his description of a 'sacrificial economy', his neglect of Vattimo's understanding of modernity's appeal to the 'foundational' calls the complete application of this critique into question. Is it possible in any sense to describe contextual theologies in terms of a recovery or renaissance of a European 'origin'?

Vattimo's advocacy of the postmodern is simply left aside in Long's critique. However, in positing his thesis of 'the end of modernity' Vattimo's advocacy of what is truly 'post' and alternative is crucial. In relation to this, contextual theologies do seek to posit alternatives to Eurocentrism, whether these are constructed consciously in relation to a notion of postmodernism or not. What then remains at issue is not so much the 'sacrificial economy', or Long's critique *per se*, but rather the ontological, epistemological and linguistic implications, particularly in relation to Feuerbach's proscription.

In his more detailed exposition of 'sacrificial economy' Long draws upon the work of René Girard[26] on mimetic desire and Julia Kristeva's critique of first-wave feminism.[27] Through the exposition of the dependence of Kristeva's critique of first-wave feminism upon Girard's conception of mimetic desire, Long is able to produce a further level of analysis of contextual theologies. He is concerned in particular to interpret the present political situation, and the counter-cultural politics of contextual theologians in relation to Girard's theories of desire, rivalry and sacrificial economy. In doing so, Long argues that 'the proliferation of contextual theologies – far from producing a true theological difference – lends itself to a theological indifference that colludes with the same object it rejects [i.e. Eurocentrism].'[28] Long's thesis that the adoption of counter-politics by contextual theologians reinscribes the politics it seeks to destroy is closely argued and based upon the self-criticism of first-wave feminism. This element in his critique of contextual theologies is more sustained than his appeal to Vattimo, and clearly demands closer attention in our assessment of the implications for contextual theology and its effect upon ecclesiology. In particular the understanding that 'opposition to certain forms of power collude with them precisely in our opposition',[29] is potentially a telling indictment of much counter-cultural, counter-establishment theologizing about the church *qua* institution.

The general acceptance by theologians of a progressive understanding of modernity and its politics, whereby the new emerges at the expense of the old, has particular linguistic consequences according to Long. He expounds the view that it is now understood to be a given that all language about God is limited by its context.

> This *a priori* limit requires the sacrifice of any theological knowledge that thinks or speaks God outside the space to which 'God' is confined by western metaphysics. This confined space in which we can think or speak God was given its most definitive articulation in Feuerbach's work where theological predications are predications about our own being. Only by thinking of, and speaking about, ourselves can we think or speak 'God'. This establishes a limit no one can cross.[30]

Thus the fundamental notion of the liberation of theology from the hands of the West and of professionals into the hands of ordinary, the poor, the non-European, is utterly compromised by the fixed linguistic limit which contextual method (unwittingly) imposes upon the outcome of its own processes. If we were to accept Long's diagnosis here, then more questions would be raised in relation to the use of contextual methods. Does the method used by contextual theologies collude with Feuerbach's proscription? In one sense it matters not whether this is done intentionally or not, if the outcome is sustained. Long insists that it is. He argues that the effect of using the sacrificial economy of modernity leads inevitably to a Feuerbachian concept of reality, in which the content of 'God' is merely human projection.

> if God loves man, man is the heart of God – the welfare of man his deepest anxiety. If man, then, is the object of God, is not man, in God, an object to himself? is not the content of the divine nature the human nature? If God is love, is not the essential content of this love man? Is not the love of God to man – the basis and central point of religion – the love of man to himself made an object, contemplated as the highest objective truth, as the highest being to man?[31]

Long argues that these are the limits of theological discourse espoused in the method used by contextual theologians. Whether intentionally or not the designation of context as the primary or only arena for theological enquiry and reflection leads to a limitation of language, which Long designates as univocal for each context. Each univocal language for God is essentially Feuerbachian in content and extent. And thus each context is unable to dialogue with any other, and has sacrificed the mainstream ontological and metaphysical claims of the Christian tradition. Long concludes that 'The only theological task at the end of modernity is to constantly give existence to *new* conceptions of divinity that fit better our political and cultural needs.'[32]

Long's diagnosis of the method and outcome of contextual theologies presents a considerable case to answer. His argument remains at a highly cognitive level, which is primarily, perhaps exclusively, philosophical in its force. In order to judge Long's thesis we need to seek answers to the questions raised in his argument: Do contextual theologies go on reinscribing the political powers and systems they seek to replace? Do contextual theologians view God as a projection of the human? Does contextual theology provide an alternative? Does it liberate? Does it empower? Answers to these questions will inevitably be complex and possibly contradictory. One of the prime issues here is the notion of the end of modernity and the emergence of the postmodern. Long uses arguments borrowed from this debate but neglects to address the central question: is the sacrificial economy overcome by alternatives? He implies that this cannot happen; others clearly believe that it can and does. Long has raised fundamental issues about the method and outcome of contextual theology. We will need to take this seriously as we proceed with our assessment of the implications of contextual theology for doing ecclesiology. However, despite a closely argued thesis, Long's conclusions may be challenged, at both a philosophical and a more practical/pragmatic level.

3 Relating the outcome of context-based theology to quest for ecclesiology in systematic theology

In this section we shall pursue our quest for a frame of reference to facilitate the exchange between contextual and systematic theology, in relation to understanding what the church is (for). We will begin our quest with an examination of the implications and possibilities suggested by Elaine Graham's appeal to the work of Jürgen Habermas, in particular to his understanding of *ideal speech communities*. From this emerges a distinctive role for community, which will be set alongside Derrida's deconstruction of text. Out of these various and diverse agendas it is our endeavour to craft a frame of reference, which will be rooted in a dialectic between ideality and deconstruction.

In her appeal to community, Elaine Graham[33] relies heavily upon the Frankfurt school, and in particular on the work of Habermas.[34] Much of what Habermas has to offer to the contextual theologian rests in his understanding of language (i.e. 'the corporate and communicative nature of language'):

> Language entails and ensures sociability: any speech-act implies a desire to communicate and a commitment to the possibility of the creation of mutual understanding and shared meaning. Such conversations can be harnessed in the service of emancipatory principles and practices, by acting as the testing ground for rationality and political strategy. Speech therefore establishes relationship and reveals intentions to forge *moral-practical* or *aesthetic-practical* reason . . .[35]

While Habermas rejects hegemonic institutions and belief-systems, he nonetheless seeks to describe and value *ideal speech communities*. It is within these, he argues, that intersubjectivity emerges and functions. Thus Elaine Graham bases her argument for a role for community in pastoral theology on the basis of the *adaptation* of the rationality of the Enlightenment, rather than a rejection of it. Her position, rooted in the thought of Habermas, values and uses praxis as a significant element in the construction of notions of language and thus of community. This construct of community can provide valuable insights for contextual and systematic theologians seeking to craft understandings of church. While the contribution of Habermas is no doubt a crucial ingredient, his vision of language and community will need to be set alongside that of post-structuralists.

The position taken by Pattison,[36] and echoed by Graham, to situate pastoral theology in the local context, also recognizes the need to take cognizance of the large-scale effects of the wider global context which impinges upon people in their immediate context just as much as particular and local factors of that context. Thus the question emerges: What contribution can contextual theology make to the development of our understanding of the relationship of church and world? In order to pursue this line of thought we need to investigate emerging understandings in the world, from a variety of sources. One source is the understandings of language and text held by Jacques Derrida. The implications for 'shared understanding' in the thought of Derrida need to be taken into consideration just as much as those of Habermas. On the whole, Derrida's writings on religion have been considered more by biblical scholars than by systematic and pastoral theologians. His 'return' to religion is surely something which should elicit a response, particularly in relation to understandings of the church,[37] although the challenge which Derrida presents should by no means be underestimated. As Gil Anidjar writes:

> The Abrahamic does more than harangue us towards a prophetic and messianic future that, more often than not, comforts because it presents, destroys, or steals no more than the images of the other. The Abrahamic breaks and tears as it utters words that break from their context, finding again a speech that cuts and unbinds.[38]

In the essay 'Des Tours de Babel'[39] Derrida sets forth his understanding of the complex diversity of human language, which nonetheless holds the 'promises [of] a kingdom to the reconciliation of languages'. So it will be crucial that any reflection on human community and church community takes account of Derrida's thought.

In our exploration of understandings of human community and the public sphere in the work of Habermas and Derrida and their possible bearing upon attempts to understand the Church we shall begin with a critique of the work of Habermas and then turn to Derrida.

Through his reworking of the tradition of critical theory and his appeal to communication Habermas offers a potential revisioning or reconstructing of concepts of community at local and international levels. This endeavour in Habermas's thought is based upon Kant's conceptions of world citizenry and cosmopolitan right. It is Kant's exposition of the universal community in which all are entitled 'to present themselves in the society of others by virtue of their right to the communal possession of the earth's surface',[40] which remains at the heart of Habermas's commitment to and vision of the reconstruction of community. Kant's exposition of the universal community rests entirely on an appeal to the rationality of humankind, which is conceived as unrelated to place and time. This aspect of Kant's legacy is something which Habermas seeks to rework, arguing that community is a contextual category.

While Habermas himself does not make an explicit appeal to Hegel,[41] it is Hegel who sought to re-establish the credentials of 'context'. He argues that reason is not a-contextual but that it is bound up with history. Reason is not an abstract mental faculty, an inherent part of each individual, which may be affirmed on autonomous grounds. Rather, for Hegel, reason grows out of the way in which the individual understands herself as part of a community. Thus Hegel argued that the ability to reason is shaped by time and culture. Indeed for him, only the study of history could disclose one's place in the world. The interpretation of the relationship between context and reason has considerable bearing upon how personal responsibility and freedom are to be understood, and thus the conceptualization of community. If reason precedes context, then each person, as a rational agent, can be considered an already autonomous unit, pursuing her own choices and needs. However, Hegel (followed by Marx and Freud) deemed that such understandings are illusory. In answering the question: 'Why do individuals make the choices that they do?' Hegel perceived that choices are limited by each person's access to resources: i.e. economic, cultural, educational, psychological, religious and technological resources.

Despite Kant's conceptualization of the universal community and its progress towards perpetual peace, and Hegel's earthing of reason in history and context, the events of the twentieth and twenty-first centuries demonstrate that contrary forces remain to be combated and overthrown. Philosophy and theology need to recognize and make allowance for the extreme fragility of human laws and institutions which facilitate and uphold human community, including church. The threats to community in totalitarianism, fundamentalism and terrorism each relate to those perceived to be 'different'. For instance, one interpretation of totalitarianism is the eradication of difference in people: i.e. their individuality and capacity for autonomous action.[42]

Habermas roots his quest for a reconstruction of community in the light of totalitarianism, the Holocaust and now terrorism in the struggle for the best form of democracy, which he perceives offers the solution to apparently insurmountable problems. Thus democracy in its structural perfectibility is both the means and end of individual and social emancipation. Kant has argued that emancipation was a process of civic maturation, which provided the individual with self-confidence to use her own reason and understanding. Maturity is seen as the key prerequisite for participating equally and freely in community understood as a political structure (i.e. constitutional democracy). Habermas sees maturity and emancipation in terms of self-experience, which issues in self-understanding and true autonomy. However, Habermas does not take individual autonomy for granted. This is not a 'given'. Rather individual autonomy is to be understood as a function of interpersonal exchange. Thus autonomy is rooted in the equality of all individuals in their participation in community. He expresses this in particular in relation to the requirement of 'symmetry' between human subjects in their participation in communication and community.

Habermas sets the discussion and formulation of what autonomy and participation are within his understanding of everyday communication.[43] We learn who we are as autonomous agents by relating to others. The most basic relation between human beings is the act of communicating through language. Habermas argues that the substance of communication must be mutual understanding, without, of course, mystification or manipulation. Thus communication requires a commitment to telling the truth on behalf of both speaker and listener. On this basis communication is categorized as rational practice, which enables the formation of consensus. Habermas's understanding of communication is therefore to be seen as structurally analogous with democratic deliberation. Furthermore, when what I am saying is understood to be (or claimed to be) valid (true, right, truthful), then Habermas understands that 'a bit of ideality' enters our ordinary existence. Communication can of course be distorted and is open to manipulation. However, Habermas argues that the category of lying requires a concept of truth. The net achievement is that Habermas has reconstructed Kant's understanding of emancipation in terms of a unique historical event. If, as he argues, everyday communication produces even a little 'ideality' then emancipation is (potentially) relocated in every act of speech. A consequence of this means that Habermas's idealism does not rest on the classic understanding that the task of philosophy is to craft the requirements for a well-ordered and just society. Rather, following in the tradition of critical theory, philosophy is to diagnose those ills of society that prevent effective communication.

Habermas remains dependent upon Kant for the basis of his understanding of the 'public sphere'. However, he is not uncritical of Kant, whose understanding he sees as limited by his context, particularly in terms of bourgeois values and male predominance. Habermas identifies the advent of mass communication as a major change since the time of Kant. This is seen to expand the public sphere; however, expansion in quantity is interpreted as a decrease in quality. The speed of mass communication is understood to place power in the hands of those who select and distribute information at the expense of those who receive it. The advocates of critical theory have generally been preoccupied with the negative effects of mass culture. Their diagnosis is that while it may be that more people are able to participate in the public sphere, the expansion is often forced and/or manipulated. Further, the growth in the availability of information is interpreted as having brought atrophy to democratic functions and institutions. Nonetheless Habermas poses again the question of the legitimacy of the public sphere; thus setting a new agenda for critical theory. He argues that late-capitalist/post-industrial mass democracies can only claim continuity with the concept of the liberal constitutional state if they live up to their mandate to deliver a public sphere that fulfils political functions, as he understands them. The main problem, which emerges for this new agenda is to set in motion a critical process through the means of mass communication. Habermas seeks to formulate a concept of the 'public sphere' on a new foundation, which is his theory of communicative action.

Habermas pursues his critique of Kant's notion of the public sphere in terms of what he designates as 'monologism'.[44] In so far as Kant's context predates mass communication and the current processes of globalization, it is inevitable that there needs to be readjustment. Kant's construction of the public sphere was based upon an understanding that the individual's participation in it rested on the sharing of opinions which were already constituted. Thus participation in the public sphere was in effect like a hypothetical conversation with oneself. The elements of Kant's monologism are twofold:

1. The solitary nature of the categorical imperative indicates that it is in reality a mental experiment in which one interrogates oneself concerning the universal application of one's ideas and actions.
2. The priority of subjectivity over intersubjectivity rests upon Kant's concept of individual autonomy. That is to say, autonomy is a natural given rather than a product of rational communicative exchange.

In place of Kant's conceptuality Habermas argues that personal opinions and moral decisions are shaped through intersubjective dialogue. This is a fundamental shift from the subject-centred paradigm of monologism. 'While in the monological model the individual speaker preexists intersubjective communication, for Habermas intersubjective communication is the condition of the possibility for the individual speaker.'[45] Thus an individual speaker is not to be understood as a freestanding agent but as an agent within a community of speakers. Habermas designates this conceptuality in terms of 'universal pragmatics'.[46] In other words an individual is incapable of establishing the rules of communication alone. Such conceptuality rests upon the understanding that an act of speech and the modalities of communication depend on a plurality of users, which is manifested in rules of grammar and commitment to consensus. Habermas extends this to every speech act. Each time we communicate with one another we automatically commit to the possibility of a freely achieved dialogical agreement in which the 'better' argument will 'win'. Thus for Habermas all communication is at least potentially emancipatory. That is, it may yield a resolution of disagreements and therefore produce 'ideality'. His conceptuality moves towards an inter-subjective understanding of community, away from Kant's monologism. However the idea that all disagreements and every plurality of conviction can be brought to a future resolution remains problematic and a weakness of his 'new' conceptuality.

Habermas reinforces his understanding in a rejection of any resort to relativism. While committed to an emphasis on the concrete and particular, he does not concede relative value to each position. For him rationality is not to be rooted in personal preference. Thus he stands out against Richard Rorty's 'neopragmatism', in which he holds that each belief has equal validity. Habermas argues that if one holds a position, then one must do so rationally, i.e. it must be rationally defensible. Upon this basis individual belief and public consensus can be held together. Habermas here is appealing to the Socratic distinction between knowledge and opinion. That is to say he draws a distinction between temporary utilitarian agreement and what is to be designated 'proper consensus'. Thus he opposes rational consensus over against the volatility of subjective feelings.

The conceptuality of communication and thus of community which Habermas sets out provides close parallels with the thought of a number of theologians and philosophers who have sought to expound a theoretical basis for either church or human community. An instance of such a parallel is to be seen in the work of John Zizioulas on the conceptuality of the human person and the divine hypostases in relation to the category of *koinonia*.[47] However, it should also be noted that the understanding of the cosmopolitan, the right to the earth, and the public sphere, as set out by Habermas, is a challenge to the very notion of the distinctiveness of the church as community.

In seeking to posit a framework for an exchange between contextual and systematic theology rooted in a dialectic between ideality and deconstruction, we now turn to examine the work of Derrida. The springboard for Derrida's deconstruction of community is close to the underpinning concepts of Habermas's endeavour. Derrida prompts awareness of the historical and textual connections of words, and points out how often we use language unreflexively. Much of the import of those connections remains hidden, and we are left to reiterate normative assumptions. He raises questions concerning our assumptions about the phrase: 'the human being' and member of the 'human species'. He argues that the words 'human' and 'species' are terms 'that branch out in historically constructed mazes that broaden and indefinitely complicate the semantic spectrum of this phrase'.[48]

He goes on to argue that as 'species' are generally understood to be evolutionary, where does that leave the designation 'human'?

Derrida identifies what he describes as the 'anthropologism' of thought relating to 'human being' from the Renaissance onwards, by which he understands a shared notion of the 'unity of man'.[49] Jean-Paul Sartre sought to redefine 'man' and 'human reality' as a subject which could not be understood apart from the world, thus positing an interdependence between subject and world.[50] However, Derrida argues that the existentialists' questioning of the meaning of 'man' did not succeed in deconstructing the classical ideal of the 'unity of man'. This, he argues, was because they did not sufficiently pursue the practice of a 'history of concepts'. Thus the history of the concept of 'man' has never been examined. Once the concept of man is given historical, cultural and linguistic boundaries, then, Derrida argues, it is much harder to resort to essentialist understandings of 'man'. Derrida's contribution to the debate about context adds weight to the need to make context the primary starting place for theological enquiry as much as for any other concern. Derrida's argument lends a further dimension to the questioning of Long's critique of local language, suggesting that the notion of univocity is itself to be called into question. If we were to accept such a contention, then this element of Long's argument is removed immediately.

What then of an appeal to anything as a universal? Despite the events of the twentieth century Habermas maintains that the Enlightenment has not failed as a project, and defends the universal values of republicanism and democratic participation. But Derrida challenges and deconstructs this appeal to universalism or universal values as givens. Rather, he argues, these are what republican institutions and democracy struggle toward through the quest for justice. In Derrida's view, republicanism, democracy, institution and participation are not absolutes but constructs whose validity evolves with time, so that our understanding of them requires constant revision.[51]

Each understands the task of philosophy differently. Habermas follows in the tradition of critical theory, which bestows on philosophy the diagnostic function of identifying the ills of society and pursuing an intellectual discourse on the causes underlying them. This function of philosophy is focused on the ultimate goal of emancipation, which Habermas claims is the 'unfinished project of modernity'. This endeavour is based on a belief in principles of universal validity, which cross historical and cultural specifics. Derrida pursues the quest for deconstruction, which draws upon the intellectual lineage of Nietzsche, Heidegger and Freud. Derrida claims that 'many of the principles to which the Western tradition has attributed universal validity do not capture what we all share or even hope for'.[52] Rather, these principles have tended to impose a set of standards that benefit some and disadvantage others. Thus for Derrida 'demarcating the historical and cultural boundaries of such principles is a precondition for embracing the Enlightenment demand for justice and freedom for all'.[53]

To these central ingredients of deconstruction Derrida adds a further dimension, which he designates 'a responsibility before alerity and difference'. This means listening to and taking note of that which is beyond the boundaries of description, excluded and silent. On the basis of his appeal to alerity and difference

Derrida argues that the Enlightenment demand for universalism can be pursued and achieved. Thus both Habermas and Derrida as interpreters of the Enlightenment project remain committed to its core values in relation to community, but seek to take it forward by different means.

4. Community and communion (koinonia)

In this final section we shall pursue our quest for a frame of reference to facilitate the exchange between contextual and systematic theologians by relating the dialectic between the local and the universal, and between ideality and deconstruction, to the debate over the use of toleration and hospitality, and in doing so we shall seek to posit the possibility of sociality as a transcendental. We shall argue that such a possibility emerges in relation to the ontological conceptuality invested in the category of *koinonia* by theologians who seek to expound an ecclesiology of communion.

The possibility of an appeal to transcendentals does not overturn the criteria of context and the pre-cognitive, because it is made in relation to the diverse conceptualities of language and community identified in the appeal to either ideality or deconstruction. The positing of sociality as a potential transcendental is offered not as a synthesis but as ground common to the poles of each dialectic (local/cosmic, ideality/deconstruction), which therefore enables an exchange between theory and practice. We begin our investigation of the concepts of tolerance and hospitality with the recognition that these characteristics of human community are central features in the Enlightenment quest for universalism. However, as we have noted already, Derrida deconstructs any claims for a universal applicability of ideas, which is reinforced by his plea for a recognition of 'a responsibility before alerity and difference'. Thus the claim for sociality as a transcendental, is to be built not on universalism but on the ongoing dialectic between ideality and deconstruction.

A particular focus of Derrida's deconstruction of 'community' applies to the concept of 'tolerance'. On his understanding, this is no neutral concept but rather the remnant of a paternalistic gesture in which the other is neither regarded nor treated as an equal. Derrida is suspicious of tolerance, particularly because of its Christian origin. For him this means it can never have or gain universal validity. He remarks on various linguistic usages of tolerance and acceptance; particularly as they are used in relation to the tissue of a transplanted organ. Thus for Derrida tolerance is the opposite of hospitality. Derrida finds the roots for his appeal to hospitality in the work of Kant. Here again we see that he is not rejecting the Enlightenment agenda but seeking to reappropriate and expand it. In Derrida's understanding, social critique and ethical responsibility require the deconstruction of anything that is falsely claimed as neutral and has hegemonic ideals. Thus deconstruction does not curtail the demand for universal justice and freedom; rather in his view it renews the demand infinitely.

At the other pole of the dialetic, Habermas continues to work with the concept of tolerance in relation to ethical and legal issues. Tolerance, for him, comes from the concept of constitutional democracy as the only political possibility which is able to deliver free and uncoerced communication and facilitate the formation of a rational consensus. Habermas acknowledges the religious origin of tolerance and that its threshold is easily understood to belong to the existing authority. However, he argues that this is overcome if tolerance is practised in a properly participatory public sphere. Whether one embraces tolerance or hospitality (or both) an intractable problem emerges in relation to participation in the face of globalization. The issues that emerge centre around where power is held and who is participating in what. While the possibilities for global participation seem to grow, yet the threshold of tolerance and openness to hospitality seem to recede. Indeed it may be argued that globalization brings the illusion of participation and reciprocity.

Thus both Derrida and Habermas argue for a need to leave behind nation-states and to pursue the possibility of transforming classical international law into a new cosmopolitan order. This order would rest upon an understanding of hospitality, which would replace enmity. This hospitality would not be a new form of philanthropy, but would be based upon the right to share the earth's surface, becoming members of a universal cosmopolitan community. Here then is the challenge for theologians, whether in pastoral or systematic theology, in their crafting of understandings of the church. It is a challenge to all forms of sectarianism, and to any concept of the human subject which produces conflict in the human community.

How can the church respond to demands for tolerance and/or hospitality? How can the church facilitate participation and reciprocity in a universal cosmopolitan community? One way in which to overcome the tension between the local/contextual and cosmic dimension of the divine purposes in creating and redeeming, would be to posit an understanding of certain concepts and realities as trancendentals. This would also be an answer to Long's critique of the deficiencies of contextual theologies in the sense that an appeal to transcendentals would stem the ongoing problem of the 'sacrificial economy' and the issue of univocal local expression. Hardy argued that 'sociality' should be understood as a transcendental in his essay, 'Created and Redeemed Sociality'.[54] Gunton distanced himself from this understanding, arguing that an ontological conceptuality of relationality did not make 'sociality' a transcendental.

> Communion is being in relation, in which there is due recognition of both particularity and relationality. But that does not make sociality a transcendental ... It is a doctrine of the personal, and leaves unresolved the question of the relation of human society to the material context within which it takes shape. It is therefore ideal rather than transcendental.[55]

However, Kant's understanding of 'transcendental' as that which provides the possibility of experience may resonate more nearly with Hardy's concept of 'sociality' than an 'ideal' with its resonance with perfection. Nonetheless it may be possible to forge a link between Gunton's understanding of sociality and relationality as an ideal and Habermas's concept of each speech-act releasing 'ideality', and overcome the utopian connotations of 'ideal'. For Habermas's claim is made upon the ground of 'the relation of human society to the material context within which it takes shape', understood in terms of a rigorous understanding of human communication.

Kant argued for the particular status of Categories of Relation, as I have argued elsewhere.[56] For Kant, such categories are, 'pure concepts of the understanding which apply *a priori* to objects of intuition in general',[57] and the Category of Community (reciprocity between agent and patient) 'is not conceivable as holding between things each of which, through its subsistence, stands in complete isolation'.[58] In Kant's view, the isolated subsistence of the individual thing is transcended by its relationality in 'community'. If, as Hardy argued, that 'transcendentals should be understood as the basis for the real', which are to be understood as 'necessary notes of being' and 'the presupposed basis for the establishment of knowledge through argument and agreement'[59] there is support in Habermas's conceptuality of the *ideal speech community*, for an understanding of sociality as a transcendental.

Instances of a coincidence or parallel understanding with Habermas's view of intersubjectivity can be found in John Macmurray[60] and Alistair McFadyen,[61] as well as in the thought of John Zizioulas and others who espouse communion ecclesiology. It would be mistaken to suggest that Habermas's understanding of intersubjectivity has an immediate correspondence in Zizioulas's ontology of the person.[62] However, the priority which Habermas gives to intersubjectivity over subjectivity is an area of overlap with Zizioulas's conceptuality of the *hypostasis* and the ontology of *koinonia*. Thus Habermas's understandings of community and communication provide a basis for the discussion of the church as an instance of human community, particularly in relation to his understanding of the relation of these concepts to emancipation and ideality. An exploration of the implications of this conceptuality for notions of the church as a caring or healing community and a community of salvation may prove fruitful. Also Habermas's notions of the public sphere, republicanism and democracy may yield interesting parallels with the church's own quest to find an ecumenical hermeneutic.[63]

Our discussion in this section has led us to posit an overlap of interest and understanding between Habermas and theologians in relation to discussion of community. Habermas's concept of *ideal speech communities* as instances where intersubjectivity emerges and functions in a symmetry of relationships, and where it is understood to manifest its priority over subjectivity, demonstrates close parallels with the endeavour of pastoral and contextual theologians and those who espouse an ecclesiology of communion, to describe church and wider society in terms of *koinonia*. This parallel is further supported in Habermas's understanding that community is a contextual category. In other words the ideality, for which he argues, is rooted in the local and contextual. For ideality emerges from what is said, situated in the context of ordinary existence. It is out of this everyday communication that 'ideality' promises emancipation.

Thus there emerges a conceptuality of contextual speech communities, which leads us to be able to posit a cogent set of connections between context and community and church. By identifying ideality and emancipation with these speech communities we can see pathways which connect the local context and the cosmic implication of the divine purposes in creating and redeeming. It is on the basis of such connections that it is possible to support Hardy's claim that sociality is more than an 'ideal', but is indeed a transcendental which does deliver the prerequisite of the basis for establishing knowledge through argument and agreement. This is rooted in Habermas' conceptuality of intersubjectivity, manifested in ideal speech communities. Thus the contextual category of community is able to support the epistemological prerequisites for sociality to be understood as a transcendental. This does not mean that a localization of language is made redundant. Rather the interrelatedness of language, inter-subjectivity and community, which offer the potential of ideality in ordinary speech acts, suggest that Long's critique of the univocal nature of 'local' language is to be set aside.

The appeal to sociality as a transcendental also provides an answer to Long's critique of the deficiencies of contextual theologies in terms of what he deems the ongoing problem of the 'sacrificial economy'. Habermas's concept of each speech act potentially releasing 'ideality' is made upon the ground of his conceptuality of 'the relation of human society to the material context within which it takes shape'. Thus the *ideal speech community* is rooted in the contextual category of 'community', while also facilitating the emergence of ideality and emancipation. Long's critique that contextual theologians may collude with or repeat the very factors they seek to overcome does not preclude the notion that they do achieve something new and local and contextual. The sociality of the community is both contextual and universal (cosmological), in the sense that each person stands by right together with all others upon the face of the earth, in the *cosmopolis*. The localization of theology thus need not in any sense divorce it from the cosmic dimensions of the divine purposes in creating and redeeming.

In our quest to craft a possible frame of reference to facilitate an exchange between context, practice and the systematic theologian, we have pursued a variety of different avenues and critiques. In recognition of the status which context and practice now occupy in the theological endeavour we have sought to draw upon the insights of philosophy to support the role of context and community. The pursuit of different schools of philosophy to elucidate our theological quest has enabled us to hold together the local with the cosmic dimensions of what it means to be church. This has largely been possible on the basis of upholding Habermas's concept of ideality in relation to intersubjectivity to support an appeal to sociality as a transcendental. The challenge which this presents to the church and to systematic theologians in terms of both theory and practice is enormous. However, what emerges from this dialogue between philosophy and theology, and between contextual and systematic theologians, is a potential secular metaphysics which may form the basis of a frame of reference to enable an ongoing exchange between theory and practice.

Notes

1. Nicholas M. Healy, *Church, World and the Christian Life: Practical-Prophetic Ecclesiology* (Cambridge: Cambridge University Press, 2000).
2. E.g. Clodovis Boff, *Teoria do método teológico* (Vozes: Petrópolis, 1999).
3. Howard Clinebell, *Basic Types of Pastoral Care and Counselling: Rresources for the Ministry of Healing and Growth* (London: SCM Press, 1984).
4. S. Pattison and J. Woodward, *A Vision of Pastoral Theology: In Search of Words that Resurrect the Dead*, Pastoral Monographs No. 4 (Edinburgh: Contact Pastoral Trust, 1994).
5. Ibid., pp. 17f.
6. Ibid., p. 24
7. Alasdair MacIntyre, *After Virtue: A Study in Moral Theory* (London: Duckworth, 1985).
8. See the works of Stanley Hauerwas and D. Stephen Long: e.g., *A Community of Character: Toward a Constructive Christian Social Ethic*, (Notre Dame, IL: University of Notre Dame Press, 1981); *The Goodness of God: Theology, the Church and Social Order* (Grand Rapids, MI: Brazos Press, 2001).
9. E.g. Colin E. Gunton, *The One, the Three and the Many: God, Creation and the Culture of Modernity* (Cambridge: Cambridge University Press, 1993).
10. Such tools might be found in the work of H.-G. Gadamer, *Truth and Method* (London: Sheed & Ward, 1979).
11. Laurie Green, *Let's Do Theology: A Pastoral Cycle Resource Book* (London: Mowbrays, 1990 and Continuum, 2001).
12. See Emmanuel Lartey, 'Practical Theology as Theological Form', in James Woodward and Stephen Pattison (eds), *The Blackwell Reader in Pastoral and Practical Theology* (Oxford: Basil Blackwell, 1999).
13. See Pattison and Woodward, *A Vision of Pastoral Theology*, pp. 14f; and Lartey, 'Practical Theology', pp. 132f.
14. Avery Dulles, *Models of the Church: A Critical Assessment of the Church in all its Aspects* (Dublin: Gill & Macmillan, 1988).
15. I am indebted to Yuri Koszarycz, a senior lecturer within the School of Theology at the Australian Catholic University, McAuley Campus, Brisbane, Australia, for this synthesis of Dulles' models. See http://www.mcauley.acu.edu.au/~yuri/ecc/chap3.html
16. See Dietrich Bonhoeffer, *Letters and Papers from Prison* (London: SCM Press, 1953).
17. D. Stephen Long, 'Fetishizing Feuerbach's God: Contextual Theologies as the End of Modernity', *Pro Ecclesia*, 12.4 (2003): 447–72.
18. Gianni Vattimo, *The End of Modernity: Nihilism and Hermeneutics in Post-modern Culture* (Cambridge: Polity Press, 1988).
19. Long, 'Fetishizing Feuerbach's God', p. 449
20. Ludwig Feuerbach, *The Essence of Christianity* (London: Kegan Paul *et al.*, 1893).
21. Long, 'Fetishizing Feuerbach's God', p. 450.
22. Ibid., p. 448.
23. Ibid., p. 449.
24. Ibid., p. 460.
25. Vattimo, *The End of Modernity*.
26. E.g. René Girard, *Violence and the Sacred* (New York: Athlone/Continuum, 1988).
27. See Julia Kristeva, 'Women's Time', in Toril Moi (ed.), *The Kristeva Reader* (Oxford: Basil Blackwell, 1986).
28. Long, 'Fetishizing Feuerbach's God', 452.
29. Ibid., p. 452.
30. Ibid., p. 450.
31. Feuerbach, *The Essence of Christianity*, p. 58.
32. Long, 'Fetishizing Feuerbach's God', p. 456.

33. Elaine L. Graham, *Transforming Practice: Pastoral Theology in an Age of Uncertainty* (Eugene, OR: Wipf and Stock Publishers, 2002), Ch. 7.
34. E.g. Jürgen Habermas, *Knowledge and Human Interests* (London: Heinemann Educational, 1972).
35. Graham, *Transforming Practice*, p. 146.
36. Pattison and Woodward, *A Vision of Pastoral Theology*.
37. E.g. Kevin Hart, *The Trespass of the Sign* (Cambridge: Cambridge University Press, 1989) and Hugh Rayment-Pickard, *Impossible God: Derrida's Theology* (Aldershot: Ashgate, 2003).
38. Gil Anidjar, 'Introduction: Once More, Once More', in Jacques Derrida, *Acts of Religion* (New York & London: Routledge, 2002), p. 9.
39. In Derrida, *Acts of Religion*, pp. 104–33. (The essay dates from 1980.)
40. Kant also assumed that such conceptions of the universal community would lead (eventually) to 'perpetual peace'. I. Kant, *Zum ewigen Frieden. Ein philosophischer Entwurf* (Könisberg: Friedrich Nicolovius, 1795, 1796).
41. G. W. F. Hegel, *The Philosophy of History* (New York: Dover Publications, 1956), pp. 79–110.
42. E.g. Hannah Arendt, *The Origins of Totalitarianism* (London: Allen & Unwin, 1967).
43. Jürgen Habermas, *Theory of Communicative Action*, 2 vols (Boston, MA: Beacon Press, 1984).
44. Other commentators have challenged the view that Kant champions the individual over community: see Allen Wood, 'Rational Theology, Moral Faith and Religion', in Paul Guyer (ed.) *The Cambridge Companion to Kant* (Cambridge: Cambridge University Press, 1992), pp. 407–8; and Gerard Mannion, *Schopenhauer, Religion and Morality: The Humble Path to Ethics* (Aldershot: Ashgate, 2003), ch. 5.
45. Giovanna Borradori, *Philosophy in a Time of Terror: Dialogues with Jürgen Habermas and Jacques Derrida* (Chicago, IL: Chicaco University Press, 2003, p. 60.
46. See Jürgen Habermas, 'What is Universal Pragmatics?' in *Communication and the Evolution of Society* (Boston, MA: Beacon Press, 1979), pp. 1–68. See also Karl Otto Apel, *Understanding and Explanation. A Transcendental Pragmatic Perspective* (Cambridge, MA: MIT Press, 1984).
47. J. D. Zizioulas, *Being as Communion: Studies in Personhood and the Church* (London: Darton, Longman & Todd, 1985), pp. 17ff.
48. Borradori, *Philosophy in a Time of Terror*, p. 12.
49. Jacques Derrida, 'The Ends of Man', in *Margins of Philosophy* (Chicago, IL: University of Chicago Press, 1982).
50. Anchoring human reality in responsibility toward one's world seemed the necessary antidote for the inhumanity of totalitarianism. See Borradori, *Philosophy in a Time of Terror*, p. 12.
51. It would be a misconception to draw from this that while Habermas explicitly defends the Enlightenment project, Derrida rejects it. Thus it emerges from this understanding of Derrida's thought that it would be an oversimplification to identify him with 'postmodernism'.
52. Borradi, *Philosophy in a Time of Terror*, p. 15
53. Borradi, *Philosophy in a Time of Terror*.
54. In Colin E. Gunton and Daniel W. Hardy, *On Being the Church: Essays on the Christian Community* (Edinburgh: T&T Clark, 1989), pp. 21–47.
55. Colin E. Gunton, *The One, the Three and the Many*, p. 223.
56. See Paul M. Collins, *Trinitarian Theology West and East: Karl Barth, the Cappadocian Fathers and John Zizioulas* (Oxford: Oxford University Press, 2001), pp. 187f.
57. Immanuel Kant, *Critique of Pure Reason* (London: Macmillan, 1929), p. 113.
58. Kant, *Critique of Pure Reason*, p. 255
59. Hardy, 'Created and Redeemed Sociality', in Gunton and Hardy, *On Being the Church*, p. 27. Hardy quotes K.-O. Apel, *Towards a Transformation of Philosophy* (London: Routledge & Kegan Paul, 1980), p. 138, in support of his argument.
60. John Macmurray, *Persons in Relation* (London: Faber & Faber, 1961).

61. Alastair I. McFadyen, *The Call to Personhood: A Christian Theory of the Individual in Social Relationships* (Cambridge: Cambridge University Press, 1990), pp. 176–8.
62. See John D. Zizioulas, *Being as Communion*, pp. 27-49
63. World Council of Churches (WCC) Faith and Order paper no. 182, *A Treasure in Earthen Vessels* (Geneva: WCC, 1997).

Chapter 8

ECCLESIOLOGY: WORSHIP AND COMMUNITY

Paul M. Collins

The discussion of the role of worship in the life of church is raised by two rather contrary indications. On the one hand worship is such a commonplace factor in the life of the churches that it seems inevitable that one should discuss worship in a set of essays on ecclesiology. On the other, regular worship is an activity which is becoming the preserve of the few, so much so that the need for an adherent to the Christian faith to be a worshipper is being questioned.[1] Thus the place of worship in the life of church is called into question. Another manifestation of the questioning of worship relates not so much to the activity *per se* but to the sacramental in particular. This emerges from what one might call a neo-functionalism, which colludes with the notion that sacramental worship is exclusive, while non-sacramental is inclusive. However, in a secular context, where worship is an activity rarely encountered by the masses, all kinds of worship are as likely to be perceived as alienating and inaccessible. A further manifestation of this neo-functionalism may be seen in the composition of hymns and songs, which contain no (explicit) reference to the divine or transcendent.[2] These are clearly to be identified with contemporary culture and may be said to be an expression of the concern raised by Long[3] that contextual theologies work with a univocity of language, which can be an expression of Feuerbach's diagnosis that 'God' is in reality a projection of human values. Such a critique of contemporary hymnody may also be expressed in relation to 'all-age' or 'family' worship which can often rely too much on entertainment value, or to much 'modern' worship which fails to convey any sense of the transcendent or numinous.[4] During the twentieth century a considerable effort was made towards the renewal of Christian worship, so does this rather bleak picture of the situation of worship today do justice to the aims and outcomes of that attempt in the Liturgical Movement in the churches of the West?

Any assessment of a movement as broad and widespread as the Liturgical Movement is inevitably going to be partial. However, let us begin by identifying the main concerns of the movement. The Liturgical Movement was as much concerned with the consequences of worship for the life of the church, as it was about rites and ceremonial. It was essentially an ecclesiological movement and its main focus was on the church understood in terms of the metaphor of the Body of Christ.[5] In seeking to renew the liturgy, the protagonists of the movement sought the renewal of the church. And in this and a renewed interest in patristic sources and scholarship, the Liturgical Movement shared much in common with the ecumenical movement, and indeed there was much reciprocal influence between the two. In seeking the renewal of the church and its activity of worship, there was a central appeal to the intelligible and rational as well as the sacramental and mystical. It became clear to those who sought to renew its rites that part of the kerygmatic office of the church needed to be focused in pedagogy. Thus, as well as making provision for the renewal of the various rites themselves, there would need to be catechesis and mystagogy as well. This is particularly to be seen in terms of the revival in various traditions of the adult catechumenate in relation to initiation.[6] Another central feature of the renewal of the liturgies of initiation and the eucharist was a clear focus on the paschal content of these rites.[7] St Paul's letter to the Romans, ch. 6, became a proof text of the movement; and this secured the function of worship, and by extension of the church, to the divine purposes in creating and redeeming not only the human race but the whole cosmos. It becomes evident that the situation we began by describing bears little relationship to the aims and intentions of the liturgical movement. Does this mean that the movement has failed or become irrelevant? Some might argue that this is the case, and might do so in part by pointing to a lack of connection between the effects of the movement and the reality of the contemporary sociocultural context of the West. However, before we designate the Liturgical Movement as a failed project, we should reflect that a movement so radical and far-reaching may take longer than we have yet seen to be 'received'. As Cardinal Walter Kasper[8] has argued in recent times in relation to the Vatican II, the process of reception has barely begun.

The process of reception of the ecclesiological as well as of the liturgical factors of the Liturgical Movement may benefit from further reflection upon the possibility of an appeal to the metaphysical and ontological, and thus to transcendentals. Von Balthasar, in his project *Herrlichkeit*, sought to explore and offer such possibilities, and the reception of the movement may find a new imperative by revisiting von Balthasar's proposals for a theological aesthetic.[9]

We will pursue our discussion of worship under two main headings: anaphora and anamnesis. 'Anaphora' means 'offering' and refers in current liturgical usage to the Encharistic Prayer; 'anamnesis' means 'memory' and refers to the encharistic memorial of Christ. We will investigate the implications of both offering and remembering for the life and purposes of the Christian community, particularly as they relate to God's purposes for the cosmos. And we shall return at the end of this investigation to reflect on the potential for a theological aesthetic in relation to the worshipping community today.

The activity, which distinguishes the church from other gatherings of human beings, is the activity of worship. However, in making such a claim, we need to understand from the outset, that we are claiming more about this activity than that which can be analysed empirically. In other words, in making this claim that the distinguishing mark of the church is worship, we understand that there is a transcendental dimension to this activity, which is outside the scope of empirical verification. Thus the distinguishing or defining mark of the church entails an epistemological and ontological claim, outside the generally accepted norms of contemporary Western conceptualities, just as belief in God does. What do we mean in suggesting this? First of all, we might say that worship is an/the activity in which a collection of human beings makes an 'offering' to the divine. Secondly, we might say that what gives meaning to such activity is a sense of reciprocity between the human and the divine, understood in the Judaeo-Christian tradition in terms of a 'covenant' relationship. The people doing this are God's people; and the people offering this are doing so to 'their' God. These two claims in themselves are prerequisites for the transcendental claim, but do not constitute it *per se*. What constitutes the transcendental claim is a third claim, in which the exchange between human and divine is understood in terms of the bestowal by the divine upon the human beings of what is usually described as 'grace' – gift – *charis*.

The distinguishing characteristic of worship is not therefore the empirically verifiable activity undertaken by human beings, but a bestowal upon them by the divine, usually understood as a consequence of the activity, whether that be understood primarily in terms of the preaching of the Word or the celebration of the sacraments. This immediately places our discussion of worship as the distinguishing mark of the church in the realm of faith. We are not here primarily concerned with the phenomena of worship or liturgical rites. We are concerned with the meaning invested in them by the collective we call the church at its various levels of existence and manifestation. The discussion of 'meaning' and by extension of 'value' also places our claim for the transcendental in the context of hermeneutics. Thus our discussion of the worship offered by the Church will be founded upon the recognition that what we are dealing with is a variety of epistemological and hermeneutical claims or traditions, which in turn are founded upon a complex set of preconceptions, that are at least in part metaphysical claims.[10]

In our discussion we shall therefore be making the assumption that worship as an activity is to be understood as a reciprocity of human offering and divine bestowal. The action is both divine and human: this is what constitutes our designation that worship entails a transcendental claim. The transcendental is recognized and claimed by those who have 'faith'. However, the scope of the claims consequent upon that recognition are not primarily personal or devotional, but rather noetic, ontic and cosmic.

At the centre of this claim is the appeal to 'grace': the gift of God to the human community we call 'church' in particular in relation to the activity of worship. Grace is itself variously understood. Two different emphases may be distinguished: one in which 'grace' is seen as something imparted to or bestowed by God on the recipient(s) for particular, usually salvific, purposes; the other in which 'grace' is understood as the gift of God himself. At this stage, this distinction need not detain us; indeed it is perhaps a distinction which is pursued less in current debate, as a result of ecumenical dialogue on 'justification'.[11] Leaving aside for the moment whether or not 'grace' is to be identified with the divine *per se*, it is crucial at this juncture to consider its role in the Christian claims for the church community. I shall relate the investigation of this role to two key Pauline texts, which focus on the term *koinonia*. The first is 2 Cor. 13.13 and the second

1 Cor. 10.14–22. These texts will form the basis for all the ensuing discussion of worship and the Church community.

The text of 'the grace' places three notions alongside one another: grace (χαρις), love (αγαπη) and fellowship/communion (κοινωνια). We might interpret these as: gift, reciprocity and sociality. To do so is to structure and interpret the sentence beyond the immediate words of 2 Cor. 13.13, and to place a strong priority upon gift; gift becomes the basis for the reciprocity of love and sociality of communion. This is suggested as at least a legitimate option for the interpretation of the sentence: to see the gift of Jesus Christ as foundational for the offer of love and communion. The second text from 1 Corinthians 10 further situates the outcome of gift in communion, within Paul's discussion of the Lord's Supper. Here κοινωνια is connected directly to the activity of the Lord's Supper, to worship, and thus to the 'one body'. The intimacy in Paul's thought between worship, eucharist, church and communion will thus become the basis for the ensuing discussion of worship and church; and will focus primarily upon the action of the eucharist: an event I shall assume to encompass both Word and Sacrament.

In this short exposition of my positioning of our discussion of worship and church, we have already encountered prime and determinative epistemological and hermeneutical decisions. We are working with an epistemology based upon faith, and a consequent hermeneutical tradition of the concept of divine gift or grace. From these two decisions a complex of metaphysical claims is already emerging. These are metaphorical and ontological claims about the church community and its eucharistic worship; which are centred upon the metaphor of the 'body' and the category of 'communion'. As the discussion proceeds it will be crucial to retain our connection with these decisions and their consequences, and in particular with the contingent provisionality of this nexus of epistemological, hermeneutical and metaphysical claims. For all too often this provisionality is forgotten or disregarded and the transcendental claim is itself either forgotten, and the activity of the worshipping community is simply treated as a collection of human phenomena; or it is too easily appropriated and the activity is treated as a 'divine reality' with little or no perceived connection with the ordinary or the general public sphere – either in terms of epistemology or culture.

Inculturation

We are seeking to treat the activity of worship as a/the distinguishing mark of the human community of the church; and we are doing so in relation to two themes: anaphora and anamnesis. Before we proceed with any detailed analysis of each of the themes there are a number of provisos to consider. They relate in the main to the epistemological and hermeneutical claims outlined above, but to the metaphysical/transcendental claims as well. The nature of these provisos is driven by a concern for what might be called apologetics, or indeed inculturation, of this activity 'worship' in relation to the contingency and provisionality of the claims the church makes about worship.

We begin with what is potentially a fundamental blow to the whole edifice of claims which I have constructed above. Martin Stringer[12] has argued that claims about the meaning of worship, particularly worship which uses a set form of words, are highly disputable. He argues that whatever the intentions about meaning of those who composed the liturgy, whether that be historic, contemporary, or indeed *ex tempore*, the participants or recipients of the worship will make and assimilate their own meanings irrespective of the original intentions. Stringer's critique, which is rooted in postmodern understandings of communication and text, relies upon different understandings of personal perception, reception and interpretation, such as a hermeneutic of reader response. Undoubtedly there is much to commend Stringer's analysis of what happens during an act of worship: there are after all no thought police. People's reception of a sermon, as well of the other words, actions and symbols in worship, will always be on an individual basis. However, does this mean that the notion of *lex orandi, lex credendi* is discredited? Or is the idea that a congregation is formed through the collective experience of worshipping together regularly to be jettisoned?

Stringer's critique is undoubtedly something which all composers of liturgy should be aware of in the production of texts. His argument certainly relativizes some of the more grandiose claims about the effects of worship.[13] However, if the notion of shared meaning arising from a shared experience of the use of liturgical texts is questionable, does that also invalidate the collective experience of the activity of worship, in its actions and symbols and shared 'tasks' such as collective singing. It is usual to claim that collective activity does 'form' those who participate. One might argue this in relation to attendance of a club's supporters at football matches, as much as for those who attend worship; and there are both implicit and explicit learned expectations, values and meanings in these events. But these are learned. They are either learned by experience, by shared conversation about norms and meanings, or indeed by catechesis. Thus a primary element in the church's own claims about the (shared) meaning of the activity and content of worship resides in the processes of catechesis. Thus we might say that *lex orandi, lex credendi* needs also to be understood as *lex credendi, lex orandi*. The meaning and value invested in the activity of worship by the church also requires the formation of the participants through catechesis as much as through simply attending. Thus an understanding of worship depends on the church's office of proclamation and teaching for its meaning and value; these are not self-evident or self-authenticating. And this is particularly the case in a context where the Christian tradition and the experience of worship are less well known and less practised than in previous generations in the West.[14]

This brings us to a more detailed discussion of the relationship between context and worship. The outcome of the work of contextual theologians relates not only to the process of theological reflection and social action but also has implications for the activity of worship. One possibility for contextualization would be to encourage specific usage in each locality, or even for each congregation. To some extent this occurs 'naturally' as worship reflects its social, cultural and geographical environment. However, some would argue that this process needs to be embraced consciously in relation to liturgical texts, actions and symbols. The practice of liturgical inculturation was endorsed in the decrees of Vatican II[15] and has been promoted in some provinces of the Anglican Communion,[16] and in other Protestant traditions[17] too. These experiments in adaptation expose a tension between local custom and the questions of meaning and value.[18] We are brought back to the issue of the interplay between meaning associated with the action of worship and the need for catechesis. The tension between the local (contextual) and universal often surfaces at its strongest in relation to the inculturation of worship.[19] How does one ensure the truth of the Gospel and of the tradition in the local context without the central or universal authority structure becoming (too) predominant? Or in terms of Long's critique of contextual theology, how does one prevent or overcome the univocity of the local language of each context?[20]

Perhaps the notion of ideal speech communities put forward by Habermas[21] can offer some way out of this impasse. His understanding of the intelligibility of communication in terms of the rules of grammar offers us greater hope about the possible outcomes of dialogue than Stringer's critique of a worshipping community's interaction with its liturgical texts. If we accept Habermas's claim that everyday speech acts can potentially be instances of 'ideality', can this be applied to the activity of worship? The circumstances, for which Habermas envisages the emergence of ideality are rooted not only in dialogue but also in the symmetry or equality of the dialogue partners. On the face of it, one might argue that worship does not conform to Habermas's criteria, or that the practice of worship is at the least sharply challenged by them. However, on closer inspection, the liturgy of the eucharist is essentially a dialogical event in which all fully participate as baptized 'members' of the royal priesthood of the Body of Christ. The eucharist understood in this light suggests that the criteria for ideality are in place even if in practice they are sometimes obscured: the challenge for a worshipping community is to live them out. Habermas's secular notion of ideality also meets head on the church's transcendental claim. This confrontation of ideologies could easily be destructive; however there is certainly a place for the mutual interpretation of these two understandings of reality which could enhance and facilitate the relationship between worship and the public sphere.

In seeking to investigate the potential for enhancing the relationship between worship and the public sphere, we can usefully reflect on the difference of understanding between Habermas and Derrida on the place of dialogue and democracy in relation to the achievement of the ideal cosmopolis and perpetual peace for humankind.[22] Habermas assumes that dialogue and democracy are straightforwardly the instruments which will deliver the sought goals; while Derrida is much less confident about them, seeing them only as two among other means necessary in the ongoing struggle to achieve the goals. This difference concerning political means is echoed in their difference over tolerance and hospitality, which we have discussed more fully above.[23] Each of these differences can be applied to the activity of worship, with the effect of clarifying further the provisionality of the church's claims.

The difference concerning the status of dialogue demonstrates on the one hand the usefulness and necessity of certain liturgical texts and norms and dialogical practices, contexts where ideality and transcendence are to be perceived, while on the other suggesting clearly that texts and norms are not magical formulas which inevitably deliver up the divine into human hands. The further difference concerning either tolerance or hospitality also challenges the practitioners (lay and clerical) of worship to examine the limits imposed upon worship, whether those limits be explicit or implicit. To what extent is worship an event at which any one is welcome? On what basis is that welcome extended? As a paternalistic tolerance, or 'symmetrical' tolerance, or as absolute hospitality? If the church is to claim that worship is a transcendental activity which manifests and facilitates true human sociality, then much more consideration needs to be taken of the philosophers' understandings of both tolerance and hospitality.

The outcome of dialogue and hospitality in the Kantian tradition, which both Habermas and Derrida inhabit but variously rework, is the achievement of perpetual peace in the ideal *cosmopolis*.[24] It is interesting to reflect that this has a strong resonance with the Christian tradition's understanding of the City of God: i.e. the reign or kingdom of God. It has become commonplace to suggest that worship, particularly eucharistic worship, is to be understood as the sign, instrument and foretaste of that reign.[25] This claim rests upon a complex set of conceptualities and metaphysical claims which we shall need to investigate further. This is an understanding which historically has been rooted in the tradition of the Eastern Orthodox churches. In their view, suggested by the iconography of the Byzantine tradition, the transcendental aspect of worship is not an additional extra, consequent upon the various human activities undertaken during worship. Rather the human community assembles to become united with the heavenly community of the church triumphant already worshipping and in communion with God. This dimension of understanding is not absent from Western traditions, and is expressed in particular through the singing of the Sanctus. However, the Orthodox tradition in its iconography, ritual and textual provision gives a much clearer emphasis and articulation not simply of the transcendental but of what this means: i.e. the connection of worship to the whole purposes of God in creating and redeeming and their outcome in the reign of God as all in all.[26]

Community and anaphora

The designation of the eucharistic prayer as 'anaphora' is a clear indication that worship is an activity, a 'doing', but what is done? Is it simply a matter of the human community or its ministers offering up something to God? Or is the conceptuality more complex and nuanced than that? At the time of the Reformation it was certainly the case that the Reformers found the commonplace assumptions about the Mass an easy target, which was articulated in their polemic against 'the sacrifice of the Mass', to which was usually added 'for the living and the dead'. The Reformers' anxiety concerning the Mass relates to a nexus of preconceptions. Their primary concerns are focused in the doctrine of justification. If salvation is God's gift (grace) received by faith (alone), then the notion of 'doing' something, i.e. 'offering' to God, is a contradiction of the pure doctrine of justification. In other words, the polemic of the Reformers was that the Mass had become a 'work', an opportunity whereby human beings could 'earn' salvation. This dispute was re-examined by the Doctrine Commission of the Church of England,[27] and also through a series of essays and pamphlets published by Grove Books.[28] In these various publications the two sides of the Reformation dispute are replayed, and the complex preconceptions behind the description of the eucharist in terms of offering/sacrifice explored. Two crucial understandings emerge from these publications: firstly, many designations of the eucharist as a sacrifice 'start too far up the conceptual ladder',[29] and are supported by a whole series of nuanced understandings beneath it (the implication being that much of this had been 'forgotten' by the time of the Reformation). Secondly, that the designation of the eucharist as a sacrifice or offering also relates to where it is perceived that the eucharist fits into the life of the church.[30] In other words, any understanding of the eucharist as offering implies or requires that the eucharist take the central place in the life of the church. For those who do not see the eucharist as central, the designation of it as offering is always likely to be mystifying at the least.

Thus our claim that the church is a community of offering already assumes that the eucharist is central to the life of the church. The church is both the company of the baptized and the eucharistic community. These are not in any sense to be seen as competing designations of the church. For the eucharist is the final component of Christian initiation, which, unlike baptism and confirmation, is repeated.

What then are the implications for understanding the church as a community of offering and what are the preconceptions? Is the activity of worship, in particular of the Eucharist, a 'work'? Is it a matter of the human community 'doing' something to God? The simple answer is, of course not; and this was never meant to be the case. The misunderstandings about this have to some extent been clarified recently in the various ecumenical statements on justification.[31]

The ground upon which the community of offering is founded is not in its own doing, but in Christ's action. The 'offering' in the eucharist is not any human re-immolation of Christ, but Christ's own self-offering to the Father. This self-offering is to be understood in two different but complementary ways. Christ's self-offering is revealed on the Cross, but that historical action is a revelation of the eternal self-offering of the hypostasis of the Son to the Father in love.[32] Thus the action of offering in worship is nothing less than that offering of the Son to the Father in love. The worship and offering of the human community are to be understood in relation to the action of hypostases of the Holy Trinity in their eternal perichoretic communion. Thus when we pray such prayers as the Prayer of Oblation, in the Book of Common Prayer, and say 'And here we offer and present unto thee, O Lord, our selves, our souls and bodies, to be a reasonable, holy and lively sacrifice unto thee' we do so not in our own right, not on our own initiative, but because we stand in Christ, having received Christ in Holy Communion. In other words, the offering we make is in and with and through Christ to the Father. Thus the eucharistic offering and the church understood as community of offering (anaphora) rests only upon an understanding, indeed a complex and nuanced understanding, that this claim relates to the inner life of the Trinity. The understanding of the life of the church as centred upon the eucharist, and thus as eucharistic community, is an understanding which sees the church as part of the continuum of the divine purposes in creating and redeeming the world. The church is wholly caught up in the *exitus* and *reditus* of the processes and purposes of creation and redemption, through which God will become 'all in all'[33].

These understandings are both complex and sophisticated. One response might be to ask how they relate to the simplicity of the Gospel? While the Gospel may in some sense be 'simple' its implications are profound and cosmic, as well as personal and local. And as well as there being dangers in making things too complex, there are also dangers inherent in oversimplification. In seeking to understand the church as a community of offering, we are claiming an epistemology rooted in faith, grace and 'revelation', through which we are establishing an appeal to the doctrine of the Trinity. Through the establishment of the conceptual ladder, which is both epistemological and metaphysical, we are accessing a highly nuanced understanding of the nature and activity of God, which we then use to refer to and describe the church as community. In making these claims we are then situating the local worshipping community within the processes and purposes of God in relation to the cosmos.

Another dimension of the understanding of the church as a community of anaphora relates to the offering of praise. Thus alongside the cosmological can be set the doxological content of offering. This relates to the human element, to the human response to the cosmological offering focused on the *Logos-Christos* and his eternal self-offering of which we become part and by which we become empowered to offer the sacrifice of praise: in both words and deeds:

> We now obey your Son's command ...
> Made one with him, we offer you these gifts
> and with them ourselves,
> a single, holy, living sacrifice.[34]

The oblation of praise, the material oblation of the gifts of altar and the oblation of our lives are all caught up in the cosmological and trintarian offering, instantiated on the Cross, and together are given expression in the offering of praise and thanksgiving – the eucharist.

The doxological content of the eucharistic offering, and by extension of the Church as community of anaphora, may be seen at least initially in terms of human response to the divine purposes in creating and redeeming. The doxological is to be seen neither as additional to nor indeed in competition with the cosmological. The opening words of the Westminster Confession of Faith remind us that doxology is imprinted upon the cosmos in God's purposes:

> *Q:* What is the chief end of man?
> *A:* Man's chief end is to glorify God, and to enjoy him for ever.

The offering of praise and the giving of glory (δοξα) and worship to God are not optional extras, nor are they simply matters of human response to God: they are fundamental to God's purposes in creating and redeeming. They are part of the vocation imprinted in each human being, in what the Christian tradition understands as the *imago dei*. If, as Zizioulas argues, the divine image in us is not simply to be understood in terms of rationality but also in terms of relationality,[35] then the vocation to glorify God is one way in which that relationality is to be expressed. Furthermore. if the *imago dei* is understood in relational terms, then the doxological calling can not in any sense be understood in individualistic terms. Once it is understood that the calling to offer praise and glory to God is intrinsic to the divine purposes and is also an expression of the calling to relationality with the Creator and fellow creatures in the creation, then the church as community of anaphora, as eucharistic community, can no longer be thought of as a side-show, an optional extra, but is rather an instantiation of the destiny for which human beings are created and to which they are called. As we have already noted above, the community makes its offering of praise and thanksgiving in communion with the church triumphant, of which the singing of the Sanctus is the major articulation. Furthermore, in so far as we are called into communion with all things in God, then worship may also be seen as an occasion through which all creation gives praise to God.

> Countless hosts of angels stand before you to do your will;
> they look upon your splendour
> and praise you, night and day.
> United with them,
> and in the name of every creature under heaven,
> we too praise your glory as we sing: [36]

The offering made by the church in its worship, and in particular in the Eucharist, is an offering not just for Christians or believers, or even human beings. It is the offering made to articulate the human vocation to communion and to doxology, which are primary expressions of God's purposes in creating and redeeming the cosmos; thus worship is part of the process of the accomplishment of the *exitus* from God and *reditus* to God.

> Τα σα εκ των σων σοι προφερομεν κατα παντα, και δια παντα
>
> ... offering you your own from your own, in all, and for all,
> we hymn you, we bless you, we give thanks, Lord, and pray to you, our God.
> We offer you also this reasonable and bloodless service, and we pray and beseech, and
> entreat you, send down your Holy Spirit on us and on these gifts set forth ... [37]

These words from the anamnesis/oblation of the Anaphora of St John Chrysostom, remind us that the offering is cosmic in its extent and meaning, and that the liturgy reinforces the trinitarian context of the eucharistic offering in connecting as closely as possible the offering with the epiclesis of the Holy Spirit.

Finally, in considering the community of anaphora in terms of doxology we should pause to reflect how the vocation to offer glory relates to the God who is glory. Von Balthasar, in expounding his theological aesthetics, in terms of the divine glory, sets before us another potential dimension of understanding of the community of anaphora. This would become possible through the exploration and exposition of a metaphysical framework for understanding the church, its worship and its value and meaning, in terms of the categories: αληθες (clear/true); αγαθον (good); καλον (sound, beautiful).[38] The development of such a metaphysical framework would need to be founded, as von Balthasar argues:

> In the biblical revelation [where] the object of contemplation is not an ordering between God and man but first the living God as the *only subject* of the act of revealing, law-giving and the bestowal of grace – and only then can the man who is the object of God's action become a subject whose action is a reply to God.[39]

On such grounds a metaphysics of worship could also contribute to our conceptuality of anaphora, further clarifying the role of the church community as the agent of God in the achievement of his purposes for the cosmos, as the bearer of the transcendentals of sociality and glory in the world now.

Community and anamnesis

The discussion of the notion of anamnesis in relation to the eucharist was one of the most significant features of both liturgical composition and eucharistic theology in the twentieth century. The discussion in part focused on the issue of the possible connection between the act of anamnesis and the act of oblation. We have noted already that for some any idea of a material oblation was anathema, and indeed remains so. However, as our investigation has demonstrated, it is possible to understand the act of oblation as an expression of our primary human vocation. The discussion of anamnesis focused on the twin poles of the past and the future. The 'remembering' of the future remains a challenge to the logical tradition of many in the West, and we shall return to this later in our analysis of the anamnesis of the Christ event, including the parousia. The discussion of the possibility of 'remembering' the past was also contentious. And a variety of hypotheses were developed in terms of the eliding of the past and present into one another.[40] We will investigate this below more fully. However, the anamnetic quality of the worshipping community is something shared, at least to some extent with any ongoing human gathering or community. It is after all an anamnetic factor that in part gives community its identity. Shared memory ties people together, and informs who they are and how they became that, and thus it sustains their collective self-understanding. This is as true for the worshipping community, which the church is, as for a club of football supporters. The anamnetic quality of human collectivity is something which shapes all our lives, and can of course be either supportive and constructive, or competitive and potentially destructive. This again is clearly evident in the life of the churches, and this competitive feature of the churches' existence is something which has provided the imperative for the ecumenical movement. That imperative arose from concern about the fractured witness which the competition between denominations produces. However, the fundamental issue is not witness *per se*, but rather that to which witness is given: i.e. the Gospel, or the divine purposes in creating and redeeming the cosmos. Thus while the anamnetic quality of the worshipping community is a phenomenon shared with all different expressions of human communal identity, the Christian tradition suggests that it is not simply to be understood in these terms. Rather the anamnetic quality of the worshipping community is also part of the transcendental claim we make for the church. For the anamnesis made in the eucharist is not simply the anamnesis of the experienced memory of those gathered, but the anamnesis of the divine purposes in creating and redeeming, particularly focused in Christ, and is therefore a cosmic remembering or 'memorial'. This does not in any sense preclude actual remembering by the participants. Indeed, one of the deficiencies of most eucharistic celebrations is the lack of opportunity for the local community to make its own anamnesis, or indeed its own thanksgivings. Liturgical provision and composition seems not to want to recognize the legitimacy of such expression, thus denying the role of the local and contextual in the offering of the eucharist. In other contexts it is often recommended that 'our' story needs to be incorporated in 'the' story.[41] This remains a challenge for those who compose liturgical rites, as well as for those who celebrate them. This lack of opportunity contributes to the widespread misappropriation of the anamnetic quality of the worshipping community. In turn this leads to an over-valuing of local tradition at the expense of 'universal' Tradition. Christian identity becomes focused in the denominational and its local manifestations rather than in the shared tradition and its cosmic significance. Such misappropriation also threatens the reality of the transcendental claim for the church.[42] In the discussion which follows we shall investigate the various ways in which the church makes anamnesis and their implications for understanding the church and its relationship to God's purposes. In doing so we shall bear in mind the concept of ideal speech communities and the appeal to sociality as a transcendental, and by extension to the twin characteristics of community: tolerance and/or hospitality.

The primary focus of the anamnesis in the eucharistic prayer has been christological. The memorial which is commanded was after all 'to do this in memory of me' – (τουτο ποειτε εις την εμην αναμνησιν).[43] However, the constituents of what is to be 'recalled' have been enumerated quite differently by different traditions. Thus the Roman tradition makes memorial of '*tam beatae passionis, necnon et ab inferis resurrectionis, sed et in caelos gloriosae ascensionis*':[44] the Passion, Resurrection and Ascension of Christ. These three constituents of the anamnesis are all 'events', which are understood to have happened in the past. However, the Byzantine tradition in making the memorial of Christ is:

Μεμνημενοι τοινυν της σωτηριου ταυτης εντολης,
και παντων των υπερ ημων γεγενημενων,
του Σταυρου, του Ταφου, της τριημερου Αναστασεως,
της εις ουρανους Αναβασεως, της εκ δεξιων Καθεδρας,
της δευτερας και ενδοξου παλιν Παρουσιας,[45]

the Cross, Tomb, Resurrection, Ascension, Sitting at the Father's right hand and the Parousia of Christ.

The latter of these in 'ordinary' experience remains an event in the future, and thus the notion of making anamnesis of the future adds a further dimension to the issue of what is meant by 'making anamnesis'.

During the twentieth century various attempts were made by Western theologians and liturgists to explain the dynamics of making this memorial of Christ. This entailed using metaphysical concepts to make certain epistemological and ontological claims. This process was often not discussed, or at least remained implicit. As a consequence various rather implausible theories of anamnesis were propounded. Max Thurian's two volumes on the eucharistic memorial[46] sought to borrow from Jewish understandings of the Haggadah of the Passover to set forward the notion that events of the past are brought into the present by means of ritual and liturgical celebration. The metaphysical implications of this claim remained unclear, and while many commentators were less than convinced, it is only recently that a convincing critique and alternative to his views has been put forward.[47] To a certain extent Thurian's proposal and similar attempts at constructing a theory of anamnesis, which related to the past orientation of the liturgical anamnesis evident in the Roman/Western tradition, has been overtaken by the wholesale dominance of the Eastern tradition of anamnesis cited above, with its future orientation.[48] This dominance is demonstrated in the general acceptance of the motif which has emerged from ecumenical dialogue, that the eucharist and the church are each to be understood as 'sign, instrument and foretaste of the Kingdom of God'.[49] This is not necessarily an adequate statement of the Eastern tradition, for, as Zizioulas argues, in that tradition church and eucharist are empowered by the offices of the Holy Spirit 'from the future'.[50] Nonetheless the introduction of the clearly eschatological thrust of 'sign, instrument and foretaste' has changed the topology of many Western eucharistic rites. In general the newer Western eucharistic liturgies stop short of 'remembering' the parousia, but it has become *de rigueur* 'to look forward to his coming in glory'. The thrust of the Western rites remains oriented to the past, while the Eastern rites are empowered from God's future. These different orientations in terms of eschatology and making the anamnesis of Christ are not necessarily rooted in utterly different conceptualities surrounding the interpretation of the divine purposes in creating and redeeming the cosmos. But they do reveal that the eucharist and the church are understood to occupy different 'places' in the scheme of God's purposes. This can also be seen in terms of how the church and eucharist are understood to relate to the hypostases of the Trinity. Zizioulas argues that in the West the emphasis on the christological dimension of both, at the expense of a pneumatological dimension, means that church and eucharist are set in linear or progressive view of history, which is driven from the past,[51] while the more epicletic view of church and eucharist evident in the Eastern rites, suggests that history is less a matter of progress, and is seen more in terms of the achievement of the divine purposes in the eschaton, which in God's eternity is understood in a certain sense to have arrived already.[52] This difference of understanding of the 'place' of the church and the eucharist also relates to the difference between the East and West concerning what 'salvation' is, the West focusing on notions of atonement, while the East focuses on *theosis*. The former has often meant that salvation remains a transactional and rather extrinsic reality, while the latter is more likely to produce understandings which are intrinsic and participative. Thus the anamnetic worshipping community may be perceived in two rather distinct ways. In each, however, it is the divine purposes in creating and redeeming which are the content of the anamnesis, and thus give the community its cosmic significance. We now turn to examine the dynamics through which this significance emerges.

Sign, instrument and foretaste

The dynamics of the anamnesis of a Byzantine anaphora are not to be understood without reference to the oblation and epiclesis. The 'being mindful' (Μεμνημενοι τοινυν της σωτηριου ταυτης εντολης, και παντων των υπερ ημων γεγενημενων)[53] which designates the anamnesis, is not something which occurs in its own right, or independently of the oblation or epiclesis which follow on immediately from it. Thus the Parousia is recalled alongside the other events which 'have come to pass for us': i.e. the Cross and Resurrection. The conceptuality of the anaphora takes for granted the preconception that the parousia, while yet to be accomplished historically *in tempore*, has happened in the eternity of the divine counsel of the Trinity. On this basis the offering to God of God's own from all and for all is made; and the Holy Spirit is invoked 'on us and the gifts', so that the gifts being changed, those who partake of the gifts, may receive, 'vigilance of soul, remission of sins, communion of the Holy Spirit and fulfilment of the Kingdom of the heavens': Ωστε γενεσθαι τοις μεταλαμβανουσιν εις νηψιν ψυχης, εις αφεσιν αμαρτιων, εις κοινωνιαν του Αγιου σου Πνευματος, εις Βασιλειας ουρανων πληρωμα'.[54] The outcome of the anamnesis/oblation and epiclesis in the reception of the Holy Communion is trinitarian and eschatological. The *koinonia* of the Spirit, is also communion with and in the Trinity, and together with *pleroma* of the Kingdom, we are left in no doubt that the participants are receiving nothing less than the cosmic and eternal outcome of the divine purposes in creating and redeeming. Such a claim is certainly transcendental in its character, meaning and value. The dynamics of the making of anamnesis in this tradition are empowered, as Zizioulas argues, by what from our mortal perspective is the future: for the achievement of the goal of the divine purposes, in the return of all things to God that God may be all in all. The *anamnesis* is the being mindful of that which constitutes the *exitus* and *reditus* of creation and redemption. This is a conceptuality, which depends on a metaphysics of eternity, which is understood from the perspective of the divine counsel to include the simultaneity of all things.[55] Thus the parousia of Christ, heralding the completion of all things, is both now and future: it is something yet to come and also a *par-ousia*, a presence, a future-oriented ontology.[56] Thus the ontology of the Real Presence is itself transformed from a metaphysics of being reliant upon the ideal world of forms, to a renewed state of being, which God achieves through the Incarnation of the Word, and the vocation of all human beings to become partakers of the divine nature. Thus the anamnesis of the parousia of Christ, is the 'being mindful' of the calling and destiny of all human beings in *theosis*.[57] The anamnesis which the worshipping community makes is thus an anamnesis which establishes its identity intrinsically and ontologically, in the orientation of the community's celebration to God's future, through the epiclesis of the Holy Spirit.

The dynamic of the anamnesis of the Byzantine anaphoras and its implication for our understanding of the worshipping community is quite distinct from either Thurian's conceptuality of the bringing of the past into the present, or of the ecumenical motif of 'sign, instrument and foretaste'. The conceptuality of *anamnesis* to be found in *Baptism, Eucharist and Ministry*[58] was formulated largely in the light of Thurian's notion of actualizing the past in the present, and the document appeals to what is understood to be a 'biblical idea of memorial', which 'refers to this present efficacy of God's work when it is celebrated by God's people in a liturgy'.[59] The document is clear that the implications of a eucharistic celebration are cosmic,[60] and that Christ in granting communion with himself, means that 'The eucharist is also the foretaste of his *parousia* and of the final kingdom.'[61] However, what remains less clear are the metaphysical preconceptions underlying this claim. The act of *anamnesis* is designated as 'both representation and anticipation',[62] which is further qualified as 'the Church's effective proclamation of God's mighty acts and promises'.[63]

The dual designation of anamnesis as 'representation and anticipation' is further qualified in terms of the activities of thanksgiving and intercession.[64] While these claims concerning *anamnesis* indicate a considerable step forward in the possibility of multilateral consensus, nonetheless in order to be sustainable there would need to be considerable clarification regarding the allusion of the 'biblical idea of memorial', as well as to the further designations, and perhaps in particular the appeal to 'anticipation'. On the whole, the dynamic of the *Baptism, Eucharist and Ministry (BEM)* document in terms of the making of memorial feels rooted in the past; thus the claim is made that 'the Holy Spirit [is] the One who makes the historical words of Jesus present and live'.[65] Although it is also claimed the Holy Spirit 'gives a foretaste of the Kingdom of God: the Church receives the life of the new creation and the assurance of the Lord's return'.[66]

Thus the dynamic and conceptuality of 'sign, instrument and foretaste' remains implicit and ambiguous in the *BEM* document, and part of this difficulty rests in its appeal to an understanding of the dynamic of *anamnesis* akin to Thurian's notion. The conceptuality of the original Anglican–Roman Catholic International Commission (ARCIC) I document on the eucharist made explicit appeal to the notion of *anamnesis* as the making effective in the present an event in past.[67] However, in the *Elucidation* this was challenged, and a clearer, perhaps more sustainable claim was made by an appeal to the work of the Holy Spirit in making *anamnesis*, as well as to the understanding of participation in the movement of Christ's self-offering to the Father.[68] In making this fundamental shift in conceptuality the ARCIC document pursues a theological metaphysics more rooted in the tradition, and sustainable as an explication of the making of and effects of *anamnesis*. However it becomes evident that a greater transparency in relation to the claims made about *anamnesis* and the dependent conceptuality of

'sign, instrument and foretaste' would enhance not only ecumenical dialogue but
also all endeavour to explicate the connection between church and Kingdom.

Re-membering

We turn now to examine another understanding of anamnesis, which relates
particularly to the metaphor of the Body of Christ. The worshipping community
by making the memorial of its Lord and Saviour, are incorporated afresh into
Christ; into his Body, which is also the church. The re-membering of the Body is
achieved through the making of anamnesis, by which the individuals who
constitute the members of the Body are renewed in their membership of the Body
by the celebration of the Passion and Resurrection and Parousia of Christ. Just as
in baptism the individual is baptized into Christ's death and resurrection, and
becomes a member of the Body of Christ, so also in the repetition of the eucharist,
a reincorporation of the Body's members is achieved in the making of anamnesis.
This is a conceptuality which underlies the theologizing that the eucharist makes
the church, as well as the church makes the eucharist.[69] The understanding that
the eucharist makes the church in turn bears fruit in ecclesiologies of communion.
Thus the community of anamnesis not only celebrates but also participates in the
anamnesis of Christ. The anamnetic community of the church is thus formed by
its participation in the Christ Event, including the parousia/presence of Christ,
and acquires the transcendental significance and value which it claims. The
collective dimension of this is reinforced in Zizioulas's understanding that Christ is
not to be understood as an individual.[70] The conceptuality of the re-membering of
the Body of Christ furthermore clearly points towards an unavoidable centrality of
the eucharist in the life of the church, in which the church is seen to play a intrinsic
role in the achievement of the divine purposes for the cosmos.

Human community/Church community

In our discussion of the church as an anamnetic community we have noted on the
one hand that anamnesis is associated with identity, while on the other it is
associated with God's purposes for the cosmos. These associations are potentially
(and often in practice) held in tension. It is a tension that is not always
immediately constructive. In making anamnesis, the worshipping community
establishes its identity in relation to the Christ event. This is begun in baptism, and
reiterated in the repeated celebrations of the eucharist. Individuals are incorporated
into Christ, into his dying and rising, and into the outcome of God's purposes in
creating and redeeming through their encounter with the parousia/presence of
Christ. Making anamnesis is thoroughly christological and thus depends mainly
on the metaphor of the Body of Christ to give meaning to the collective experience
of anamnesis. This can easily be interpreted in exclusive terms. Most ecclesial
groups make this interpretation to some extent. For example, even those
denominations who claim to operate an 'open table' policy in relation to who is

invited to receive Holy Communion, usually suggest that one should 'love the Lord Jesus'. In the secular context of the West this is by no means an invitation to all. For those who require baptism and possibly confirmation or preparation for first communion as prerequisites for receiving Holy Communion, the boundaries of the identity of the anamnetic community are clear enough. If one adds to this the layers of identity which worshipping communities accrue simply through their shared experiences, traditions and memory, then the actual extent of exclusivity quickly becomes apparent. On the whole this exclusivity is neither ignored nor decried by the denominations, rather it is put forward as a virtue. It is often defended on moral grounds, be those personal or matters of social or political justice, and in the name of truth.[71] If then the making of anamnesis inevitably delivers an exclusive worshipping community, how is the relationship of the community of the church with the human community to be construed? Is the church to be interpreted in terms of the metaphor of the 'Ark of Salvation', removing people from the sphere of danger: *extra ecclesiam nulla salus*.[72] In which case, what are we to make of the claims for the church in relation to ideality and the transcendental of sociality – where does an exclusivist stance leave our appeal to tolerance and hospitality? The answer to these questions will lie, in part, in the extent to which an emphasis is placed upon the cosmic dimension of the anamnesis, and also how this is interpreted. The questions of interpretation relate of course not only to the welcome extended to individuals but also on a wider front to the relations between the church and other faiths and ideologies. A detailed discussion of these matters is beyond the scope of this essay, but it is evident that the outcome of such deliberations should define a denomination's self-understanding of its place in the divine purposes.[73] In the circumstances of a denomination understanding that there is truth (and revelation) to be discerned in the world faiths, it becomes incumbent upon that denomination to articulate this not only in interfaith dialogue, but also in its making of anamnesis, and in the expression of tolerance/hospitality in its worshipping communities generally.[74]

In our discussion we have sought to suggest how the situating of the worshipping community is to be understood in relation to God's purposes in creating and redeeming. But we also need to ask how the situating of the worshipping community is to be understood in relation to the human community. The answer to this latter is to be found in the former. If the worshipping community occupies a central place in the achievement of the divine purposes in creating and redeeming the cosmos, then it must also surely have a central place in the human community. The issue for us in the West is how is this to be understood and achieved in the secular context of the present day? The answer to this lies for some in the remodelling of the community as a mission-shaped church.[75] This is understood in terms of the deconstruction of current models of the church, and their replacement with new models rooted in contemporary culture. Such a proposal is open to critique on the basis of the old adage that he who marries the spirit of the age is soon widowed. However, on a more serious note, the emphasis on inculturation does not necessarily deliver a sustainable model for other reasons. The adaptation of church structures and institutions to become more contextually and culturally appropriate is one thing, but that does not of itself create models by which the church can express itself and offer worship which give clear articulation to its situating and calling in relation to the divine purposes for the cosmos. The community which makes the anamnesis of Christ, and thus of creation and redemption of the cosmos, need look no further than that which it celebrates to discern a model for its relationship with the human community. The understanding of Christ's role in creation and redemption in terms of a priestly role is something which has informed ecclesiology from the outset.[76] The role of the anamnetic community in relation to the human community may still be understood in terms of a priestly role today. The worshipping community offers to the human community an experience and example of the sociality and fellowship (*koinonia*) to which all people, as God's creatures, are called and destined. The anamnesis, which is sign, instrument and foretaste, is such not only for the worshipping community itself, but for the whole human community. The ideality which emerges from the dialogical experience of worship is something not to be possessed, but rather something to be shared in its emancipating power with all creation. This clearly lays a challenge before all worshipping communities to discover and actualize means by which to practise this sharing. Tolerance and hospitality both present theoretical opportunities which need to find concrete expression in each local context. In doing so each anamnetic community of the church will be offering the wider community access to an experience of the *exitus* and the *reditus* which characterize the divine purposes in creating and redeeming the cosmos. This then is the calling of the worshipping community in terms of its participation in the *missio dei*.[77] The facilitation by the worshipping community of tolerance and hospitality in each local context is one possible fulfilment of its priestly and missionary role.

Theological aesthetic, worshipping community and mission

This statement of understanding of the church's participation in the *missio dei*, is made only on the explicit acceptance of the modern unknowing of God.[78] One way by which to confront and challenge this unknowing is as von Balthasar argues to posit a transcendental aesthetics. If we accept this diagnosis and seek to apply it to the church's activity of worship, we do so in the sense that this is another way to understand the church's priestly participation in God's mission in and for the cosmos. An understanding of the church's activity of worship may be set forth within the framework of von Balthasar's three primary concepts that delimit his quest for a theological aesthetic. The first concept of the *epiphaneia* of the divine to man,[79] which is understood to break man open to grasp this appearing, may be seen as a primary dynamic of the activity of worship, particularly when we seek to claim it as a transcendental reality. The second concept relating to the ordering of world rests upon what is just, fitting and right (*dike, themis*). Its manifestation in the *polis* of God relates to the ordering of the church community through its pneumatological empowerment from God's future, as a sign and foretaste of the destiny of humankind and the cosmos. Finally, the third concept of the world revealed as *charis* (a free grace) may also be applied to the worshipping community, as an instance of the divine initiative in which *charis* is bestowed as the ground of *agape* and *koinonia*. These three concepts are the foundation for a theological aesthetics rooted in a doctrine of *seeing* which leads to a doctrine of *rapture*, of *being brought out*.[80] This conceptuality provides a further basis for our transcendental claims for the worshipping community, as well as offering a framework out of which to endorse and ratify our metaphysical and ontological claims. Thus the priestly people of God, in the transcendental activity of worship, extend God's invitation to the cosmos to share in the glory of the divine *koinonia*, that God may be all in all.

Notes

1. See Helen Cameron, 'The Decline of the Church in England as a Local Membership Organization: Predicting the Nature of Civil Society in 2050', in Grace Davie, Paul Heelas and Linda Woodhead (eds), *Predicting Religion: Christian, Secular and Alternative Futures* (Aldershot: Ashgate, 2003).

2. E.g. Richard Gillard, 'Brother, Sister, Let me Serve you'.

3. D. Stephen Long, 'Fetishizing Feuerbach's God: Contextual Theologies as the End of Modernity', *Pro Ecclesia*, 12.4, (2003): 447–72. See also in 'Ecclesiology: Context and Community', ch. 7 of this vol., p. 14–44.

4. See J. D. Crichton, *Christian Celebration: The Mass* (London and Dublin: Geoffrey Chapman, 1971), ch. 11, 'Liturgy and the World'.

5. E.g. A. G. Hebert, *Liturgy and Society: The Function of the Church in the Modern World* (London: Faber & Faber, 1935; 1961).

6. E.g. (Roman Catholic) *Rite of Christian Initiation of Adults* (London: Geoffrey Chapman, 1987); and (Episcopal Church of the United States of America) *The Book of Occasional Services* (New York: The Church Hymnal Corporation, 1988; 2nd edn), pp. 112–26.

7. Louis Bouyer, *The Paschal Mystery: Meditations on the Last Three Days of Holy Week* (London: Allen and Unwin, 1952).

8. Walter Kasper, *Nature and Purpose of Ecumenical Dialogue*, http://www.vatican.va/roman_curia/pontifical_councils/chrstuni/card-kasper-docs/rc_pc_chrstuni_doc _20030227_ecumenical-dialogue_en.html

9. Hans Urs von Balthasar, *Herrlichkeit: Eine theologische Asthetik*, English trans, *The Glory of the Lord: A Theological Aesthetics* (San Francisco, CA: Ignative Press, 1982–89).

10. See 'Hermeneutical Investigations', ch. 4 of this vol. pp. 63–90.

11. E.g. Second Anglican–Roman Catholic International Commission (ARCIC), *Salvation and the Church: An Agreed Statement* (London: Church House, 1987); Lutheran World Federation and the Catholic Church, *Joint Declaration on the Doctrine of Justification* (London: Catholic Truth Society, 1999).

12. Martin Stringer, 'Text, Context and Performance: Hermeneutics and the Study of Worship', *Scottish Journal of Theology*, 53.3 (2000): 365–79.

13. E.g. Duncan Forrester, James I. H. McDonald and Gian Tellini, *Encounter with God* (Edinburgh: T&T Clark, 1983); Susan J. White, *The Spirit of Worship: The Liturgical Tradition* (Maryknoll, NY: Orbis Books, 2000).

14. E.g. Grace Davie, *Religion in Britain since 1945: Believing without Belonging* (Oxford: Basil Blackwell, 1994), and *Religion in Modern Europe: A Memory Mutates* (Oxford: Oxford University Press, 2000); also Davie *et al.*, *Predicting Religion.*; Callum G. Brown, *The Death of Christian Britain: Understanding Secularisation 1800-2000* (London: Routledge, 2001).

15. Third Instruction, 'For the orderly implementation of the Constitution on the Sacred Liturgy of the Second Vatican Council': *Liturgicae Instaurationes* (Vatican: Sacred Congregation for Divine Worship, 1970); also 'Inculturation and the Roman Liturgy', *Varietates Legitimae*, Fourth Instruction for the Right Application of the Conciliar Constitution on the Liturgy (Nos 37–40), Congregation for Divine Worship and the Discipline of the Sacraments on 29 March 1994.

16. E.g. David Gitari (ed.), *Anglican Liturgical Inculturation in Africa: The Kanamai Statement with Introduction, Papers from Kanamai and a First Response* (Nottingham: Grove Books, 1994); *A New Zealand Prayer Book* (London: Collins Liturgical, 1989).

17. *The United Methodist Book of Worship* (Nashville, TN: United Methodist Publishing House, 1992) – see 'A Family Hour or Wake', pp. 168f.

18. E.g. the processes of inculturation in the Indian subcontinent raise profound issues of caste which relate to the culture that is to be 'borrowed' for adaptation.

19. See, for example, above issues relating to Dalit Christian awareness; the Zaïre Rite for Mass (1975) and other African examples which recognize the place of the Ancestors; and the use of dance in eucharistic celebrations in Papua New Guinea.

20. See Long, 'Fetishizing Feuerbach's God'.

21. Jürgen Habermas, *The Theory of Communicative Action*, vol. 1 (Cambridge: Polity Press, 1984); vol. 2 (Boston, MA: Beacon Press, 1987).

22. Jürgen Habermas, 'Kant's Idea of Perpetual Peace, with the Benefit of Two Hundred Years Hindsight', in James Bohman and Mathias Lutz-Bachmann (eds), *Perpetual Peace: Essays on Kant's Cosmopolitan Ideal* (Cambridge, MA: MIT Press, 1997), pp. 113–54; and Jacques Derrida, *Politics of Friendship* (London: Verso, 1997) and *Of Hospitality*, (Stanford, CA: Stanford University Press, 2000).

23. Jürgen Habermas, 'Wann müssen wir tolerant sein? Über die Konkurrenz von Weltbildern, Werten und Theorien', Festvortrag zum Leibniztag der Berlin-Brandenburgischen Akademie der Wissenschaften, 29 June 2002, http: //www.bbaw.de/schein/habermas.html; Derrida, *Of Hospitality*.

24. See 'Ecclesiology: Context and Community', pp. 151–4 of this volume.

25. E.g. *God's Reign Our Unity*, report of the Anglican–Reformed International commission, 1981–84 (London: SPCK, 1984).

26. 1 Cor. 15.28 and Col. 3.11.

27. Archbishop's Commission on Christian Doctrine, *Thinking about the Eucharist: Papers by members of the Church of England Doctrine Commission* (London: SCM Press, 1972).

28. R. C. P. Hanson, *Eucharistic Offering in the Early Church* (Nottingham: Grove Books, 1976); Rowan Williams, *Eucharistic Sacrifice: The Roots of a Metaphor* (Nottingham: Grove Books, 1982); Colin Buchanan (ed.), *Essays on Eucharistic Sacrifice in the Early Church* (Nottingham: Grove Books, 1984).

29. Leslie Houlden, in *Thinking about the Eucharist*, Ch. 6, p. 96

30. Houlden, *Thinking about the Eucharist*, Ch. 6, p. 97

31. E.g. Second ARCIC report, *Salvation and the Church: An Agreed Statement*; Lutheran World Federation and the Catholic Church, *Joint Declaration on the Doctrine of Justification*.

32. See the *Lambeth Conference Report 1958* (London: SPCK and Seabury, 1958), §§2.83–2.8; also ARCIC, *The Final Report* (London: CTS and SPCK, 1982), p. 20.

33. E.g. Maximos the Confessor, '*Ambigua*', Migne PG 91: 1228A.

34. The Eucharistic Prayer: Anamnesis/Oblation, *Scottish Liturgy 1982* (Edinburgh: General Synod of the Scottish Episcopal Church).

35. John D. Zizioulas, 'On Being a Person. Towards an Ontology of Personhood', in C. Schwöbel and C. E. Gunton (eds), *Persons, Human and Divine* (Edinburgh: T&T Clark, 1991), esp. pp. 37–44.

36. Eucharistic Prayer IV, *Roman Missal*, 1970 (International Committee on English in the Liturgy trans).

37. Anaphora of St John Chrysostom, *Prayers of the Eucharist: Early and Reformed*, ed. R. C. D. Jasper and G. J. Cuming (New York: Pueblo, 1987), p. 133.

38. Hans Urs von Balthasar, *The Glory of the Lord: Volume IV: The Realm of Metaphysics in Antiquity* (Edinburgh: T&T Clark, 1989), p. 12.

39. Von Balthasar, *The Glory of the Lord*, vol. 4, p. 24.

40. See e.g. Max Thurian, *The Eucharistic Memorial*, vols 1 and 2 (London: Lutterworth Press, 1960, 1961).

41. See John Barton and John Halliburton, 'Story and Liturgy', in *Believing in the Church: The Corporate Nature of Faith*, the Doctrine Commission of the Church of England, (London: SPCK, 1981).

42. See John D. Zizioulas, *Being as Communion: Studies in Personhood and the Church* (London: Darton, Longman & Todd, 1985), ch. 7.

43. Lk. 22.19.

44. The Roman canon of the Mass: 'his passion, his resurrection from the dead, and his ascension into glory'.

45. Anaphora of St John Chrysostom: 'We, therefore, remembering this saving commandment and all the things that were done for us: the cross, the tomb, the resurrection on the third day, the ascension into heaven, the session at the right hand, the second and glorious coming again' (Jasper and Cuming [eds]. *Prayers of the Eucharist*, p. 133).

46. Thurian, *The Eucharistic Memorial*.

47. Aelred Arnesen, 'The Myth of Anamnesis', *Theology*, 105.828 (November/December 2002): 436–43.

48. E.g. Zizioulas, *Being as Communion*, pp. 160f.

49. E.g. World Council of Churches (WCC), *Baptism, Eucharist and Ministry* (Geneva: WCC, 1982), pp. 11f.

50. Zizioulas, *Being as Communion*, pp. 114–22.

51. However, see *Ecclesia de Eucharistia*, Pope John Paul II, April 2003, §§23 and 24, where explicit reference is made to the Eastern tradition's understanding of the role of the Holy Spirit in the eucharist.

52. See Alexander Schmemann, *The Eucharist: Sacrament of the Kingdom* (Crestwood, NY: SVS Press, 1988), pp. 34f.

53. See n. 45 above.

54. Anaphora of St John Chrysostom.

55. See Karl Barth, *Church Dogmatics*, vol. II.1 (Edinburgh: T&T Clark, 1957), pp. 608–77: Barth expounds his understanding of 'pure duration' or the divine simultaneity (*Gleichzeitigkeit*).

56. See Eberhard Jüngel, 'The World as Possibility and Actuality: The Ontology of the Doctrine of Justification', in *Theological Essays* (Edinburgh: T&T Clark, 1989).

57. See Maximus the Confessor, *Mystagogia*, 24:704D–705A.

58. WCC, *Baptism, Eucharist and Ministry* (hereafter *BEM*).

59. *BEM*, Eucharist §II B 5.

60. Ibid. §II B 6.

61. Ibid. §II B 6.

62. Ibid. §II B 7.

63. Ibid. §II B 7.

64. Ibid. §II B 8.

65. Ibid. §II C 14.

66. Ibid. §II C 18.

67. ARCIC, *The Final Report*, §5, pp. 13f.

68. Ibid., Elucidation, §5, pp. 18ff.

69. E.g. Paul McPartlan, *The Eucharist Makes the Church: Henri de Lubac and John Zizioulas in Dialogue* (Edinburgh: T&T Clark, 1993).

70. Zizioulas, *Being as Communion*, p. 108.

71. E.g. Catholic Bishops' Conferences of England and Wales, Ireland, Scotland, *One Bread, One Body: A teaching document on the Eucharist in the life of the Church, and the establishment of general norms on sacramental sharing* (London: CTS, 1998); Stanley Hauerwas, *Christian*

Existence Today: Essays on Church, World and Living in Between (Durham, NC: Labyrinth Press, 1988).

72. See St Cyprian (*Epistola* 73, 21; PL 1123 AB); the Fourth Lateran Council (DS 802); the Bull *Unam Sanctam* of Boniface VIII (DS 870); and the Council of Florence (Decree for the Jacobites, DS 1351). See also Karl Rahner, 'Christianity and the Non-Christian Religions', in *Theological Investigations*, vol. 5 (London: Darton, Longman & Todd, 1966), pp. 115–34. Rahner argues that nowhere is '*extra ecclesia*'.

73. E.g. Second Vatican Council, *Lumen Gentium* 16; *Nostra Aetate*, 1, 2; *Ad Gentes*, 3, 9, 11, 18; *Gaudium et Spes*, 28, 92.

74. See for example, *Dominus Jesus*, Congregation for the Doctrine of the Faith, August 2000, §8.

75. See General Synod paper no 1523, *Mission-Shaped Church* (London: Church House, 2004).

76. 1 Pet. 2.

77. Thomas Aquinas, *Summa Theologiae*, pt 1, Q.43

78. Von Balthasar, *The Glory of the Lord*, Vol. 4.

79. Ibid., pp. 21f.

80. Ibid., vol. 4, p. 24

Chapter 9

GOVERNANCE AND AUTHORITY: THE BASIS OF FAITHFULNESS

Gareth Powell

Questions relating to governance and authority have to be addressed, not through some desire to be introspective but because on a practical level they are being asked. The questions are posed from two general perspectives; firstly from inside the church; and secondly by those who are really rather relieved to find themselves outside it. From the latter perspective, questions are often set against a backdrop of wondering what on earth the church is for, it having apparently lost credibility in terms of taking context seriously. This is mirrored internally by a perceived inability to order its own affairs with any degree of coherence and confidence. The church seems to slip away into some far-off country called the past. From within (and occasionally from those who may be interested in a return), the questions are asked by way of making a passionate enquiry about God, acutely aware of the need not to chase the prized goal of postmodern relevance but simply and crucially to be faithful. The manifestation of such faithfulness having an impact on the good order of the church is most clearly expressed and revealed in terms of teaching, caring and worshipping. This is not to say that such people are not interested in the future of the church as having something to contribute to society – quite the opposite. A good deal of the questioning from within is born out of a desire to speak of the grace of God in a way which takes seriously both the fountain of our salvation and the human framework of society. The complexities of the latter are both liberated and bound by a range of interconnected norms and systems from localized issues of political devolution, to the impact of far-off economies which have the possibilities to change the present in a very localized manner. Far from issues of governance enabling a retreat into a holy club they are explored here in order to ensure that the 'order' is just that, in order and thus responsive to God.[1] Such a context for questioning is the very opposite of a holy retreat, for the encounter with the living God is the transformation which enables the church to be that which God calls and directs. We are concerned with the community in which those called to the royal priesthood work out not only a personal salvation but also fulfil the command of the Risen Christ, the head of the body. Seen in this light (and I am not at all sure that this is worth addressing if it is not seen in this light), questions of governance relate to, and in the answering rely upon, conversations undertaken under the broad headings of ethics and pastoral theology.

Addressing questions of governance is not to be seen as a last-ditch attempt to claim supremacy for canon lawyers or questions on church order, tempting as that may be when faced with decline, misunderstanding, or threat from forces beyond one's control. Rather the issue of governance is addressed so as to ensure that the church is faithful and diligent in the expression of the bonds of love which unite and sustain. This requires a twofold approach.

Called into being by God

Beginning with God is, as we have seen in Part 1 of this book, crucial to the whole enterprise of the Church working out its calling in the world, let alone its place in salvation history and the divine economy. This could, to put it in terms of governance, become a perfectly acceptable enquiry as to where the church finds the source of its authority. But already that all sounds very human. It sounds as if the protection and defence of that which successive generations have created must be defended and preserved at all costs, even through, or at the cost of, pastoral theology and moral discourse. It slips easily into responsiveness to human interpretation which could be called obedience, when in fact it is not about obedience to God (or faithfulness for that matter), but rather the translation of authority cast as an exercise in good or necessary instruments of governance. Such a view causes Nicholas Lash to observe, 'issue after issue ... has been abstracted from its pastoral or doctrinal context, and debated predominantly in terms of the formal structure of authority'.[2]

Coming to terms with God as the source of authority and consequent impact upon the structures of governance requires the recognition that the agenda is not human. This can present us with particular problems when thinking about the nature of the church. Certainly there will be the human side; there will be the teaching of Jesus of Nazareth; the call to discipleship; the Communion of Saints; and the enrichment of human relationships. But at the first and last the source of authority, and as such the grounding of all governance, from creation to the command that proclamation is fundamental to discipleship, is God's love for the world. Far from being an abandonment of reason and rational thought, this is a call to use the gifts of creation and the talents of the human community to embody the grace of God in such a way that is faithful to God's will and embrace. The centrality of God is the source of good government in the church and the foundation of all that the church will want to say and do in terms of ethical comment, teaching, pastoral care and thought, issues of mission and liturgy. Understanding God to be supreme is not to deny the effectiveness of human society and order. Far from removing the responsibility away from human beings, centring on God ensures our effectiveness as humans called into being by God for that which God wishes to see for his world.

For those who comment on church order from outside the ecclesial structures, the charge (and very real experience) of bad order is something that needs to be taken into account because of what can be heard in those comments and experiences about the separation of order and faithful living. For many people the difficulty is not God but the way in which churches go about the practice of living as God's holy people. The church as the community of the faithful, the Body of Christ, is not in the pursuit of good order being asked to adopt a management technique that has been of proven worth. We are not in the business of dealing with faith only to treat order as if it comes from an altogether different source, or for that matter has no role in responsible pastoral relationships. There will certainly be things to learn from other communities and organizations, but not at the expense of prayerful living and faithful discipleship. There will be requirements placed upon churches by civil authorities and state laws. Those issues are to be dealt with by a community clearly and diligently focused on responding to God. Thus the order of the church is as much a part of life and experience as the worship which is offered to God and a sacramental view of the church, its nature and character, raises questions about its organisation and structure. The enquiry about the ground of governance has to be set very firmly within the sacramental experience. This is to ensure that we really do begin with God and that the activity of the community of faith on earth is infused with such an awareness of God that the governance of the Church really is a faithful product of the divine economy, albeit enriched by a serious understanding of human society. At its worst, failure to ensure this aspect of godly living becomes a microversion of sacred and secular, as if to say that the presbyters will be presbyters and the lawyers will look after order. Not only does this raise serious questions about pastoral responsibility and oversight, it also results in a failure to see the body as being in communion and as such invited to participate in all its forms in the activity of a loving and redemptive God.

> . . .where God shall be all our love and every desire and effort, every thought of ours, and all our life and words and breath and that unity which already exists between the Father and the Son, and the son and the Father, has been shed abroad in our hearts and mind.[3]

Monasticism may not offer a perfect vision for a Christian community, but it does offer a pattern of God-centred community life. What the monastic way does is to establish a rule or pattern that is focused on God so as to ensure that prayer and action become part of the same. At the heart of the community is worship from which everything else flows. Worship infuses the domestic round as well as the ordering of communal life. In terms of the *Rule of St Benedict* it would probably be most unfair to claim supremacy for worship as if to suggest that other aspects of life were not capable of revealing grace. After all, 'even when he [the Abbot] is dealing with the control of real wickedness, it is never stern regulations that matter to him but the ultimate supremacy of prayer and love'.[4]

The notion of being in communion is very much more than simply getting along with one another or recognizing something of a common faith and set of values in those whom we know we ought to love. What we might call the action of communion on the part of the believers is in response to the reality of the community of faith, that is the church seeking to live in love and peace with all whom Christ has called. However, the vocation of those who are called into the fellowship of the church, by the proclamation of the love of God, is itself to be rooted in the grace that is God. The responsibility to be in communion is now much more than a desire to live peaceably. The notion of being in communion is itself about living in the grace of God. Here is the ground of communion and the foundation of community; as Jean-Marie Tillard observes, 'their common foundation – the socio-religious condition of the people of God'.[5]

Tillard goes on to use the description of the olive tree in Rom. 11.16–24 as the basis for this understanding. The means of nourishment are not the activities or righteousness of the other believers. The branches, new and old, have a common root and that alone is the source of sustenance: 'it is not you that support the root. But the root that supports you.'[6] 'The entire olive tree grafted together'[7] not only represents a call to communion but also lifts the sights beyond the possibilities of thinking that this is simply about disciples learning to live together.

Raising this notion of being in communion is not an attempt to build walls around the church so as to keep it pure and free from the forces of daily living. The consequences of a sacramental view of the Church simply do not permit that, for the very nature of such a view requires Christians both to pay attention to God and to the context of service. Failure to do so will see the business of offering love and grace becoming a very one-sided affair and falling into the trap of assumption and self-reliance. (Self-reliance either in terms of thinking that the Christian community can go it alone without God, or a sort of self-reliance that claims the Christian community can just get on without attention to the world.) Beginning with God is crucial to the whole enterprise of the church working out its calling in the world, let alone its place in salvation history and the divine economy. Coming to terms with God as the source of authority requires the recognition that the agenda is not human, as such thinking about the nature of the church presents particular challenges to frail humanity. The challenge of this sacramental view is that one comes both face-to-face with salvation and yet is still able to look upon human weakness and find the ability to act and respond in grace.

This is the call to use the gifts of creation, and the talents of humanity to embody the grace of God in such a way that is faithful to God's will and embrace. The centrality of God is the foundation of all that the church will want to say and do. Far from removing the responsibility away from human beings, centring on God is to ensure our faithfulness as a people called into being by God for that which God wishes to see for his world. It is important that the undoubtedly justifiable charge levied by Lash becomes a regrettable reference to history and not a prediction for the life of the church. As such it is important to make some comment on the why and how of governance and order.

Confidence in the task

Perhaps the first thing to say is that if taken seriously the task of ensuring that faithful ecclesiastical governance is in place requires confidence. This is not confidence in any given structure, although clearly there has to be confidence in structures. This is confidence in the very task of being faithful to the mercies of

God as churches and Christian communities set about ordering their affairs. It is by God's grace that Christians embark on the exploration of all that is. This in turn enables the asking and answering of all sorts of questions. As well as being the sort of environment in which such exploration takes place, the Christian community is also called to be a place where hospitality is exercised. All of this is to represent inquisitive minds and the challenge of the Risen Lord: feed my lambs; tend my sheep; follow me.[8] It is then important that the ordering of communities takes this into account from the outset. Confidence in the task is important not only because it keeps us true to our calling but also because well-tempered confidence enables us to be aware of weakness and strengths and the fundamental tasks of a Christian community. It is what the sales person would call, being clear about the USP (unique selling-point).

There is a danger here. Not in having a clear understanding of God, although that can easily become a sort of fundamentalism which far from encouraging conversation actively sets about ensuring that it does not take place. The danger is that confidence becomes absolute belief in the given moment. In turn there is a failure to see the longer perspective or be open to the work of the Holy Spirit as we are called to new possibilities in the divine economy which the Christian community is trying to live out on earth. It simply will not do to cling to positions which clearly reflect the needs or activities of a given time in the face of considerable human change, let alone the call of God which seems to be saying something very different about the need to be open to new possibilities. This is not to be unconcerned about the long-term future of the church; it is not an attempt to undermine authority and leadership; it is not to deny the possibilities of the church as a God-given community, quite the opposite in fact. It is the realization that this is the business of God. 'Renewing any institution requires revitalizing its core, its reason for being. Unless this core is refocused and funded afresh, renewal becomes a matter of strategy for survival'.[9]

Obedient government: responding to the love of God

The Church as the body of Christ is to understand its authority in relation to what we know of God and what God calls us to be; this in itself requires considerably more attention than the 'what would Jesus do?' school of moral theology. A crucial if not fundamental point becomes the question of how to be obedient given God as our primary source. Answering that question (without reference to what Jesus would do) will not only require confidence but awareness of the issues raised in consideration of pastoral and moral issues. What Clive Marsh says about our ethical consideration could just as easily be applied to the question of church order and governance: 'The working out will at least include argument with Christians and others, worship and prayer, theological reflection, political protest, and thoughtful ethical conduct.'[10] Seen in this light there will be the need to construct a way of being as the obedient community which is responsive to the sorts of conversations required under the heading of moral and pastoral reflection. This is to acknowledge that the exercise of good governance is both about the ability of the

Church to teach and to form appropriate patterns of communal life and action that furnish and enable the task of proclaiming the Lord's song – in all sorts of seemingly strange lands. Of course the various 'lands' ought not to be strange if the pastoral dimension to this work is taking context and culture seriously enough to employ a language which pays due respect to the situation. The sort of obedience required is not to impose the language and grammar of God so as to get the right result; it is to enable the church to be prophetic and pastoral whilst all the while being understood, because what we have to say is understandable. For John Wesley, this theme was at the heart of his first conference of preachers held in 1744. The agenda consisted of three questions: What to teach? How to teach? What to do? (i.e. how to regulate doctrine and exercise discipline and practice). Aside from the fact that Wesley was the one who both asked and answered the questions, the second and third questions seem to be as reliant on the experiences of the people of God as they are on any understanding of God's own self. This is particularly the case in the context of Wesley seeking not to disrupt the order of the Church of England for the sake of being a protesting Christian, but instead to be faithful to what he saw as basic, fundamental requirements and duties placed upon the people of God. In particular there are responsibilities central to the life of those who have understood their vocation as priests.

Obedience then is not simply about God as if churches can pray and the question of discipline or finances will sort themselves out. In all of this there needs to be an acute awareness of the context in which ministry and community formation takes place. The task of application becomes as crucial here as it does in consideration of hermeneutics, ethics and pastoral theology. In seeking to keep our Christian communities in order we must also hold together the requirements of state law and the essential nature of the Gospel. More importantly, the order of our communities must always point to the command of the Risen Christ which stands at the heart of the Christian community.

All of this points to what is required of the actualities of governance as churches fulfil their tasks and responsibilities. What do we want our canon law to do? What do we say about our money and how we use it? What sort of leadership makes this possible? Rather than address the specifics of any one tradition it is worth making some general observations about the life of churches, assuming our Risen Lord as having provided the unique selling-point.

Canon law and leadership

The exploration about good governance and faithful obedience must 'never lose sight of what canon law is for: the advancement of God's kingdom and the holiness of God's people'.[11] Clearly John Wesley, in simply phrasing his questions, was not averse to the use of rules and structures to aid the task of the early Methodist communities. He himself formulated rules for those who met together to deepen their Christian experience. The purpose of such rules was straightfor-wardly to help those who sought to follow Christ. Christian discipleship is not divorced from discipline, and neither is the corporate activity of communities. It may be that we can trace some common strands of particular traditions through canon law;[12] it may be that canon law provides a framework in which are enshrined certain basic principles which reveal and describe the particularity of a denomination or tradition. Such a definition should not stifle the work of God but rather ensure that faithfulness to the cause is ever before the people. The emphasis on prayer in the *Rule* of Benedict is an example where nothing is left to chance. Regrettably it must not be assumed that the Christian community will always seek to be faithful in prayer. That in itself is a salutary reminder of the weakness of human communities, even those raised up by God. It is the responsibility of the community to be open to God and not open to corruption or manipulation. In that sense canon law and discipline provide a corrective, even if the thrust of the *Rule* of Benedict is not totally democratic. However, the other side to this is that canon law becomes the only principle, the one by which everything is measured, even the word of God, the activity of the Spirit. Clearly there are extremes here and their mere existence often prevents a useful and constructive conversation about authority and governance. The canon lawyers are seen as stifling new developments whilst those with bright ideas are riding roughshod over tradition and good order. The measured tone of conversation was never more required. Even in less dramatic climbs conversation would be good. The Church of England and the Methodist Church are exploring what it means to be in a covenant relationship. The covenant makes claims such as: 'We affirm that one another's ordained and lay ministries are given by God as instruments of God's grace' and 'We affirm that one another's ordained ministries posses both the inward call of the Holy Spirit and Christ's commission given through the Church'.[13] Yet the discipline of the churches has yet to enable much more than a rather basic sharing in some cases or curiously in others just something akin to a localized version of interchangeability of ministries. Clearly in terms of theological consistency some work is necessary. Canon law may provide some of the framework, so too will the essence of the Covenant which the denominations believe to be a response to the call of God.

The good ordering of the community of the faithful is more than adherence to well-framed canon law. The bonds of love that enable and encourage faithful living have to express the nature of the Gospel in the exercise of care embodied in the ministry of our Lord. When churches are sufficiently faithful and confident to be places of hospitality and welcome it is vital that they offer protection and safety to those at risk. The way in which such protection is ensured has as much to do with the principles of community life as it does with the ability of those whom the churches appoint to positions of leadership.

Avoidance of judgement and condemnation are two important principles which begin to reflect the experience of those who encounter the offer of salvation in the Gospel account of the life of Jesus of Nazareth. All the while this has to take into account that shepherds do not simply cuddle lambs, at least not good shepherds who exercise care and, when required, correction of the flock. Such care is not always about being nice to all of the people all of the time. For every sentiment of the ordination charge, 'you are to watch over one another in love',[14] we must remember the reality that

Christ has many services to be done:
some are easy, others are difficult;
some bring honour, others bring reproach;
some are suitable to our natural inclinations and material interests,
others are contrary to both;
in some we may please Christ and please ourselves;
in others we cannot please Christ except by denying ourselves.[15]

That said, this is not to be used as justification of having to issue punishment. Jesus of Nazareth is much more to be found offering grace as a correction rather than the relatively straightforward act of exclusion which results in a denial of responsibility as much on the part of the one who excludes as it does on the excluded. That seems a long way from the open arms of redemption and subsequent model for Christian communities. 'Christian believers find themselves ordered in a certain form of society precisely by the message which they believe and are charged to proclaim. And the decisive character of their order ... is that it maintains the teaching of the truth of the gospel.'[16]

In all of this there are implications for leadership and those who hold office in which they are required to exercise leadership and in some case administer discipline and justice. The answer is not necessarily to avoid personal leadership in the life of the Christian community and assume that councils of the Church are free from a desire to exercise power or less likely to be influenced more by professional career development than vocational service.

Questions of personal leadership can be addressed in light of the same principles we have sought to establish for any enquiry about governance and order. Self-sacrificial giving has as much to do with the exercise of leadership as it is in the offering of one's self for a leadership role. Indeed, it could be argued that those who exercise leadership most faithfully are those who do not seek it. That is something of a generalization, but one which churches cannot afford to lose sight of as the effects of the increase in the average age of ordinands works itself out in the sort of experience available to churches as they look for leaders. What is of crucial importance in all of this is that leaders are aware of the place they occupy in the household of God's faithful people. Walter Kasper illustrates the point in a discussion on the relationship between deacons and bishops: 'The Bishop does not have full authority over either the ordination itself or the ordinand; the sacrament of orders gives the ordinand an immediate relationship to Christ, which entails a certain autonomy and responsibility that the bishop must respect.'[17] The example of episcopal office does not mean that this principle exempts non-episcopally ordered churches from needing to understand all models of leadership as being under the authority of God and thus exercised in a collegial style and manner which helps to advance the rule of God.

A confidence to use all aspects of common life and discipleship may yet hold the crucial insights that will enable us to be the people of God more faithfully. A humility to recognize that we have much to learn both from the imperfections of our own systems and the riches of other traditions will ensure that we help one another to see the possibilities which God offers us. We might ask whether we use the instruments of governance in order that we may centre ourselves on God and thus be strengthened in our mission to speak of God. Then again we may need to discover a greater humility and reflect on Herbert McCabe's reminder that 'What we labour to achieve was already *given* to us. Now *that* is grace.'[18]

Suddenly the task before us is more clearly cast in the presence of God as guide and strength. What are we waiting for?

Notes

1. Compare this to the history of the Holy Club founded by John and Charles Wesley. The club was formed in order that the activities of those who heard the call of the Risen Lord could be explored with credibility and honesty. As the movement developed, John's apparent preoccupation with order was for the singular goal of 'spreading scriptural holiness'.
2. Nicholas Lash, *Voices of Authority* (London: Sheed & Ward, 1976), p. 113.
3. John Cassian, cited in Gordon S. Wakefield, *Groundwork of Christian Spirituality* (Peterborough: Epworth Press, 2001), p. 39.
4. Patrick Barry OSB, 'Saint Benedict's Rule: A Short Introduction' in *The Benedictine Handbook* (Norwich: Canterbury Press, 2003), p. 4.
5. Jean-Marie R. Tillard, *Church of Churches: The Ecclesiology of Communion* (Collegeville, MN: Liturgical Press, 1992), p. 83.
6. Rom. 11.18.
7. Tillard, *Church of Churches*, pp. 84ff.
8. Jn 21.15, 16, 19.
9. Leander E. Keck, *The Church Confident* (Nashville, TN: Abingdon), p. 25.
10. Clive Marsh, *Christianity in a Post-Atheist Age* (London: SCM Press, 2002), p. 85.
11. Rowan Williams, in a foreword to Norman Doe, *The Law of the Church in Wales* (Cardiff: University of Wales Press, 2002), p. xiii.
12. See Norman Doe, *Canon Law in the Anglican Communion* (Oxford: Oxford University Press, 1998).
13. The Anglican–Methodist Covenant was signed on 1 November 2003. See *An Anglican–Methodist Covenant* (Peterborough and London: Methodist Publishing House and Church House, 2001), pp. 60ff.
14. From the Ordination of Presbyters, *The Methodist Worship Book* (Peterborough: Methodist Publishing House, 1999), p. 302.
15. From the Covenant Service, *Methodist Worship Book*, p. 289.
16. Oliver O'Donovan, *On The Thirty Nine Articles* (Exeter: Paternoster, 1986), p. 118.
17. Walter Kasper, *Leadership in the Church* (New York: Crossroad, 2003), p. 17.
18. Herbert McCabe, *God Matters* (London: Mowbrays, 2000), p. 179.

Chapter 10

AFTERWORD: THE GIFT OF MISSION

Paul M. Collins and Gareth Powell

Throughout this book we have often touched upon the divine purposes in creating and redeeming the cosmos. We have celebrated the cosmos as the context for understanding God's being and action and our human response, and as the context for understanding the purpose of the church. In this afterword we return to make a brief investigation of the church's relationship with and participation in the *missio dei* ('the mission of God'). Mission has come to take pride of place on the churches' agenda at the present time – but how are the churches imagining 'mission' in the light of Bosch's endeavour to claim a paradigm shift in their conceptualization and praxis of 'mission'?

Mission as recruitment

As denominations have sought to respond to the dual challenge of major shifts in the cultural, ethnic and sociological changes in British culture, and the sharp decline in church attendance, the question of what constitutes relevant mission has increasingly taken a central position in the life of the churches. The current understanding of 'mission' in both ecclesial and non-ecclesial usage relates primarily to the concept that an organization promotes itself and undertakes its activities in order to increase its financial viability, turnover, client-base or membership. In other words, the primary conceptuality is one of increase or recruitment.

Such an understanding in ecclesiastical settings may possibly be rooted in one interpretation of the 'great commission' in Mt. 28.16–20:

> [16]Now the eleven disciples went to Galilee, to the mountain to which Jesus had directed them. [17]When they saw him, they worshiped him; but some doubted. [18]And Jesus came and said to them, 'All authority in heaven and on earth has been given to me. [19]Go therefore and make disciples of all nations, baptizing them in the name of the Father and of the Son and of the Holy Spirit, [20]and teaching them to obey everything that I have commanded you. And remember, I am with you always, to the end of the age.'[1]

It is noteworthy that in the Greek text what is translated by an imperative 'Go' in verse 19 is a participle, just as baptizing and teaching are. Thus a translation closer to the Greek might be, 'As you go [on your way] make disciples ...' This changes the tenor of the passage and opens it up to different interpretations other than the received 'Western' understanding that this is about a deliberate policy of 'recruitment'. Such an 'open' translation is further supported by Kenneth Cracknell's work on the concept of the 'nations' in both Old and New Testaments.[2] In particular he argues that 'the nations' is an important motif, which has considerable implications for understanding 'mission' particularly in a pluralist context. In his exegesis of Rev. 21.3, he expounds textual variations to support his case that the invitation of *the nations* into the Kingdom of God, and to the Messianic banquet is an invitation into diversity and difference rather than recruitment into a uniform homogeneity.[3]

So how did the current mainstream understanding of 'mission' emerge? It is generally accepted that until the sixteenth century the Latin word *missio* was used only in reference to the divine persons of the Trinity, in relation for instance to St Thomas Aquinas's concept of the *missio dei* (the mission of God).[4] However, during the course of the sixteenth century the word 'mission' came to be used in relation to activities with the intention of making converts.[5] From this change in usage, and its accompanying conceptuality, the church increasingly came to understand itself as a sending agency with the explicit notion of making more Christians. This conceptuality emerged at the same time as a number of far-reaching changes were taking place in Western Europe. Two areas are of particular interest in relation to mission. Firstly, the newly emerging European nation-states began a period of overseas conquest and colonization, and secondly those nation-states became embroiled in the political outworkings of the Reformation. Thus Jesuits and others followed the Conquistadors to the Americas and Asia, seeking to convert indigenous peoples to the Christian faith, so that conquest and colonization became indistinguishable in many instances from a programme of Christianization. This firmly established the concept of the church as sending agency. It may be argued that in the emergent Protestant kingdoms and city-states such ideas of mission took longer to take root. However, developments in England demonstrate how deepseated the notion of 'mission' as an externally directed activity became. Following the Elizabethan Settlement, the laws of England enshrined the conceptuality of a nation of wholly Christian, Protestant people. Thus if 'mission' were to happen anywhere, it could logically only be somewhere else. Such an understanding of 'mission' was forged in a climate of fear, repression and explicit intolerance.[6] Out of this climate would also eventually emerge the events of the Pilgrim Fathers' expedition (1620), the English Civil War and the Commonwealth. Later 'missionary' activity would accompany English colonial endeavours in the Americas and Asia, and was organized in 1701 with the formation of the first Church of England 'sending agency', the Society for the Propagation of the Gospel.[7] By that time other Protestant/European agencies had developed, further evidence of which may be seen in the Wesleys' visit to the Americas (1736–38). Thus while in general terms we should not in any way doubt the integrity of individual missionaries, it is essential to recognize that missionary activity was closely bound up with the ambitions of the European nations in the eras of colonialism and imperialism. Furthermore, it should also be recognized that this often led to the churches endorsing or being complicit in the use made by the colonists of slavery. Against this background it is crucial to reassess what can be claimed as authentic 'mission' by Christian churches today.

In seeking to discern such 'authentic mission' we may make appeal to the traditions, which have shaped our thinking in all that we have said about the life of the church and the nature of theological engagement. For these also offer some reflections on the nature of mission, both in the sense of the activity concerned with the growth of church communities and the theological understanding of mission as it relates to, underpins and directs ecclesial self-understanding.

As the Second Vatican Council considered the nature of the church it gave definition to mission in *Ad Gentes Divinitus*, the decree on the church's missionary activity. The decree sets out the assertion of mission as growing out of the nature of the activity of God as expressed in the calling of the church as the people of God: 'The Church on earth is by its very nature missionary since, according to the plan of the Father it has its origin in the mission of the Son and the Holy Spirit. This plan flows from the 'fountain like love [the love of God the Father]'.[8]

Whilst the essence of the church's mission, and all consequent missionary activity, is clearly concerned with the proclamation of the word of God, that is not to suggest that the task of mission is to extend the life of the church for the sake of the church or any local community. 'Its aim is to open up for all men a free and sure path to full participation in the mystery of Christ.'[9] The ability to offer such participation, and thus be faithful to God in the revelation of grace, makes demands on the church itself. The human community called to service and love must bear the marks of love: 'then the Church, urged on by the Spirit of Christ must walk the road Christ himself walked, a way of poverty and obedience, of service and self-sacrifice even to death, a death from which he emerged victorious by his resurrection'.[10] The expression of mission as evangelism and social action will only be authentic if understood against such principles.

Such views have been echoed in similar terms by other traditions. The British Methodist Church offers its most explicit understanding of mission as part of the statement *Called to Love and Praise: The Nature of the Christian Church in Methodist Experience and Practice*.[11] In addition to describing the task of the church as participation in God's mission, and requiring that the expression of personal discipleship carries with it a commitment to justice and care for the integrity of creation, the statement goes as far as to say that 'To make numerical growth the primary object of evangelism is to distort the nature of the Christian mission.'[12] A clear link is drawn between the nature of God's love as experienced through Methodist tradition (i.e. largely Arminian) and the responsibility of the church to manifest that love and nature in its own life and order as a sign, witness, foretaste and instrument. Such an understanding would appear to be embedded in the whole of Methodist tradition as is evident not only in the first attempts of John Wesley to reform existing Christian communities (that they might be more faithful) but also in contemporary international Methodist-Roman Catholic conversations.[13] A common understanding of the prophetic role of the church as a consequence of being called into existence by God, whose nature the church is called to proclaim, is reached in the 1996 report of the conversations entitled *The Word of Life*. The report makes the point that 'the Church is missionary by its very nature; mission is by its very nature ecclesial'. The importance of such a statement in an ecumenical text is not that it gives permission for the local community to exist as it sees fit, pursuing its own understanding of discipleship and order, but that the conversations underline a commitment to the church as God's, and as such mission is the expression of the *missio dei*, in which the church participates at the invitation of God.

Mission has featured in a range of ecumenical conversations at a number of levels. Many local ecumenical partnerships see the need for unity in mission as the driving force for greater cooperation. Unity establishes a clearer and more effective sense of presence and a more responsible use of resources. On a wider scale, the World Council of Churches' study programme *The Nature and Purpose of the Church* understands mission as crucial to the life of the church not only as a means to greater ecumenical consensus but also because of the 'vocation of the whole Church to be the servant of God's design'.[14] This offers opportunity to develop further the need for churches to focus on participating, by the call to discipleship, in the activity of God. That of course is not quite the same as uniting in order to have a more credible mission in the community; laudable (and in some cases financially sensible) as that might be, it would hardly seem to reflect the unity at the heart of the Gospel, to say nothing of God's desire for his creation. Dialogue between the Anglican Communion and the Reformed tradition not only reaches a similar consensus as we have seen in other dialogues but suggests that mission, when understood as 'the sovereign action of the Holy Spirit',[15] can be a means by which we gain a better understanding of each other's traditions and perspectives. 'It is within this missionary perspective that we can begin to overcome the partial understandings which have kept our two communions apart.'[16] Here we see the need for honesty in mission, not only in order that churches hear the word of God but also that they hear each other and, more importantly, listen to the context in which God has set them. Fundamental to all of that, as we saw in Part 1 of this book, is a focus on God.

Clear understandings of participation in the *missio dei*, in turn reflected in the understanding that 'The Church is not incidental to but a central part of God's gracious purpose',[17] appear to be relatively constant in a range of texts from a variety of confessional traditions, yet the application of mission in the local context is not always so well defined, so aware of humility, so focused on the gracious purpose, that it is able faithfully to address the enormity of human lifestyles and contexts.

Mission deconstructed

The context in which the reassessment of 'mission' takes place is one in which pluralism is a central feature, in which at least the 'old' colonialism is gone, and in which the insights of philosophers such as the postmodernists and poststructuralists cannot, indeed should not, be avoided. The deconstruction of 'mission' as recruitment is overdue. Such a perception is not new: Bosch, in claiming a paradigm shift, made this claim over a decade ago.[18] However, the overcoming of such a deepseated conceptuality may take several more decades to become accepted generally. Bosch argued that the churches needed to understand that they were not sending-agencies, but were themselves sent, participating in God's mission in God's world. And he offered a number of different ways in which this might be understood and become consciously adopted as working models. Churches have sought to respond to the challenge Bosch laid before them, but it remains to be seen how far they have managed to jettison the old concept of 'recruitment'. It becomes necessary not only to deconstruct the current concept of 'mission' but also to reconsider and reappropriate what may be understood as the 'mission of God'.

Mission derives from the Latin word: *missio*, ' I send'. Before the sixteenth century, as we have seen already, it was customary to think in terms of the *missio dei*: the mission of God. This was understood to refer to the divine initiative and purposefulness in creating and redeeming the cosmos. God, in overflowing love, bestowed existence on everything seen and unseen. Very much in parallel with the modern mythology of the big bang God is understood to have sent matter and existence tumbling out across the vast expanse of the universe; one day to return to God, again in terms of modern cosmology, it will coalesce through entropy. It is fascinating how closely modern cosmology expressed in the laws of thermo-dynamics parallels the insights of those great theologians of the church in the East and West: Maximos the Confessor and Thomas Aquinas. They envisage the divine purposes in creating and redeeming the cosmos in terms of an *exitus* and a *reditus*: a going-out and a returning of all things to the Creator God, the Holy Trinity. This for Maximos and Thomas constitutes the *missio dei*.[19] The whole of creation has gone out from God and will return to God.

In one sense each life lived is an *exitus* and *reditus*, a journey from and to God. And it might be said that the life of the church in the world is parallel to this. Underlying this paradigm of 'mission', God, Father, Son and Holy Spirit, whose very life is fellowship, is also a journeying in the created cosmos. The cosmos is created through the Son, the Word (Jn 1.3), and is brooded over by the Holy Spirit from the beginning (Gen. 1.1). And in the fullness of time the Father sent the Son (Gal. 4.4) to bring the world back, and Christ in turn prays the Father to send the Spirit, the Comforter to complete this mission and this return of all things (e.g. Jn 14.16). So it is God, the Holy Trinity, who is always the primary sending-agent, and the church itself is sent, rather than being a sending-agency. So ideas of 'mission' in terms of conversion and recruitment need to be re-evaluated in the light of the ultimate goal of God's cosmic mission: 'that God may be all in all'.[20] So the question emerges how does the church participate in God's purposes of creating and redeeming the cosmos? St Paul offers a vision of the church's sharing in God's purposes:

> So if anyone is in Christ, there is a new creation: everything old has passed away; see, everything has become new! All this is from God, who reconciled us to himself

through Christ, and has given us the ministry of reconciliation; that is, in Christ God was reconciling the world to himself, not counting their trespasses against them, and entrusting the message of reconciliation to us. So we are ambassadors for Christ, since God is making his appeal through us; we entreat you on behalf of Christ, be reconciled to God.[21]

One way in which to describe the ultimate outcome of all of this activity, this *exitus* and *reditus*, is of course the reign of God: the return to God as all in all is expressed in the Kingdom. But all too often church and Kingdom have become too closely identified with one another. What more can be said of the outcome of God's mission in creating and redeeming the cosmos? There is a much-neglected passage in the second letter of Peter:

[God's] divine power has given us everything needed for life and godliness, through the knowledge of him who called us by his own glory and goodness. Thus he has given us, through these things, his precious and very great promises, so that through them you may escape from the corruption that is in the world because of lust, and may become participants of the divine nature.[22]

If the ultimate goal of the divine mission is that God shall be all in all, that also means that each person is called to become a participant in the divine nature. This is God's purpose in creating. Sharing in God's mission, expressed in terms of *theosis*,[23] may be understood in terms of the conforming of the human will with God's will, human deeds and human energy being conformed to and empowered by God's energy: to participate in God's nature and in God's mission is to live in a synergy with God.

The divine purposes in creating and redeeming the world are that all should share in the life of God, Father, Son and Holy Spirit; that all should enter into the divine fellowship of the Trinity and should mirror that fellowship in individual lives and the lives of the communities to which each belongs. In doing this it may be said that the church is participating in and living out God's cosmic mission in the world today. However, such understandings of mission and the divine purpose need to be related to the world today, its pluralism and it permeating philosophies. A present-day reception of two key twentieth-century writers may assist in discerning how to situate understandings of the *missio dei* today.

Rahner's discernment of the need for a more 'missionary and mystagogic theology' is rooted in his analysis and interpretation of his context as one in which secularism and pluralism are permanent and determining features.[24] Here a parallel with Bonhoeffer's concerns with the need for an *Arkandisziplin* may be discerned. In Rahner's understanding the foundational discourse of theology has become no longer credible. 'Rahner thus shares with post-structuralism an acute consciousness of the novel situation of contemporary thought and the need to "think otherwise".'[25] Rahner's appeal to 'mystagogic' theology is then an attempt to enable people to 'experience ... their own characteristically modern experience as, on the one hand, open and oriented to God as "holy mystery" and as, on the other hand, already addressed by the "holy mystery" drawn near in a saving self-communication'.[26] Thus John McSweeney, in his recent article drawing parallels between Rahner's method and post-structuralism, argues that 'by breaking down the antagonism between the modern and the Christian, by revealing the contingency of the prevailing "order" of both modern and Christian discourses, the act of Christian faith is rendered intelligible'.[27]

Certainly there are strong parallels in Bonhoeffer's writings with the endeavour to render the 'act of Christian faith intelligible'. And there are also strong parallels to be discerned between Bonhoeffer's endeavour and that of post-structuralist philosophers to disrupt the existing order, to open up new possibilities of thought through destabilizing the claims of that order. McSweeney argues that Rahner may be said to seek to recover the 'unsaid'[28] in his appeal to the 'mystagogic'. Such retrieval is also crucial in the endeavour to challenge and destabilize the current theological paradigm in order to craft an alternative. It is possible to interpret Bonhoeffer's endeavour in a similar way. In his appeal to the *Arkandisziplin* to deliver the Christian mysteries from profanation or manipulation, he is also seeking to retrieve the 'unsaid' in order to craft an alternative theological paradigm for the world come of age. Both Rahner and Bonhoeffer may be said to have presented a serious challenge to the prevailing theological structures of their day and to have provided a viable alternative. However, in line with post-structuralism this present endeavour is not simply an attempt to reiterate the thought of either Bonhoeffer or Rahner, but to ask how their appeal for a new theological paradigm may be related to Bosch's claimed paradigm shift in understanding mission. The churches are called to 'think otherwise' and to listen to the 'unsaid' in their participation in the divine mission in the world. How, we may ask, are the churches living out this calling in the present day?

Mission revisited

In British Methodism and the Church of England much attention has, in the last few years, been given to the nature of mission and evangelism. This has been born out of concern about declining numbers, as such it would appear that the purpose of such reflection is concern about numerical strength and the need to make more disciples so that what we might call the provisionality of the church in any given setting (be that a local or the long- to medium-term future of a denomination) may survive for a little longer. One of the four main emphases of the *Our Calling*[29] process of the British Methodist Church states that 'The Church exists to make more followers of Jesus Christ.' In an age much concerned with targets and goals we should not be surprised that this is followed by the question, 'What are our plans and targets for making more followers of Jesus Christ over the next year?' This is not quite the same as another priority, which would seem to have a greater awareness of the understanding of mission expressed elsewhere in Methodism and other streams of Christian theology, 'The Church exists to increase awareness of God's presence and to celebrate God's love.' From within the Church of England there would appear to be much the same emphasis on numerical expression in *Mission–shaped Church*.[30] Not only does this imply that the act of participation in mission is an additional responsibility, rather than a core feature of the life of the community of the faithful, but the stress on church-planting appears to lay all the emphasis on the physical reality of local communities rather than a sense of wider fellowship and participation in the *missio dei*. The Fresh Expression initiative[31] is both a response to decline and an attempt to engage in more overtly mission-orientated activity by mainstream churches. The range of these so-called 'fresh expressions', amongst them Cell Church, Café Church, Liquid Church and Network Church, are invariably an attempt to 'make more disciples' in a context which has little connection to anything more than the locality of believers, or indeed the activity of evangelism. 'Cell church offers a seven-day a week system that mobilizes and multiplies every member for discipleship, ministry, leadership and expansion'.[32]

The desire to offer fresh expressions of church seems to have little awareness of the tradition of *the* church into which at baptism we are welcomed and as members of the body of Christ called to share in the mission of the church, the mission of God's gracious purpose. Rather they are made in a desire to be faithful, as we know the faithfulness of God whose enterprise this is that we might bear witness to the possibilities of truth and not that we might invent new things or act in the presumption that we are the only group who have anything to give. The responsible action of the Christian community is much more about drawing attention to the possibilities of grace as agents rather than construction as would-be directors. If we are to take seriously the task of participation in the *missio dei* then we shall need to employ resources to enable us to be faithful. That is not simply about being faithful in response to the call of God and the challenge of the Gospel, but faithful as we watch over one another in love and care. In his forward to *Mission-Shaped Church*, Rowan Williams notes that as people encounter the Risen Jesus there is plenty of room for diversity, 'so long as we have ways of identifying the same living Christ at the heart of every expression of Christian life in common'.[33] A rigour of theological language and exploration will be as important here as in any other aspect of ecclesial life.

Our concerns are not to argue for the preservation of existing patterns, nor even to urge the return to an oft-perceived golden era. The areas explored in this book provide the foundation for reflection on mission in that we understand such reflection to be concerned with the nature and the function of the church. Grounded in an understanding of God as Creator, churches have to ensure that future developments are understood as belonging to God's nature and time. The consequences of this are, as Rahner can be seen to hint at, considerably greater than seeking a return to the notion of revival as the answer to the problem. Drawing attention to God and thus not seeking to invent an artificial environment for the purpose of divine activity would appear to be crucial if denominations are to be taken seriously, if God is to be taken seriously and if context and culture are to be respected. The sense of awakening so often associated with the growth of the Christian community needs to be far less about numbers and far more about enabling the God-given potential of each human being to be realized. Thus the activity of the churches becomes deeply aware both of the activity of God and activities within cultures and context. Justice and mercy are not restricted to the campaigns for trade justice, important as these might be. The desire to build upon such values requires that they become the very watchwords of the churches as they seek to participate in the task of establishing the kingdom of heaven. The central character in Philip Pullman's trilogy *His Dark Materials* is wrestling with a rather closed Christian faith which has sought to control and manipulate. The young Lyra realizes that this is not quite the republic of heaven that could be more than a possibility:

> but then we wouldn't have been able to build it. No one could, if they put themselves first. We have to be all those difficult things like cheerful and kind and curious and brave and patient, and we've got to study and think, work hard, all of us, in all our different worlds, and then, we'll build ... The republic of heaven.[34]

We might add that in fact that is precisely what the Gospel demands.

When churches appear to be concerned with numbers and the pension fund many will see them as having lost confidence in the ability to converse with and be attentive to God. The task of bearing witness to the vital presence of God requires diligence and breadth, even the costly obedience to faith which will manifest itself in an ethical system (and more) which might not be the system conducive to human ease and profit. Churches have to raise their sights a little higher not to ignore but to bear witness to the infinite possibilities of truth.

Denominations face the challenge of decline, not least because in their present form the structures require more people. Such a view represents an understanding of the churches which is about perpetuating that which has existed. What of the call of God to be a pilgrim people? If the structures are understood as the agents of the church's divine role, the bonds of love that enable a community to order its life and work, we could see a very different set of possibilities beginning to emerge, indeed a very different understanding of the essential becomes more apparent. The challenge of mission is set down by both the context of human living and the call of God. Both are in one way or another about a mixture of humility and faithfulness. The focus is not the fresh expression of what it is to *be* the church, it is the ever new discovery of mercy, grace and the transforming possibilities which they offer. The arts, industry, commerce, science, economics and education all have to be taken seriously, not so that we make all artists Christians, but to explore the possibilities of God-given human potential, which is very much more than the number of sheep in the fold. When we do that we most faithfully reflect the sacramental nature of the body of Christ that is *the* church.

Notes

1. See Greek text:
   [16]οι δε ενδεκα μαθηται επορευθησαν εις την γαλιλαιαν εις το ορος ου εταξατο αυτοις ο ιησους, [17]και ιδοντες αυτον προσεκυνησαν, οι δε εδιστασαν. [18]και προσελθων ο ιησους ελαλησεν αυτοις λεγων, εδοθη μοι πασα εξουσια εν ουρανω και επι [της] γης. [19]πορευθεντες ουν μαθητευσατε παντα τα εθνη, βαπτιζοντες αυτους εις το ονομα του πατρος και του υιου και του αγιου πνευματος, [20]διδασκοντες αυτους τηρειν παντα οσα ενετειλαμην υμιν· και ιδου εγω μεθ υμων ειμι πασας τας ημερας εως της συντελειας του αιωνος.

2. See Kenneth Cracknell, *Towards a New Relationship: Christians and People of Other Faith* (London: Epworth Press, 1986).

3. Cracknell, *Towards a New Relationship*, pp. 51f.

4. Thomas Aquinas, *Summa Theologiae*, I.I.43.

5. David J. Bosch, *Believing in the Future: Toward a Missiology of Western Culture* (Leominster/ Valley Forge, PA: Gracewing, Trinity Press, 1995), p. 29. Bosch attributes the usage to Jesuits who were reconverting Protestants to Roman Catholicism.

6. It might be argued that this was the case in most if not all Western European states in the sixteenth and seventeenth centuries.

7. See http://www.uspg.org.uk/history.html

8. Decree on the Church's missionary activity, §2.

9. Ibid., §5.

10. Ibid., §5.

11. *Called to Love and Praise: The Nature of the Christian Church in Methodist Experience and Practice* (Peterborough: Methodist Publishing House, 1999).

12. *Called to Love and Praise*, 3.2.3.

13. International Roman Catholic–Methodist Conversations, 1967–2001.

14. *The Nature and Purpose of the Church: A stage on the way to a common statement*, Faith and Order paper no. 181 (Geneva: World Council of Churches, 1998), p. 41.

15. Anglican–Reformed Commission (1984), *God's Reign and our Unity*, para. 38.

16. *God's Reign and our Unity*, para. 38.

17. *An Anglican-Methodist Covenant: Common Statement on the Formal Conversations between the Methodist Church of Great Britain and the Church of England*, 2001 para. 83.

18. David J. Bosch, *Transforming Mission; Paradigm Shifts in Theology of Mission* (Maryknoll, NY: Orbis, 1991), *passim*.

19. See Maximos the Confessor, '*Ambigua*', PG, 91, col. 1385BC and St Thomas Aquinas, the *Summa Theologiae*, whose overall structure may be interpreted as a moving-out from and return to God, through the revelation in Christ.

20. E.g. 1 Cor. 15.28.

21. 2 Cor. 5.17–20.

22. 2 Pet. 1.3–4.

23. The Greek term *theosis* denotes a qualified sharing in the divine nature; also referred to as 'deification' or 'divinization'.

24. Karl Rahner, *Theological Investigations*, vol. 13 (London: Darton, Longman & Todd, 1975), pp. 40–2.

25. John McSweeney, 'Rahner in the Mirror of Poststructuralism: The Practice of Theology as the Venture of Thought', *Louvain Studies*, 29 (2004): 196.

26. McSweeney, 'Rahner in the Mirror of Poststructuralism', p. 196.

27. McSweeney, 'Rahner in the Mirror of Poststructuralism', p. 196.

28. See G. Deleuze and F. Guattari, *What is Philosophy?* (London: Verso, 1994), pp. 61ff., esp. p. 63.

29. A statement of purpose designed to guide the Methodist Church's thinking on the ministry of the whole people of God. The statement was approved by the Methodist Conference in 2000, when all local congregations were encouraged to use four definitions of our calling as a means to monitor and evaluate local ministry and mission.

30. *Mission-shaped Church: Church planting and Fresh Expressions of Church in a Changing World* (London: Church House, 2004).

31. An initiative of the Archbishops of Canterbury and York, supported by the Methodist Council.

32. W. A. Beckham, *The Second Reformation: Reshaping the Church for the Twenty-First Century* (Houston: Touch, 1995), p. 9.5

33. *Mission-shaped Church*, p. vii.

34. Philip Pullman, *The Amber Spyglass* (London: Scholastic, 2000), p. 548.

INDEX